MOBILIZING INCLUSION

The Institution for Social and Policy Studies at Yale University

The Yale ISPS Series

MOBILIZING INCLUSION

Transforming the Electorate through Get-Out-the-Vote Campaigns

Lisa García Bedolla &
Melissa R. Michelson

Yale UNIVERSITY PRESS
New Haven & London

Published with assistance from the Louis Stern Memorial Fund.

Yale University Press books may be purchased in quantity for educational, business, or promotional use. For information, please e-mail sales.press@yale.edu (U.S. office) or sales@yaleup.co.uk (U.K. office).

Set in Galliard type by Newgen North America.
Printed in the United States of America.

Library of Congress Cataloging-in-Publication Data

García Bedolla, Lisa, 1969–
Mobilizing inclusion : transforming the electorate through get-out-the-vote campaigns / Lisa García Bedolla and Melissa R. Michelson.
p. cm. — (The Yale ISPS series)
Includes bibliographical references and index.
ISBN 978-0-300-16678-1 (pbk. : alk. paper) 1. Campaign management—United States. 2. Voting—United States. I. Michelson, Melissa R., 1969– II. Title.
JK2281.G36 2012
324.7—dc23

2012006640

A catalogue record for this book is available from the British Library.

This paper meets the requirements of ANSI/NISO Z39.48–1992 (Permanence of Paper).

10 9 8 7 6 5 4 3 2

To our CVI babies:
    (in birth order)
Paola, Joshua, Zachary, and Micaela

Thanks for keeping everything in perspective.

CONTENTS

ACKNOWLEDGMENTS

A project of this size and scope engenders a large number of debts. Our greatest is to Don Green, our co-evaluator on the California Votes Initiative (CVI) and an incredible mentor, colleague, and friend. He provided excellent and constructive feedback all along the way, including during the experiments and through the subsequent years of data analysis. His expertise, kindness, and grace under pressure make him a joy to work with.

This project was made possible by the James Irvine Foundation, whose decision to link grant support for CVI organizations with rigorous social science evaluation allowed the academics and practitioners involved to expand not only the California electorate but also our understanding of get-out-the-vote (GOTV), far beyond what would normally have resulted from organization self-reports. As with any innovative project, our collaboration did not always go smoothly. Latonya Slack and Amy Dominguez-Arms at the James Irvine Foundation never stopped believing in the project; they provided guidance, intervention, and wisdom as needed. We applaud the foundation for taking the risk of engaging in this initiative, and we believe that the result has changed the face of California politics.

Changing the face of the California electorate and generating the findings presented in this book was the product of the efforts of the nine community-based organizations we partnered with in order to evaluate their get-out-the-vote campaigns. These groups have been working to improve their communities for decades, for little pay and, most of the time, even less recognition. We learned a tremendous amount from them about organizing, politics, and the problems facing their communities. We thank them for generously allowing us to observe their work, for listening to our suggestions, and for sharing their knowledge and optimism. We hope other groups and individuals interested in mobilizing their communities will benefit from these organizations' experiences—both the successes and the failures—as reflected in these pages.

This book would not have been possible without the tireless dedication of our research team: Jedediah Alfaro-Smith, So Yeon Cha, Kim Danh, Joanna Do, Elizabeth Fernández, Jackie Filla, David Folmer, Aida Frias, Olivia García-Quiñones, Alisha Glass, Christy Glass, María Elena Guadamuz, Marisol Gutiérrez, Jacqueline Guzmán, Lisa Hahn, Jennifer Hernández, Michael Jackson, Angela Ju, Nhi Khoan, Amanda Rose Knockaert, Carolynne Komata, Mzilikazi Kone, Christine Lee, Stephanie Loera, Gabriel Lucas, Margaret McConnell, Xavier Medina, Thien-Huong Ninh, Kim Panach, Javier de Paz, Susan Phay, Alexandra Ramos, Daisy Reyes, Jonathan Sarpolis, Betsy Sinclair, Joe Tafoya, David Tran, Diane Tran, Titi Mary Tran, Yamissette Westerband, Jaehee Yoon, and Arely Zimmerman. Those that worked as canvassing observers braved inclement weather, aggressive dogs, dangerous neighborhoods, and unfriendly voters in order to provide us with the narrative observations that form the basis of chapter 5. Ricardo Ramírez provided critical research support and coordination for the National Association of Latino Elected and Appointed Officials (NALEO) experiments. Our other research assistants helped us to organize, systematize, and analyze the reams of paper and gigabytes of data this project produced. We thank them for all their time and effort. It is a pleasure to acknowledge their extraordinarily skilled work.

Our final framing benefited from feedback from Don Green, Vince Hutchings, Jane Junn, Taeku Lee, and Rogers Smith, along with the manuscript's anonymous reviewers. We also were privileged to receive questions and comments at a variety of public presentations of the book project, including talks in the Political Science and Sociology Departments at the University of California, Berkeley, the Economics Department at Loyola Marymount University, the Political Science Department at the University of Michigan, the Department of Political Science and the Wayne Morse Center at the University of Oregon, the Political Science and Ethnic Studies Departments at Santa Clara University, the Political Science Department at Stanford University, the Stanford University Center for Comparative Studies in Race and Ethnicity, and the Political Science Department at the University of Texas A&M. The input we received in all these instances was invaluable in clarifying and strengthening our theoretical frame. Any errors or confusion that remains is, of course, our own.

We received financial assistance for the final preparation of the manuscript from the Institute of Governmental Studies, the Graduate School of Education, and the Abigail Hogden Publication Fund at the University of California, Berkeley, and from Menlo College. Melissa Michelson received support during the crucial manuscript-writing phase of the project from the Stanford University Research Institute for Comparative Studies in Race and Ethnicity, which hosted her as a Visiting Faculty Fellow from 2009–2010. William Frucht, our editor at Yale University Press, was remarkably supportive of the project from the beginning and was instrumental in making the book come to fruition. His assistant, Jaya Chatterjee, was very helpful in getting the manuscript ready for submission. Our editor, Mary Pasti, provided excellent feedback and greatly improved the quality of our prose. Overall Yale University Press has been exceptionally easy to work with and has made the publishing process remarkably smooth.

When we embarked on this project, neither of us had any idea what we were getting ourselves into in terms of time, complexity, and commitment. For almost four years, we spent large amounts of time meeting with the participating organizations, our research team, and James Irvine Foundation staff, as well as randomizing lists and collecting and analyzing large amounts of data. Three more years were spent delving into the findings and their implications. To the extended family members, friends, colleagues, and acquaintances who put up with our stress, our busy schedules, and our various demands on their time and help, we extend our heartfelt thanks. We couldn't have done it without you. We owe you all chocolates and champagne.

Our debt to our partners, José Luis Bedolla and Christopher Gardner, is especially great, particularly because between the two of us we had four babies during the course of this project. It is to our CVI babies that this book is dedicated. We hope that they gained a bit of the optimism and hope for the future that is at the core of any mobilization campaign. May the world they inherit be a little more inclusive and equitable thanks to the work of organizations like those involved in the California Votes Initiative.

A NOTE ON TERMINOLOGY

We employ a number of terms to describe the different populations being targeted by these voter mobilization efforts. We understand that all are imprecise, but for the sake of clarity we would like to explain how we are defining and using them in this volume. The word "Latino" is used to describe all individuals, male and female, foreign and U.S. born, who have ancestry in any of the Spanish-speaking nations of Latin America. We choose to use that term instead of "Hispanic," because "Hispanic" is sometimes used to include individuals from the Iberian peninsula, which is not the population targeted by the community organizations mobilizing voters in this book. We use "Asian-origin," "Asian American," or "Asian Pacific American" to describe all individuals, foreign and U.S. born, who have ancestry in the Far East, Southeast Asia, the Indian subcontinent, or the Pacific Islands. In our descriptions of the experiments, the specific national-origin groups are referenced, but we use the panethnic terms to refer to these varied national origin groups taken as a whole. We use the terms "African American" or "black" to refer to individuals, foreign and U.S. born, with some ancestry that can be traced back to Africa. We realize that the terms "Latino," "Asian American," and "African American" refer to individuals who are diverse in terms of phenotype, national origin, nativity, class, and a variety of other characteristics, and that there are important overlaps across these groups. By using these terms, we are classifying Latinos, Asian Americans, and African Americans as ethnoracial social groups. Such a classification does not require that all individuals from that group share the same interests or characteristics, but rather simply that they be similarly situated (to other group members) within the U.S. racial hierarchy in ways that affect their social, political, and economic opportunity structures (García Bedolla 2009, 4).

We choose the term "ethnoracial" to describe these groups in order to capture the intersection between race and ethnicity. Scholars have long debated which is the more appropriate term to describe group experiences. The word "race" presupposes a common biological or genealogical ancestry among people. "Ethnicity" places more of an emphasis on cultural practices than on common genetic traits. Many scholars use the terms "race/ethnicity" or "ethnorace" to describe the ways in which factors often attributed to culture, such as language, can be racialized. In other words, ascriptive attributions can be based on linguistic or cultural practices that are not "racial" (or biological), but still can have racialized consequences. Because we believe the lived experiences of the populations being mobilized in this book include both racialized and ethnic/cultural traits, we describe them as ethnoracial groups. We use "communities of color" to denote those neighborhoods and areas populated by large numbers of ethnoracial group members.

ACRONYMS

AACU	African American Churches United
ACORN	Association of Community Organizations for Reform Now
ACT	Sacramento Area Congregations Together
AGENDA	Action for Grassroots Empowerment and Neighborhood Development Alternatives
ANES	American National Election Study
APALC	Asian Pacific American Legal Center
APSA	American Political Science Association
CalPIRG	California Public Interest Research Group
CARECEN	Central American Resource Center
CBC	Congregations Building Community
CCAEJ	Center for Community Action and Environmental Justice
CVI	California Votes Initiative
FIA	Faith in Action
FIC	Faith in Community
GOTV	get-out-the-vote

ICO	(Greater Long Beach) Interfaith Community Organization
ICUC	Inland Congregations United for Change
IVE	Integrated Voter Engagement
LHA	Latino Health Access
NALEO	National Association of Latino Elected and Appointed Officials
NET	neighborhood education team
NVSC	North Valley Sponsoring Committee
OCAPICA	Orange County Asian Pacific Islander Community Alliance
OCCCO	Orange County Congregation Community Organization
PACT	People and Congregations Together
PAVs	permanent absentee voters
PICO National Network	People Improving Communities through Organizing National Network
PIRG	Public Interest Research Group
PPIC	Public Policy Institute of California
RCI	Relational Culture Institute
SCOPE	Strategic Concepts in Organizing and Policy Education
SES	socioeconomic status
SVREP	Southwest Voter Registration Education Project
TOT	treatment-on-treated (effect)

1

CONSTRUCTING VOTERS: THE SOCIOCULTURAL COGNITION MODEL AND VOTER MOBILIZATION

A man unlocked the heavy gate to let Rosa into the apartment complex; rusted metal squeaked as it swung open. Entering, Rosa found herself in a small, dusty courtyard framed on all sides by three levels of apartments. A few children were playing in the courtyard; they stopped to look at the stranger and to comment on her bright blue vest, identifying her as from the Central American Resource Center (CARECEN), a local community organization. Rosa glanced at the clipboard she carried to find the number of the first apartment she sought. She turned left up a flight of stairs and entered a dimly lit corridor. It was a warm spring evening, so many of the doors were open. The sounds of family conversations and the smells of garlic, *curtido*, and *pupusas* spilled into the corridor. A few young men were lounging in the middle of the hallway. Nervous to be the object of their suspicious stares, Rosa quickened her step, adjusted her clipboard and the handouts she was carrying, and hurried on. When she reached the apartment on her list, she knocked briskly on the door, rehearsing her get-out-the-vote (GOTV) speech in her head.

Rosa's first targeted voter was a young Latino man named Juan. He had recently become a naturalized citizen, and the upcoming election was the first in which he would be eligible to vote. When he answered the door, he was surprised to see Rosa, a stranger, on his doorstep. As he and Rosa talked, a television could be heard in the background; a young child was playing in the living room just beyond the open door. Juan was surprised that Rosa knew not only his name but that he was registered to vote, and that she believed it was important for him to cast his ballot on Election Day. Although their conversation was short, Juan was moved by Rosa's visit and did show up to vote in the June election; he became a voter. The same was true of two of the other five voters Rosa was able to speak to that evening; all turned out to vote on Election Day. This level of participation is rare in this neighborhood and a sign of the impact that mobilization conversations can have on new or low-propensity voters. That impact raises a question: How and why did Rosa's visit make a difference?

We attempt to answer that question in this book. To do so, we explore a variety of mobilization efforts targeting ethnoracial new and low-propensity voters like Juan—registered voters who are new to voting or who have chosen to sit out most, if not all, of the recent statewide elections they had the opportunity to vote in. By mobilization efforts we mean nonpartisan contacts—through indirect methods such as mailers or leaflets, through live phone banks, or through door-to-door visits—made by individuals on behalf of community-based organizations to encourage targeted individuals to vote in an upcoming election. Our analysis is based on 268 randomized field experiments that we conducted in cooperation with nine community-based organizations from 2006 to 2008 and on 3,000-plus hours of field observations from the mobilization campaigns.[1]

The campaigns were part of the James Irvine Foundation's California Votes Initiative (CVI)—a multiyear effort to increase voting rates among infrequent voters, particularly those in low-income and ethnoracial communities in California's San Joaquín and Sacramento Valleys and targeted areas in southern California, including parts of Los Angeles, Orange, Riverside, and San Bernardino Counties. The initiative also aimed to determine effective approaches by which to increase voter turnout and to share those lessons with those in the civic engagement field.[2] The participating organizations included: African American Churches United (AACU);[3] the Asian Pacific American Legal Center (APALC); the Center for Community Action and Environmental Justice (CCAEJ); the Central American Resource Center (CARECEN); the National Association of Latino Elected and Appointed Officials (NALEO); Orange County Asian Pacific Islander Community Alliance (OCAPICA); the PICO (People

Improving Communities through Organizing) National Network; the Southwest Voter Registration Education Project (SVREP); and Strategic Concepts in Organizing and Policy Education (SCOPE).[4] Overall, the CVI groups delivered indirect GOTV messages to almost 119,000 voters, had live telephone conversations with about 75,000 voters, and had face-to-face GOTV conversations with almost 45,000 voters. Table 1.1 summarizes the campaigns by tactic, targeted voter population, number of contacts, and statewide election.

We, along with a colleague, Donald P. Green, worked with these organizations in an iterative fashion across six electoral cycles (2006–2008), evaluating the impact of their efforts after each election and proposing new approaches and tactics in order to make their work as effective as possible.[5] The results of that analysis, along with a set of best practices, were published in a series of three CVI reports, which are available for download at the James Irvine Foundation's website, www.irvine.org (Michelson, García Bedolla, and Green 2007, 2008, 2009).

In this book, we expand significantly on that analysis of these campaigns by developing a theoretical frame, the Sociocultural Cognition Model of voting behavior, for understanding GOTV effectiveness. We use this model to analyze GOTV campaign impact by tactic and election type. The depth and breadth of our analysis of these efforts, combining extensive experimental and qualitative data and looking at both successes and failures, allows us to gain important analytical traction for understanding the variation we find in observed treatment effects. We explain that variation with our model of voting behavior, which delineates the cognitive and sociocultural processes that explain why, and under what circumstances, these sociocultural interactions have an impact on voter behavior.

The Sociocultural Cognition Model of Voting Behavior

In our Sociocultural Cognition Model, we argue that GOTV effectiveness is rooted in the effect it has on individual-level cognition (Brubaker, Loveman, and Stamatov 2004; Abdelai et al. 2006) and that that cognition, in turn, must be situated within its sociocultural context (Reicher 2004). By sociocultural context, we mean the social and cultural

Table 1.1. Overview of CVI Mobilization Campaigns by Tactic, Number of Experiments, and Election, 2006–2008

Indirect Methods (65 experiments)	Phone Banks (86 experiments)	Door-to-Door Canvassing (117 experiments)
June 2006 (Low Salience)—35 Experiments		
Asian Americans (4 experiments, N = 35,062)	Latinos (6 experiments, N = 76,795)	Latinos (2 experiments, N = 7,046)
Congregation-Led Efforts (15 experiments, N = 18,875)	Asian Americans (6 experiments, N = 36,479)	Mixed Ethnoracial (2 experiments, N = 9,126)
November 2006 (High Salience)—66 Experiments		
Asian Americans (13 experiments, N = 52,098)	Latinos (7 experiments, N = 70,268)	African Americans[a] (3 experiments, N = 34,192)
Congregation-Led Efforts (11 experiments, N = 21,692)	Asian Americans (13 experiments, N = 49,076)	Latinos (1 experiment, N = 6,148)
	Congregation-Led Efforts (11 experiments, N = 13,926)	Mixed Ethnoracial (3 experiments, N = 24,953)
		Congregation-Led Efforts (4 experiments, N = 4,289)
March 2007 (Low Salience)—2 Experiments		
	Latinos (1 experiment, N = 5,535)	African Americans[a] (1 experiment, N = 10,393)
February 2008 (High Salience)—31 Experiments		
	Latinos (4 experiments, N = 50,750)	Latinos (1 experiment, N = 5,180)

Table 1.1. ***(continued)***

Indirect Methods (65 experiments)	Phone Banks (86 experiments)	Door-to-Door Canvassing (117 experiments)
	Congregation-Led Efforts (3 experiments, N = 6,002)	Mixed Ethnoracial (1 experiment, N = 8,973)
		Congregation-Led Efforts (22 experiments, N = 11,025)
June 2008 (Low Salience)—48 Experiments		
Asian Americans (11 experiments, N = 58,151)	Asian Americans (12 experiments, N = 60,052)	Latinos (1 experiment, N = 5,995)
	Congregation-Led Efforts (3 experiments, N = 5,085)	Mixed Ethnoracial (2 experiments, N = 10,414)
		Congregation-Led Efforts (19 experiments, N = 27,954)
November 2008 (High Salience)—86 Experiments		
Asian Americans (11 experiments, N = 54,683)	Latinos (6 experiments, N = 129,306)	Latinos (1 experiment, N = 6,205)
	Asian Americans (11 experiments, N = 54,683)	Mixed Ethnoracial (3 experiments, N = 31,832)
	Congregation-Led Efforts (3 experiments, N = 2,987)	Congregation-Led Efforts (51 experiments, N = 28,506)

Note: For all the analyses in this volume, N = the size of the experiment (treatment group + control group).

[a]All of these attempts to organize African Americans were congregation-led.

factors that frame individual experience, including, but not limited to, ethnoracial identification(s) and social context. With this model, we are attempting to assert the role that an individual's sociocultural context plays in framing their cognitive outcomes, thus bringing the cognitive aspect of schema theory together with the sociocultural context of the individual voter to explain the effects of GOTV conversations. That is what we mean by sociocultural cognition.

Because the canvassing conversation is a narrative-based sociocultural interaction, it provides a set of social cues that lead the targeted individual to adopt a new cognitive schema as a "voter," which is what leads her or him to choose to vote. The process we are imagining is similar to Penelope Oakes's (2002, 812) conception of how self-categorizations influence behavior: "As identity varies, the cognitive, motivational, and emotional resources brought into play for interpreting the world also vary . . . It is about people creating meaning through the active use of the categorization process . . . and the consequent potential for the self to be defined and to act in collective, group-based terms." In a GOTV effort, the mobilization interaction taps into sets of categorizations that the targeted voter already has, resulting in the development of new meanings and therefore the voter's development of a new cognitive schema. Our Sociocultural Cognition Model allows for a better understanding of the heterogeneity in outcomes that arise from these GOTV conversations by underscoring the relationships among narrative interactions, individual cognitive processes, and sociocultural context (Bandura 1989; Stryker and Burke 2000; Oakes 2002; McFarland and Pals 2005).[6] Using this framing, in the pages that follow we show when, where, and why GOTV mobilization conversations work.

In our formulation, the key is the impact the GOTV conversation has on a person's cognitive schemas. The schema concept "refers to cognitive structures of organized prior knowledge" (Fiske and Linville 1980, 543). Cognitive theorists argue that human memory contains long-term memory and working memory (Fiske and Linville 1980; Morris et al. 2003). Schemas facilitate the storage and retrieval of long-term memory. These memory structures "determine how people interpret and evaluate political events and make decisions" (McGraw 2000, 807). In other words, schemas serve as the filing systems that allow individuals to access old information, incorporate new information into their cognitive self-understandings, and act upon both. As such, schemas serve as "cognitive bases for defining situations, and they increase sensitivity and receptivity to certain cues for behavior" (Stryker and Burke 2000, 286). For cognitive theorists, schemas are used to explain "how people perceive and interpret the world and . . . how knowledge is acquired, stored, recalled, activated, and extended to new domains" (Brubaker, Loveman, and Stamatov 2004, 41). Therefore, schemas are not only representations of information; they are also "processors" that "guide perception and recall, interpret experience, generate inferences and expectations, and organize action" (41). They must be "activated by some stimulus or cue" and they "are the mechanisms through which interpretation is constructed" (41–44). Thus, schemas provide the bridge between the individual and the social world. It is through cognitive schemas that individuals organize their understanding of who they are and therefore how they should act (McGraw 2000; Marilynn Brewer 2001; Brekhus et al. 2010).

This is not to say that all individuals possess the same schemas; in fact, the opposite is true. Schemas may compose the architecture of human beings' cognitive infrastructure, but the content and complexity of the schematic structure, as well as its receptivity to particular stimuli, will vary significantly across individuals. The schema construct is especially appealing to scholars interested in employing an intersectional approach to understanding the relationships among marginalization, privilege, group attachments, and behavior. Intersectional theory argues that individual identifications are multiple and mutually constitutive rather than singular and fixed (Crenshaw 1991; Cohen 1999; Collins 2000; García Bedolla 2007; Hancock 2007). That means that race and gender identities, for example, cannot be understood in isolation from one another; instead, they form part of what Judith Howard (2000) calls "the whole person."

To understand the ways these multiple identifications may affect behavior, scholars need frameworks that allow them to situate individuals and their political behavior within their relevant sociocultural and historical contexts instead of seeing them as "atomized actors floating unanchored in a homogenized stream of national mass-media stimuli, their perceptions unfiltered by constraining and validating personal relationships" (Knoke 1990, 1058). Schemas allow for that type of contextualization within an individual cognitive frame. Those self-understandings that make up an individual's schematic structure are the product of a particular life history (Stets and Harrod 2004). Therefore, an individual's receptivity to new information/stimuli will be mediated by personal historical understandings and self-subjectivity (Bagozzi and Lee 2002). In other words, the new information or suggestion will be accepted or rejected depending upon the individual's existing self-understandings and self-categorizations. Schemas therefore allow for an understanding and interpretation of individual behavior that acknowledges the importance of multiplicity and the sociocultural context for explaining behavioral outcomes within the political system. It also explains variability—why the same stimulus might work for one voter but not another and why the same stimulus might not work for that voter at another point in time. Thus, our model situates variability in GOTV outcomes within its sociocultural context and within historical time.

Our Sociocultural Cognition Model sees GOTV effectiveness as the result of a change in cognition—the adoption of a voter schema by the mobilization target—that is a product of a particular type of sociocultural interaction, namely, the conversation between the canvasser and the targeted voter. Although we are not arguing that GOTV mobilization is the equivalent of a social movement, we posit that the cognitive processes at work within a GOTV conversation are similar to the mobilization processes within contentious politics as Douglas McAdam, Sidney Tarrow, and Charles Tilly (2001) describe them: routine and contentious politics are, they say, "clearly connected" (41). For them, the key to mobilization is the "activation, creation, and transformation of collective identities" (55). McAdam, Tarrow, and Tilly see social actors as "socially embedded and constituted beings who interact incessantly with other such beings and undergo modification of their boundaries and attributes as they interact" (56). For them, mobilization is always rooted in the routines of social life and, in particular, in social interaction—"the site in which identities form, coalesce, split, transform, and intersect with other processes" (58). They argue for a need "to look at relationships between identity constructions and structures of power and how contention changes identity, which changes structures of power" (62). That is precisely what we do in this book.

We contend that a GOTV mobilization conversation (albeit not within a context of contentious politics) is exactly that type of sociocultural interaction, situated within a narrative format. Much of the literature on social identification focuses on the importance of narratives to the development and maintenance of individual identity (G. Howard 1991; Rappaport 1993, 2000; McGraw 2000; Marilynn Brewer 2001; Eliasoph and Lichterman 2003; Lawy 2003; Todd 2005; Hammack 2008; Scottham and Smalls 2009; Brekhus et al. 2010). On the most basic level, narratives are seen as the way cognitive processes are organized and interpreted (Rappaport 1993; Holland et al. 1998; Dettori and Morselli 2008; Hammack 2008, 232). Personal stories and self-understandings are what form the basis for individual-level identifications. It is therefore through dialogue with others, as happens in a GOTV conversation, that personal self-understandings are "expressed, risked, and ultimately reformulated" (Hammack 2008, 234). Those reformulations are what changes voter behavior.

The schema concept is not new in political science (for a review, see McGraw 2000). In 1973, Robert Axelrod (1973) laid out the importance of "schema theory" for understanding how individuals make sense of complex environments. Scholars have used the schema concept to examine the impact of partisan schemas on policy information (Lodge and Hamill 1986), individual assessments of presidential candidates (Miller, Wattenberg, and Malanchuk 1986), African American racial attitudes (Allen, Dawson, and Brown 1989), and political information processing and attitudes (Conover and Feldman 1984; Bolland 1985; Hamill, Lodge, and Blake 1985; Lieberman, Schreiber, and Ochsner 2003; Morris et al. 2003; Duncan 2005). Interestingly, schemas mainly have not been used to explain voter turnout per se, but rather political decisionmaking, attitudes, and candidate choice (Lau and Sears 1986a). Within political science, the frame seemed to have its heyday from the mid-1980s to the early 1990s (McGraw 2000), but recently it has experienced a small resurgence (see, for example, Lieberman, Schreiber, and Ochsner 2003; Morris et al. 2003; Duncan 2005; Rudolph and Popp 2007).[7]

Critics of the schema concept have argued that the idea is ill defined, that it provides no real improvement over such previous constructs as "attitude," and that schemas cannot incorporate feelings of affect or motivation (Kuklinksi, Luskin, and Bolland 1991). We address the affect question below. In response to the charge that the measurement of the schema concept is too "fuzzy," we agree with Pamela Johnston Conover and Stanley Feldman (1991, 1365) that schemas are metaconstructs, "theoretical devices created to help understand human behavior." As such, "their measurement must be indirect; indicators can only provide empirical evidence consistent with the hypothesized construct . . . We can only observe the empirical consequences of the schemata and attitudes, not schemata and attitudes themselves" (1365). They go on to argue that "what is critical is that researchers choose as the focus of their measures theoretically defensible indicators of a schema or its functioning" (1365). On the question of the concept's value, we agree with Susan T. Fiske and Patricia W. Linville (1980, 549) that information-processing systems "underlie much of social behavior and social perception. The links are likely to be complex rather than simple, and the underlying mechanisms are likely to be multiple. But the link between the schematic bases of cognition and behavior is an untapped gold mine" (see also Hastie 1986).

In this study, we did not set out to "test" the impact of cognitive schemas on voting behavior. Our initial research design was meant to determine which GOTV strategies were most effective in mobilizing a particular voter population. What we found was quite a bit of variation in terms of GOTV effectiveness across individuals and campaigns. We developed our Sociocultural Cognition Model to explain that variation and to provide a theoretical explanation for why such a short conversation with a canvasser would change individual voting behavior. In developing this model, we triangulated a rich and varied amount of data—hundreds of randomized field experiments targeting hundreds of thousands of voters, complemented by thousands of hours of qualitative observation—in order to develop a causal story that explains the mechanisms underlying our empirical findings. Although we cannot provide direct evidence of the schematic changes that we posit are the root cause of the behavioral changes that we observe, we can prove that the GOTV conversations had causal consequences. Our theoretical model offers the first systematic theoretical explanation for why and under what circumstances those consequences occurred. We hope that future research will build upon this model to test more explicitly its core components.

Resources, Recruitment, and Voting Behavior

We believed it necessary to develop our Sociocultural Cognition Model because previous political behavior research did not provide a clear theoretical framework for understanding why and under what circumstances nonvoters can be moved to participate. Over the past ten years, hundreds of field experiments have laid an impressive foundation of empirical evidence showing that personal contact, either in person or by phone, can have a significant impact on voter turnout (Green and Gerber 2008). These experiments indicate that door-to-door canvassing is the most powerful method of turning out voters, that phone calls from volunteer phone banks can also significantly increase turnout, and that mailers (without the inclusion of social pressure messages) and other indirect methods tend to be ineffective. Experiments also suggest that the quality of a canvassing or phone banking campaign—the sincerity and commitment of those who make contact with voters—is crucial to its success (Green and Gerber 2008; Michelson, García Bedolla, and Green 2009; Nickerson 2007).

However, even though the experiments field has done an excellent job of proving which GOTV strategies work, under what circumstances, and with which voters, the literature generally has not focused on *why* a brief conversation on the doorstep or the phone works. In other words, we know little about the underlying mechanisms that make these short sociocultural interactions so effective in changing voter behavior. In fact, what we know about political behavior from fifty years of behavioral research would lead us to assume it would not work. Research has focused on how resources, interests, and voter issue concerns and political predispositions affect turnout. Since none of those factors is, in fact, changed as a result of a short GOTV conversation, it seems counterintuitive that a short interaction would alter an individual's behavior. Yet our work and that of hundreds of other field experiments show that it does.

On the resource side, the vast majority of the behavior literature has focused on the central role that resources—socioeconomic resources or civic skills—play in predicting voter turnout. Since publication of *The American Voter* in 1960, the political behavior literature in political science has focused on the role that socioeconomic status (SES)—education, occupation, and income—plays in voter turnout (Campbell et al. 1960; Verba and Nie 1972; Verba, Nie, and Kim 1978; Wolfinger and Rosenstone 1980; Conway 1991). In *Voice and Equality*, Sidney Verba, Kay Lehman Schlozman, and Henry E. Brady (1995) move beyond the SES model to look at the effect of civic resources on individuals' motivation and capacity to engage in political life, along with the influence of the networks of recruitment within which individuals are embedded (3). With their Civic Voluntarism Model, they attempt to "separate SES into its constituent elements" in order to show that "its components are differentially relevant for different kinds of participation" (5). With regard to participation, they find that education has an especially strong effect; in their analysis, they look at how education interacts with other civic opportunity structures to enhance political engagement.

Verba, Schlozman, and Brady (1995, 138) also consider the question of recruitment and the role it plays in fostering individual participation, arguing that "any attempt to understand the roots of participation must take into account the impact of requests from others." In their analysis, they find a significant demographic gap, with whites being much more likely to be asked to participate than African Americans or Latinos. Yet their analysis of political recruitment does not include questions that address the degree to which individuals were asked to vote in an election by neighbors, co-workers, or friends. Verba, Schlozman, and Brady (147) queried respondents as to whether someone in their job, church, or nonpolitical organization had asked them to vote for a particular candidate, not whether they had simply been asked to participate (regardless of vote choice) in an upcoming election. They found such institutionally based recruitment was roughly as important in driving participation as education and civic skills, which led them to conclude that the factors underlying participation are complex but rest on a strong resource base (389–390). Unfortunately, their analysis does not provide significant guidance for understanding the importance of nonpartisan requests to vote made by local organizations, a common form of voter recruitment within the U.S. political context and the type of GOTV mobilization we examine in this book.

Another resource-based line of theorizing within political science—the literature that emphasizes the importance of information provision in increasing voter turnout—would argue that it is the provision of information, such as a voter's polling place, at the doorstep that allows voters to overcome that important cognitive barrier to voting and turnout (Abramson and Aldrich 1982; Aldrich 1993; Berinsky 2005; Wolfinger, Highton, and Mullin 2005). However, our analysis, as we shall see in chapter 2, is consistent with the vast majority of work looking at indirect methods of voter contact that did, nonetheless, provide voters with this type of information; like other researchers, we found that these efforts still were not successful at mobilizing individuals to vote (Green and Gerber 2008; García Bedolla and Michelson 2009; Michelson and Nickerson 2011). Recent experiments have shown direct mail efforts to be effective if they contain elements of social persuasion (Gerber, Green, and Larimer 2008). This supports our overall argument that it is the social and interactive aspects of canvassing that make it effective. With social persuasion, it is not the informational content of the mailing that is most important but how it relates to individuals' self-understandings and their perceptions of themselves vis-à-vis others. Thus, it is only information provision combined with a social pressure (and therefore interactive) component that has an impact on voting behavior.

The spatial model of voting also focuses on the importance of information to voting, with a particular emphasis on how issues motivate vote choice (Alvarez 1997; Alvarez and Nagler 1998; Fournier et al. 2003; Miller and Klobucar 2003; Abrajano, Nagler, and Alvarez 2005; Peterson 2005). Other work has looked at the importance of economic evaluations and candidate choice (Rudolph and Grant 2002; Lewis-Beck, Nadeau, and Elias 2008). Issues and economic evaluations also have been found to be important to the development of partisan attachments, which, in turn, have been shown to influence turnout (Fiorina 1981; Franklin and Jackson 1983; Bartels 2000; Alvarez and García Bedolla 2003; Mark Brewer 2005). Although much of this work focuses on how individuals vote, it stands to reason that if issues and/or economic evaluations are what drive vote choice, the strength of those attitudes would also have some impact on voter turnout.

This assumption about the relationship between voter attitudes and turnout serves as the foundation for much of the popular discourse around voting trends within electoral campaigns. Such analysis often frames voter engagement as driven by issue concerns or political predispositions. Much of CNN's television coverage of exit polling during the 2008 presidential primary campaign, for example, followed this logic. In more recent analysis, the rise of the Tea Party movement is often framed as a reaction to the perception of President Barack Obama as having a "liberal" stance regarding the role of government. The logic in this scenario is that individuals have particular political predispositions that become activated in response to political issues or policy changes. It is that underlying issue concern that moves them to engage politically. Within the context of an issue-based framing of political engagement, a two-minute nonpartisan conversation with a phone canvasser can be expected to do little to change a voter's underlying set of interests. Yet this is precisely the type of effort that we find can have a dramatic influence on turnout. As detailed in the following chapters, we conducted hundreds of strictly nonpartisan GOTV efforts. We found that these efforts were effective in changing the voting behavior of targeted voters even though the content of the canvassers' messages was action-focused rather than issue-focused.[8] Thus an issue-based framing of voter engagement cannot help us to understand why these conversations were effective.

Another strand of literature that may help us to understand the impact of GOTV is the work that looks explicitly at mobilization effects. Using survey data, this work has shown that mobilization (or not) is a key factor in explaining the decrease in voter turnout over the past few decades in the United States and the gaps in the participation of different groups within American society (Rosenstone and Hansen 1993; Schlozman, Verba, and Brady 1995; Leighley 2001). Steven Rosenstone and John Mark Hansen (1993, 161), contend that mobilization is "the key that unlocks the puzzle of electoral participation in America." Using pooled data from the 1952–1988 National Election Studies, they argue that fully half of the decline in voter turnout from the 1960s to the 1980s can be accounted for by the decrease in voter mobilization during that period (217). In more recent work, Jan E. Leighley (2001, 49) argues that mobilization interacts with socioeconomic status, making elites more likely to mobilize white affluent voters than poor, ethnoracial voters, a point that is consistent with arguments made by Rosenstone and Hansen almost a decade earlier. Although these studies rightly point out that mobilization works and is key in motivating individuals to vote, they do not provide an explicit model for *why* mobilization works, for whom, and under what circumstances. Again, that is the model we attempt to provide in this book.

In our Sociocultural Cognition Model of voting behavior, the mobilization conversation, because it takes the form of an interactive narrative that evokes norms of civic duty and community purpose, can intervene in an individual's existing personal narrative and modify that person's set of self-understandings, moving her or him to adopt a voter cognitive schema. Similarly, because each individual brings an idiosyncratic yet contextually based personal narrative to that conversation, the effect that the interactive discourse has on the individual's cognitive schemas will vary. In other words, our model allows for a better understanding of the heterogeneity in outcomes that arise from these GOTV conversations by underscoring the relationships among narrative interactions, individual cognitive processes, and sociocultural context (Stryker and Burke 2000; Oakes 2002; McFarland and Pals 2005). There are two participants involved in these conversations. It is the narrative interaction between their particular identities that explains the power of the GOTV conversation.[9] Our model also highlights the ways each of these interactions is, in some sense, idiosyncratic. Each dyad of individuals constructs a unique sociocultural interaction, an interaction that is, however, embedded within a common set of understandings about personal community and the importance of voting to the civic character.

This conceptualization of the mobilization conversation also helps to explain why most field experiments testing messaging effects have not shown significant results (Green and Gerber 2008; Panagopolous 2009a; Arceneaux and Nickerson 2010). Although narrative structures are key to our GOTV model, they do not make up the totality of the conversation; nonverbal communication is also occurring in that exchange, communication that is rooted in social interaction. For example, a number of our participating organizations designed experiments to test the relative effectiveness of scripts using ethnic cues to encourage voting versus using cues to emphasize civic duty. We found no significant differences in the impact of each message. One explanation for this finding is that it is not only the words that matter in a GOTV conversation but also the unspoken messages being conveyed within the sociocultural interaction. If a canvasser comes to an immigrant voter's door and speaks in the immigrant's native language, that interaction will likely cue ethnicity even if the canvasser appeals only to the voter's "civic duty." Thus, we posit that the results from messaging experiments have been inconclusive because it is very difficult to control for the nonverbal aspects of the GOTV conversation, aspects rooted in the targeted voters' understanding of themselves and of the canvassers with whom they are speaking.[10] To date, scholars have not developed adequate measures of these nonverbal aspects of GOTV conversations, thus limiting their ability to draw valid conclusions about the impact of varied conversational components, including verbal and nonverbal cues.

When a mobilization conversation is successful at moving a voter to the polls, what has happened is the targeted individual has adopted a cognitive schema as a voter. We define this voter schema as a type of "situated subjectivity": "one's sense of who one is, of one's social location, and of how (given the first two) one is prepared to act" (Brubaker and Cooper 2000, 17). We realize that within this context we are adopting Rogers Brubaker and Frederick Cooper's (2000) definition of a "self-understanding" and incorporating it into a schema. Like other schema critics cited above, Brubaker and Cooper would likely argue that a schema is purely cognitive and therefore cannot include this type of affect. We would respond that the interpretations and meanings that they contend are part of any schema are, in fact, sociocultural constructs and therefore must be influenced by the societal, group-level, and individual values attached to each (Hitlin 2003). We do not believe that a strict cognitive/affective separation is possible, particularly when considering social behaviors, such as voting, that have values attached to them (Fiske and Linville 1980, 552; Schlozman, Verba, and Brady 1995).

An important part of the values and expectations that form part of the voter's new schema, given, at least within the context of this study, that the voter is a low-propensity voter to begin with, is an increase in feelings of both internal and external efficacy. Political scientists historically have defined internal efficacy as the belief that one can understand and therefore participate in politics. External efficacy is the belief that one's actions can influence what the government does. Both are reflections of the voter's feelings of self-esteem. Within the context of voter mobilization, the development of a collective self-esteem orientation, as opposed to self-esteem at the individual level, seems especially important (Luhtanen and Crocker 1992). That is, the voter also needs to feel efficacious in relation to the larger collective—in this case, the polity. It is the change in voters' feelings of self-worth, and therefore political efficacy, that is necessary to move them toward the belief that they can and should act politically.

That change in efficacy is one of the important results of the GOTV conversation. This sociocultural interaction is able to affect how these individuals "make sense of the world" because it consists of a socioculturally situated learning interaction (Nasir and Hand 2006). In other words, a form of learning is happening on the doorstep, one that is influenced by what each participant brings, in terms of self-concept, to the conversation. Thus, this narrative-based learning process is shaped by and shapes the identity of both participants (Nasir 2002; C. Lee, Spencer, and Harpalani 2003; C. Lee 2008; Nasir, McLaughlin, and Jones 2009). In this instance, the learning interaction between the voter and canvasser creates a situation where "learning changes not just what the learner knows . . . but also who the learner is. To learn is to take up a new practice, to change one's position in a community. Thus, learning can change identity and the self" (Wortham 2004, 716). But, we must keep in mind that this learning process is nested within broader institutional structures of power. As Na'ilah Suad Nasir and Victorial M. Hand (2006, 455) point out, "Accounts of power and social structure need to be considered within a treatment of local practices, for it is in these local contexts that broader forces, such as social structure and power distribution, play out" (see also Williams, Labonte, and O'Brien 2003).

These structures of power, and the constraints they may place on political behavior, are especially important when considering the targeted voters in this study—low-propensity, mostly low-income ethnoracial voters. These targeted voters belong to those social groups that have been most excluded from the polity, currently and historically, and therefore may be the most difficult to mobilize. Rogers Smith (1997, 2004) and other scholars have shown how citizenship and inclusion in the U.S. polity was defined ascriptively in terms of both race and gender classifications (see also Jacobson 1998; King 2000; Goldberg 2002; Ngai 2004; Gardner 2009). Their studies have demonstrated the many ways these discourses of political inclusion and exclusion were the product of explicit public policies, particularly U.S. immigration policies, which were designed to maintain the United States as a white Protestant nation and to materially privilege the white population (Haney-López 1996; Lipsitz 1998; King 2000). These ascriptive understandings, in turn, have been found to have affected the development of political thought within ethnoracial communities, as well as approaches to and engagement with political and collective action (Tate 1993; Gutiérrez 1995; Jones-Correa 1998; Cohen 1999; Dawson 2000; Kim 2000; García Bedolla 2005a, 2009; Parker 2009).

Because of this historical backdrop, we would argue that individuals in the United States possess common, historically based conceptions of what voters look like, which people should be engaged in this type of activity, and what political and social meanings are attached to that engagement (Schildkraut 2007). What, in an individual's mind, a voter looks like, and how consistent it is with that individual's self-understandings, will depend on that individual's particular social location, their "situated subjectivity." That subjectivity can shift after the individual's engagement with a GOTV canvasser, resulting in a new cognitive schema for the individual. It is therefore through dialogue with others, as happens in a GOTV conversation, that personal self-understandings are "expressed, risked, and ultimately reformulated" (Hammack 2008, 234). Equally important, that shift changes the voter's broader understandings of who voters are within the American institutional context (Todd 2005).

To become voters, then, all mobilization targets must be able to incorporate a voter schema into their broader cognitive framework. That process will vary across different groups of voters because each voter's incorporation process occurs within a particular sociocultural and historical context. Because the targeted population in this study consisted of mostly ethnoracial potential voters with a low propensity to vote, we will focus here on their particular schematic processes. But we would argue that the same cognitive changes described above have to occur for any voter to be moved (or not) by a GOTV conversation (C. Wong and Cho 2005). For the voters in this study, because of the history of electoral exclusion of ethnoracial voters throughout much of U.S. history, the adoption of this schema also requires a redefinition of the individual (and the social groups with which the individual holds an identification) as a voter and therefore as a first-class citizen (Smith 1997; Olson 2008). That redefinition converts their individual act of voting into a potentially transformative redefinition of the American electorate. We see this process as a redefinition of U.S. citizenship, an example of what Arjun Appadurai (2002, 35) calls "governmentality from below": the expansion of the definition of a state's active citizenry through social and institutional interactions that occur outside formal governmental structures. Thus, it is at this intersection of individual behavior and such institutions as the community-based organizations that took part in this study that social change can happen and where the transformative potential of GOTV may be realized.

Mobilizing Inclusion: Governmentality from Below

Again, we believe that the interaction between cognitive and sociocultural practices delineated above lies at the heart of why, how, and when GOTV efforts work for any targeted voter. But when a mobilization effort is focused on incorporating a larger number of ethnoracial voters into the polity—voters from social groups that historically have not participated at rates commensurate with their proportion of the population—then it is also important to consider the potential impact that mobilization can have on the nature of the electorate and what that means for American democratic citizenship. Historically, most citizenship scholarship has focused on citizenship as the possession of a particular set of rights; scholars were concerned with ensuring that everyone was treated as "a full and equal member" of the polity (Kymlicka and Norman 1994, 354). In this formulation, the focus is on the entitlements that derive from citizenship status, rather than a conceptualization of how constructions of citizenship and citizens change over time (Olson 2008, 41).

In contrast, recent theoretical work on citizenship, using the framing provided by Michel Foucault's (2004a, b) concept of "governmentality"—the recognition of the role that government plays in defining the parameters of citizenship and who, therefore, can fit within that categorization—

has focused on how citizenship is the product of the interaction between the state and society. Rather than seeing citizenship as a static category based on a fixed set of characteristics that are "natural" or "necessary," this approach serves as a framework for understanding how citizenship and society interact to construct citizens, particularly within the context of government interests and actions (Goldberg 2002; Olson 2008). Kevin Olson (2008, 42–43) sees democratic citizenship within this framework as a "malleable identity category produced by particular regimes of thought and practice . . . The governmental perspective identifies the constructed nature of such ideas and traces the process of construction itself. The result is an epistemologically sophisticated delineation of the relations between forms of liberal-democratic thought, practice, and identity."

It is the relationships among democratic thought, identity, and practice that we explore more deeply through our analysis of voter mobilization campaigns. From a governmentality perspective, the establishment of voter registration rules and requirements can be seen as a form of census taking that expresses government control over the population and restricts membership within the political community (O'Malley, Weir, and Shearing 1997; Goldberg 2002; Foucault 2004b). True to this framework, U.S. localities developed elaborate rules during much of the late nineteenth and early twentieth centuries to keep African Americans and other ethnoracial group members off the voter registration rolls, and the federal government allowed these restrictions to stand.[11] Thus, by engaging in politics and expanding the voter population to include ethnoracial groups, the voters in this study are co-constructing, along with their mobilizers, a new, more inclusive definition and practice of U.S. citizenship.

Since voting and citizenship are strongly linked in American political discourse, an individual's adoption of a voter schema includes a self-understanding as a "good citizen." By fulfilling that schema through action, namely voting, the individual strengthens and deepens that self-understanding (Haste 2004). Given that the populations included in this study were members of marginal communities, communities that historically have been excluded from the polity, through this political practice these individuals therefore were redefining and broadening American definitions of citizenship (Smith 1997; García Bedolla 2006). They were engaging in what we call governmentality from below. They may not have been engaging in their own enumeration, as was true of the slum-dwelling Mumbai activists for whom Appadurai (2002, 35) coined the term. But these voters were making themselves present and visible vis-à-vis the U.S. state through their political practice; they were successfully contesting and transforming existing definitions of inclusion and exclusion within American politics.

Pierre Bourdieu's (1977) theory of social reproduction and Antonio Gramsci's (Jones 2006) insights regarding cultural hegemony caution us not to assume that political inclusion alone will lead to change in structures of power. These theories could lead us to expect that the new voters will make a limited difference to electoral outcomes, absent significant structural change. We consider this question more fully in the conclusion. Here we simply emphasize that if voting truly makes no difference in the distribution of power in society, then why have local and state governments in the United States gone to such lengths to exclude particular populations from the franchise? State and local governments in the United States continue to purge voter lists and pass voter identification laws that have been shown to disproportionately prevent low-income ethnoracial voters from exercising their voting rights (Overton 2007; Pérez 2008). If it were true that increasing voting among low-income ethnoracial voters could have no impact on the system, then it would be unlikely that government actors would spend so much time and so many resources on excluding those very voters. Although we are not claiming that structures of power will change overnight if the electorate becomes more representative, we do contend that, particularly at the local level, increasing electoral participation in low-income ethnoracial communities can have a significant impact on these voters' quality of life. In the following chapters, we shall see how this process unfolds, one voter at a time.

Methodology

For each campaign analyzed in this book, we conducted a randomized field experiment. What that meant in this "real world" setting is that each group decided what its targeted voter population would be. Because each group was allowed to arrive at its own definition of "low-propensity voter," we provide a description of each group's targeted pool in our analysis of each experiment. Once the group decided on its targeted population, it provided us with the universe of potential targeted voters and an estimate of the number of contacts that group leaders believed they would be able to make before Election Day. We randomized the voter lists, providing the groups with a randomly assigned treatment group of the appropriate size and setting aside the remainder of the targets as the control group. Groups were not provided with contact information for the control group, making us confident that they focused their efforts on the treatment group. The groups provided us with contact information for their targets, which we compiled within the voter file.

In determining the effectiveness of the campaigns, we calculated intent-to-treat (ITT) effects—the differences in turnout between the treatment groups and the control groups—and treatment-on-treated (TOT) effects: the effect of the treatment on those who actually received it. This distinction arose from the failure-to-treat problem, whereby some people assigned to the treatment group were not successfully contacted. Because the failure to contact is not random (some individuals are simply easier to contact and therefore possibly easier to turn out), it must be controlled for. Alan S. Gerber and Donald P. Green (2000b) describe how to correct for this problem using two-stage least-squares (2SLS) analysis with "contact" as an explanatory variable and "assignment to the treatment group" as an instrumental variable; consistent with other subsequent research using field experiments to test GOTV campaign effectiveness, we adopted this approach in all of the phone bank and door-to-door campaign analyses presented in this book. For indirect campaigns (mailings and leaflets) we assumed negligible failure-to-treat problems and calculated the effect of each effort as equivalent to the difference in turnout between the treatment and the control groups. We evaluated contact effects using validated contact data that was provided to us by the CVI groups. To determine turnout rates, we utilized validated voting data from the respective county registrars for each mobilization location, rather than relying on voter self-reports.

In our analysis of the data, we did not include covariates (such as voting history) when calculating our results. Donald Green and Peter M. Aronow (2011) argue that simple regressions with experimental data are less subject to the risk of bias than multivariate analyses are.[12] Since this study included such a large number of field experiments, for the sake of simplicity we include only our main findings in the chapter tables. The detailed tables for each tactic, group, and election can be found in appendix A.

In addition to our experimental findings, we also report on the 3,000-plus hours of qualitative field observations that formed part of this project. In our analyses of the 2006 campaigns, we noticed that many mobilization efforts that looked similar on paper had very different outcomes in practice. To discover why, during the three electoral cycles in 2008 we fielded a team of dozens of multilingual field observers to follow canvassers door-to-door and to monitor phone bank conversations as they occurred. Their narrative reports are the basis of our analysis in chapter 5. These reports give us confidence in the quality of the contact information we analyze in our quantitative analysis, and provide important insights into the day-to-day operations of these campaigns. Thus, these qualitative data comprise a valuable addition to our quantitative analysis. To our knowledge, ours is the first study to combine large-scale experimental inquiry with in-depth qualitative fieldwork.

Plan of This Book

We begin our empirical analysis in chapter 2 by looking at indirect methods of contact—those that involve no sociocultural interaction. Given the importance of sociocultural interaction for developing and changing cognitive schemas, it is not surprising that we found these methods to be ineffective in moving large numbers of voters to the polls. Participating organizations utilized a wide variety of indirect methods, including mailings, leaflets, and doorhangers. The mailings varied from information-rich *Easy Voter Guides* (versions of the sample ballot written in more accessible language) to personally signed postcards to postcards with photographs of religious icons or notes from local pastors. Only occasionally did these mailings have a significant effect on voter turnout. Reviewing sixty-five experiments in a variety of communities around the state, we found indirect methods to be mostly ineffective across different electoral contexts and regardless of the type of community organization conducting the indirect outreach. This is consistent with findings from other experimental research and supports our proposition that it is the interactive aspects of the mobilization effort, combined with narrative structures, that are key to its effectiveness.

In chapter 3 we turn to an analysis of the effects of live phone banking. Our data in this chapter come from eighty-six phone bank experiments, including the first GOTV efforts to find statistically significant (and substantively large) effects with Asian American voters. APALC accomplished this result despite the logistical challenge of organizing and conducting phone banks in up to nine languages—a first, to our knowledge, in voter mobilization work. These phone bank experiment results include the groundbreaking finding that follow-up calls made to individuals who promised in an initial call that they would vote can lead to double-digit increases in turnout (over 10 percentage points), making live phone banks possibly more efficient and cost-effective than door-to-door campaigns. This finding is of great value to organizations (such as those targeting Asian Americans) wanting to mobilize communities that are geographically dispersed or multilingual. It also may be of interest to community organizations that lack the capacity to field broad-based door-to-door campaigns.

Our findings regarding phone banks support our contention that narrative interaction is at the heart of the effectiveness of mobilization efforts. The results from the phone banking campaigns were much more consistent across the different organizations than those we found for door-to-door canvassing. We argue that this is for two reasons. First, as we discuss in greater detail in chapter 5, most phone banking is conducted in a contained space, which allows for more direct supervision and monitoring of the phone canvassers' efforts.[13] Our participating organizations therefore were able to continually refine and revise their callers' implementation of the mobilization scripts. Second, on the narrative side, because of the greater organizational oversight, the phone canvassers' execution of the phone banking scripts was more reliable than the implementation of scripts in the door-to-door campaigns. This made the actual narrative interaction between the targeted voter and canvasser more consistent, and as a result, the cognitive impact was more similar across individuals, making the phone banks' impact similar as well.

Chapter 4 explores the effectiveness of door-to-door canvassing that targeted different ethnoracial populations, rural, suburban, and urban voters, and voters in quite different electoral contexts. Our analysis was based on data from 117 door-to-door field experiments conducted by participating CVI groups from June 2006 through November 2008. Our organizational collaborators directly contacted tens of thousands of potential voters. Some of the participating groups had many years of experience in door-to-door organizing; others had never done such work before. These differences in organizational capacity played themselves out in terms of differences in how these campaigns were conducted in the field. That variation is reflected in the significant differences we found in the relative impact of these campaigns.

That variability also is a reflection of the interactions among narrative content, individual cognition, and sociocultural context. A number of the organizations that conducted these door-to-door campaigns wanted not only to get out the vote among their targeted voters but also to use that interaction to build support for their organization and their programmatic foci. Those multiple goals affected the nature of the narrative and also the ways that narrative intersected with the voter's cognitive schemas. Finally, as we see in chapter 5, there were significant differences in how door-to-door canvassers delivered the organizational message. In-the-field improvisations made the narratives more varied, leading to more variation in the overall effectiveness of the campaigns.

One of the things that makes our study unique within the field of experimental research was the fielding of dozens of multilingual observers to systematically record and analyze each group's efforts on the ground. The thousands of hours of narrative reports that they produced constitute a rich and detailed complement to the experimental findings. We analyze those reports in chapter 5. Through this analysis, we are able to open up the "black box" of the canvassing operation in order to develop a list of the necessary, if not sufficient, factors that underlie a successful canvassing operation. Our examination of this on-the-ground data shows that the CVI organizations faced a number of challenges: recruiting, training, and retaining experienced canvassers; supervising how canvassers delivered the organizational message; managing and collecting multiple forms of data; and responding to the many unexpected difficulties that arose during these campaigns. More than anything, the reports make clear how difficult this work was. The canvassers braved dangerous neighborhoods, inclement weather, angry dogs, wild geese, and rude targeted voters. Yet they continued to engage in this difficult work despite those challenges because they were committed to increasing their community's political engagement and, by extension, expanding the American electorate.

We argue the expansion of the electorate is the result of cognitive shifts within contacted voters. If we are correct and mobilization results in these sorts of cognitive shifts, then we would need to see changes in their behavior over time, not just in one election. That is the question we explore in chapter 6. Our analysis shows that voting *is* habit forming. Across different campaigns and tactics, we found that having been moved to vote in a previous election does have a significant impact on future behavior. Those individuals are about 30 percentage points more likely to vote in a subsequent election, even absent any additional mobilization. This effect is consistent across a variety of experiments and different ethnoracial populations, strongly supporting the idea that being mobilized leads to enough cognitive change that it influences subsequent behavior, absent any additional contact.

Implications

Our discussion returns us to the original goal of identifying the cognitive and sociocultural mechanisms at the heart of explaining political behavior. Arthur Miller (1991, 1369) contends that "a theory about the mental processes of human actors is necessary to answer many of the questions examined by political scientists . . . Given the central role of the individual decision maker in the political process, political scientists need a theory of how individuals perceive and structure the social world in which they participate as political actors." We believe that our Sociocultural Cognition Model provides just such a theory precisely because it situates cognitive processes within an individual's sociocultural and historical context. It allows for multiplicity to exist within individuals and can explain variation across individuals. Our model shows why a particular stimulus might work for some voters and not others; it also tells us that the same stimulus may work for a particular targeted voter at one point in time but not another point in time. Our model is dynamic, allowing for change within individuals and change over time. From a practical standpoint, our model also provides those interested in mobilization the ability to specify the most effective approaches and/or tactics for changing targeted voter behavior.

The SES model of political behavior, on the other hand, sees behavior as the result of static socioeconomic structures. As Schlozman, Verba, and Brady (1995, 525) point out, the SES model "lacks a solid theoretical interpretation as to why those high on the socioeconomic scale are so unambiguously overrepresented in participatory input." The case of India also raises questions about the mechanisms underlying the SES model. In the world's largest democracy, poor and uneducated citizens are much more likely to vote than those who are wealthy and educated, even though the poor do not necessarily receive redistributive government services as a result (Keefer and Khemani 2004). This suggests that it is not that resources simply provide the time and skills to individuals that facilitate engagement, as the political behavior literature has generally argued, but that having middle-class status, at least within the U.S. political context, provides a cognitive schema that is consistent with, and inclusive of, a voter identity. Of course, the two positions are not mutually exclusive. A person's material status, and the skill sets derived from it, will inform that person's cognitive self-understandings. However, few scholars consider how the self-identifications that result from a person's particular social position are central to understanding individual behavior. That is the contribution we are making.

This work also brings home the importance of sociocultural context to understanding political behavior. In particular, we show the importance of contextualizing individual cognitive processes. It is the combination of individual self-understandings and sociocultural context that determines how receptive targeted voters will be to the mobilization message. Not all people are created equal, nor are all voters. Much of the work in political behavior treats individuals as separate from their sociocultural context (Knoke 1990). Yet individuals are embedded within a community history, a particular sociocultural context, and a set of social networks and contain their own particular self-understandings. All those factors interact to inform their receptivity to the GOTV message. In addition, the ability of these mobilization efforts to bring new voters into the political system is what opens up the possibility that GOTV efforts can result in social change. Canvassers like Rosa engage in this challenging work because they intuitively understand the transformative potential of what they are doing. We shall see in the following pages that they *are* transforming the electorate, one conversation at a time.

2

VOTERS *WILL* THROW AWAY JESUS: INDIRECT METHODS AND GETTING OUT THE VOTE

The church leaders sat in a circle, brainstorming about how best to mobilize their congregation to vote. Since they had little money, they had decided to use leaflets for their outreach. Yet they knew that voters get hundreds of pieces of literature during each election. How could they make theirs stand out? "Aha!" they thought, "if we put a picture of Jesus Christ on the front (and the Virgin Mary on the back)—people won't just throw away Jesus." They hoped that the moment of hesitation might be enough for the targeted voter to read their leaflet and for it to positively affect the decision to vote. Unfortunately, they were wrong. After the campaign was complete, we found that voters *will* throw away Jesus after all—recipients of the leaflets were no more likely to vote than those who did not receive them, despite the powerful iconography.

This result was not unique for a leafleting or direct mail campaign. These indirect methods are appealing to political organizations and campaigns engaging in voter mobilization work because the materials are fairly inexpensive to produce and distribute, allowing organizations to reach a large number of voters quickly. But unless indirect contact includes social persuasion messages, it is rarely effective.[1] The most consistent finding coming out of the California Votes Initiative campaigns was that indirect efforts, such as mailings and leaflets, seldom have a significant impact on voter turnout. This contradicts one of the central assumptions in the political behavior literature, namely that one of the main barriers to participation is the lack of information available to voters

(Abramson and Aldrich 1982; Aldrich 1993; Berinsky 2005; Wolfinger, Highton, and Mullin 2005). All the indirect contacts undertaken by CVI groups provided some key information to voters. At a minimum, they provided recipients with their polling-place information. At a maximum, the mailings included detailed, easy-to-read information about the entire ballot, often in-language—that is, in the recipients' native language. Although providing information may have ensured that those who did vote after receiving the mailings were more informed voters, the mailings had no significant impact on turnout (García Bedolla and Michelson 2009; Michelson, García Bedolla, and Green 2009).

We believe that it is the lack of a socially embedded narrative element that keeps indirect tactics from increasing voter turnout. This contention is consistent with the recent findings in the experimental literature that mail campaigns that incorporate a social persuasion component are able to influence turnout (Gerber, Green, and Larimer 2008; Panagopoulos 2009b). An experiment by Alan S. Gerber, Donald P. Green, and Christopher W. Larimer (2008) found that mailings that promised to reveal voting behavior to others, either people in the same household or one's neighbors, significantly increased turnout. Unlike other direct mail efforts, this variation of an indirect GOTV experiment had substantively large effects on turnout, with relatively low costs, peaking at 8.1 percentage points for those who believed their participation (or lack thereof) would be revealed to neighbors.

Subsequent replications by various researchers have confirmed that voters are much more likely to vote when told that doing so is being monitored and/or disclosed. (Researchers have also explored ways of telling voters this gently, to avoid backlash effects.) Reviewing these studies, Green, Larimer, and Celia Paris (2010, 6) note: "The more social pressure a mailing exerts, the stronger the treatment effect." We would argue that this type of mailing contains an implicitly social and interactive cognitive cue; recipients are meant to imagine their future conversations and interactions with their neighbors about their tendency to vote or not. Thus, the social persuasion mailing is, in fact, a form of sociocultural interaction operating in much the same way as a direct (telephone or face-to-face) contact. It is the sense of the relationship of one's behavior to one's self-perception within a community and collectivity that makes social persuasion experiments effective. That social cue, even though it is provided in the form of a mailing, mimics the interactive processes that are present within a direct GOTV contact.

It is the narrative and interactive nature of direct GOTV efforts that allows them to influence a voter's cognitive schemas. The type of sociocultural interaction offered by a typical mailing (absent the inclusion of a social persuasion message) is simply insufficient to influence an individual's behavior. Thus, our analysis suggests that information in and of itself is not what is most crucial to voter turnout. What is key is the individual's self-categorization as a voter and the possession of cognitive schemas consistent with that self-definition. Changing those schemas requires an intervention capable of altering that self-identification—namely, a narratively based sociocultural interaction. Even with a picture of Jesus on the front or pertinent voting information inside, most mail does not possess that cognitive power or potential for social influence.

Understanding the Impact of Indirect Efforts

Prior to the launch of the CVI, a number of experiments had tested the effect of robocalls, direct mail, e-mail, mass media, and leaflets (literature dropped on the doorstep or inside the screen door of targeted voters' homes). Reviewing existing studies, Green and Gerber (2008, 55–73) conclude that robocalls, e-mail, partisan and advocacy direct mail, and mass media are generally not effective, while nonpartisan direct mail and leaflets can have weak effects.

Recent work has suggested the possibility that some indirect tactics, particularly using media and mobile technology, can have significant effects. Several experiments have generated statistically significant increases in turnout using radio advertisements and cell phone text messages. Costas Panagopoulos and Donald Green (2011) targeted Latino voters, testing the power of nonpartisan Spanish-language radio advertisements to increase voter turnout in a variety of November 2006 congressional elections. They conclude that the radio advertisements were effective in prompting voting, as well as cost effective. Their work mirrors similar research on television advertisements aimed at youth. Green and Lynn Vavreck (2006) tested the impact on turnout of thirty-second Rock the

Vote advertisements played on the USA network via cable television service providers in single ZIP code areas in several states. Although the power of the advertisements was weak, it was still quite cost effective, with an estimated cost of $14 per vote.

Several experiments have found cell phone text messages to be an effective means of increasing turnout. Alison Dale and Aaron Strauss (2009) argue that registered voters need only a "noticeable reminder" to participate, not a personal invitation; they support their theory with evidence from a randomized field experiment utilizing text messages sent to voters who were either registered in person by student Public Interest Research Groups (PIRGs) or specifically requested via a Working Assets website that they be reminded to vote via text message. Using these pools of registered voters, they found that texts increase turnout by 3 percentage points.

As noted by Neil Malhotra, Melissa Michelson, Todd Rogers, and Ali Adam Valenzuela (2011), however, these text messages were not purely indirect treatments and can better be understood as "warm" texts, offered with a link to a previous face-to-face contact (with a PIRG volunteer) or sent as a follow-up to a voter-driven request for a GOTV reminder (via the Working Assets website). By contrast, Malhotra and his colleagues sent "cold" text messages to cell phone numbers culled from a list of registered voters and found a much smaller intent-to-treat effect, of 0.72 percentage points. Again, this is a relatively weak effect, but it is still statistically significant and relatively cost effective, given the high cost of direct methods such as door-to-door canvassing and live phone banking.

Dale and Strauss (2009) call their approach the Noticeable Reminder Theory (NRT) of voter mobilization. They posit that mobilization efforts that are highly noticeable and salient to potential voters, even if indirect, can be successful. Yet experiments with text messaging, e-mail, and other indirect methods of reaching out to voters designed to be noticeable and salient continue to tend to find small or null results. Those that have found some effect on voters, including experiments with text messages (Dale and Strauss 2009; Malhotra et al. 2011) and e-mail (Malhotra, Michelson, and Valenzuela, forthcoming), are the exception rather than the rule. And it could be argued that the contacts, particularly with text messages, are more meaningful to voters because they are less common, unlike regular mail. Should text messages from strangers become more common, we assume that their impact will decrease because they will seem less like a social contact. In addition, these studies did not focus on low-propensity voters. For regular voters, it is reasonable to assume that a reminder to vote would be sufficient, given that they already see voting behavior as part of their cognitive schemas.[2] Infrequent voters need the reminder and also the type of interaction that will help them to adopt a voter schema. We posit that these kinds of indirect contacts are unlikely to have that level of cognitive impact with infrequent voters.

Indirect Methods and the CVI

The CVI organizations participating in our study used more traditional indirect tactics for their mobilization campaigns—direct mail and leaflets/doorhangers. In so doing, they were building on a long line of experiments using these approaches.

Direct Mail

Harold Gosnell (1927), the pioneer of the field, conducted the first direct mail field experiments in 1924 and 1925. Assigning alternating Chicago city blocks to treatment and control, Gosnell sent letters to thousands of Chicago residents before the presidential election of 1924 and again before the 1925 mayoral election, increasing turnout by 1 and 9 percentage points, respectively. Three decades later, Samuel J. Eldersveld fine-tuned Gosnell's approach by randomizing treatment assignments in his 1953 and 1954 direct mail and canvassing field experiments. For the 1953 Ann Arbor elections, Eldersveld randomly assigned voters in his treatment group to receive either four waves of mail propaganda or a door-to-door visit that encouraged both turnout and support for a proposed revision to the municipal charter. However, the sample sizes were very small; twenty-two voters were targeted with direct mail and twenty for door-to-door canvassing. Thus, although turnout in the mail treatment group (59 percent) was 26 percentage points higher than for the control group (33 percent), the findings are not statistically robust. Eldersveld again used direct mail as part of his 1954 experiment, which targeted "local election apathetics"—those who had voted regularly in prior state and national elections but in not local elections—for that year's local elections. This time, mail failed to move voters to the polls: turnout in the treatment group (81 voters) was 10 percent, and for the control group (107 voters) it was 13 percent. Again, the sample sizes are too small to draw reliable conclusions about any possible effect on turnout.

The next test of direct mail was in 1980, when Roy E. Miller, David A. Bositis, and Denise L. Baer (1981) conducted a precinct-level field experiment for the 1980 Illinois primary election. A pool of 215 voters was divided into treatment and control groups, with subjects targeted with either one or a combination of three basic GOTV tactics: a door-to-door visit, a live telephone call, or a letter. Overall, those targeted to receive direct mail (38 voters) voted at a rate of 55 percent, while the control group (42 voters) voted at a rate of 36 percent. Although the intent-to-treat effect of 19 percentage points was quite large, the very small sample sizes make the true effect of the campaign subject to considerable uncertainty.

Direct mail was next tested by Gerber and Green (2000b), who sent registered voters in New Haven up to three pieces of nonpartisan mail just prior to the November 1998 election. Other aspects, or arms, of the treatment tested the effects of telephone calls and door-to-door visits. This experiment was much larger than those previously described, including a control group of 11,596 individuals and direct mail treatment groups totaling 7,776 targeted voters. Direct mail was found to have small but significant effects. Turnout in the control group was 42.2 percent, compared to 42.6 percent for those targeted to receive one piece of mail, 43.3 percent for those receiving two, and 44.6 percent for those receiving three. Overall, the treatment effect was a statistically significant 0.5 percentage points (standard error [SE] = 0.3).

Following up on this work, Gerber and Donald Green collaborated with Michael N. Green to conduct a set of four mailing experiments in Connecticut and New Jersey in 1999 (Gerber, Green, and Green 2003). In Connecticut, the authors partnered with the Democratic Party challenger in a mayoral race, who used a nine-piece mailing campaign to target households that contained either a registered Democrat, a registered "unaffiliated" voter who had participated in one of three prior elections, or a newly registered voter. Of the 9,900 households in this pool, 1,100 were randomly assigned to the control group and 8,800 received nine pieces of direct mail with an overall negative tone (attacking the Republican incumbent). Despite the large size of the experiment, the mailings were found to have no measurable effect on turnout. In New Jersey, three separate mailing experiments focused on the reelection campaigns waged by two Democratic members of the state assembly. The campaigns were all positive, targeting high-turnout Democratic households (N = 6,354), low-turnout Democrats, medium-turnout independents (N = 10,200), and the rest, mostly Republicans and low-turnout independents (N = 3,000).[3] Depending on which treatment arm a household was assigned to, those targeted received either four or six pieces of mail. In all four experiments the effects were weak. The authors concluded that it takes eight pieces of mail to raise the likelihood of voting by 1 percentage point (573).

Further direct mail experiments were tested in 2002 and beyond, including some that specifically targeted members of ethnoracial groups. In a meta-analysis, Green and Gerber (2008, 186–187) report that nonpartisan mail has an average effect of 0.5 percentage points, with borderline statistical significance. Partisan and advocacy mail is not effective, with perhaps one vote generated for each 1,000 individuals targeted. These generally null results include efforts targeting African Americans in 2000 (Green 2004), Latino and Asian Americans in 2002 (Ramírez 2005; J. Wong 2005), and Latino and Asian Americans in 2004 (Gimpel, Cho, and Shaw 2005; Trivedi 2005; Matland and Murray 2012). Green and Gerber (2008, 72) therefore conclude that although direct mail is relatively inexpensive to produce, its lack of effectiveness means that it costs approximately $100 for direct mail to produce one vote, making it more expensive than phone banks or door-to-door campaigns.[4]

Leaflets/Doorhangers

Like direct mail, leaflets have long been a common GOTV strategy. Yet unlike direct mail, which is sent via the U.S. Postal Service and thus has only minimal links to a message of outreach from a live human being, leafleting involves printed materials placed on a household's doorstep, inside their screen door, or hung on their doorknob by a GOTV canvasser. Although it lacks a direct personal interaction, those receiving leaflets might feel invited into the polity in an effective way, given that someone took the time to physically visit their home rather than just placing an item in the mail (assuming, of course, that the voter understands this key difference between mail and leaflets). Prior to the CVI, six leafleting experiments had tested the effectiveness of this tactic.

In 1998, Gerber and Green (2000a) distributed leaflets with nonpartisan GOTV messages to the homes of 984 voters in Hamden, Connecticut, on the weekend before Election Day. The overall results were negligible, but examining the results separately for partisan subsamples shows that while the experiment had no effect on partisans, there was a large (7.2 percentage point) and statistically significant effect on nonpartisan voters. The same researchers replicated the experiment in 1999 for the New Haven mayoral election, with a slightly smaller sample size, but this time found no effect on any subset of voters (Green and Gerber 2008).

In 2002, David W. Nickerson, R. F. Friedrichs, and D. C. King (2006) coordinated a partisan leafleting campaign with the Michigan Democratic Party, targeting voters aged eighteen to thirty-five and including about 2,500 households in thirteen different assembly districts. Doorhangers placed at the homes of targeted individuals encouraged support of the Democratic nominee for governor, Jennifer Granholm. In ten of the thirteen districts, turnout was higher in the treatment group, with a pooled estimated treatment effect of 1.2 percentage points (SE = 0.6).

Prior to the CVI, only two leafleting experiments had been conducted targeting ethnoracial voters. It is important to consider the possibility that mobilization efforts will have different effects across different types of voters, given the substantial literature in political science showing that dominant political behavior models cannot always explain fully what drives turnout among members of different racial minority groups (Fraga et al. 2006; García Bedolla 2005a; Leighley 2001; Lien, Conway, and Wong 2004; Michelson 2005; Tate 1993). Two partisan leafleting experiments targeting African American voters in Florida were conducted in 2004, in cooperation with the Democratic Party (Azari and Washington 2006). The pool of voters included African Americans living in Miami

Dade County (Miami and Hialeah) and Jacksonville, two areas subject to voting irregularities in the 2000 presidential election. Leaflets emphasized "election protection" and included contact information for a Voters' Hotline. The experiments included 661 blocks in Miami Dade (N = 6,504) and 223 blocks in Jacksonville (N = 4,996), each of which was roughly divided in half for treatment and control. Neither experiment increased voter turnout.

In March 2006, a nonpartisan leafleting experiment conducted in Philadelphia for a special election focused specifically on Latino voters (Frey and Suárez 2006). A pool of 15,550 registered voters was randomized at the block level, with 24.5 percent of the blocks assigned to the treatment group. The treatment consisted of double-sided bilingual (English and Spanish) doorhangers that encouraged voting to give Latinos a voice in the district. No measurable effect on turnout was found.

In sum, leafleting experiments conducted before 2006 indicated that partisan doorhangers were effective for increasing youth turnout but were not proven effective using nonpartisan messages or messages targeting ethnoracial voters. Given the strong results from the Nickerson, Friedrichs, and King (2006) experiments, however, there was considerable reason to believe as the CVI was launched that such methods could be used effectively to increase turnout among low-propensity voters.

This chapter is a review of the indirect methods pursued by several CVI groups, including most prominently those implemented by various affiliates of the umbrella organization known as the PICO (People Improving Communities through Organizing) National Network (PICO). We also look at mailings to Asian American voters by the Asian Pacific American Legal Center (APALC) and the Orange County Asian Pacific Islander Community Alliance (OCAPICA). While the vast majority of the experiments utilizing these tactics failed to significantly increase turnout, a review of the details of those efforts is valuable for two reasons. First, it underscores the overall message of this book, which is that a narrative sociocultural interaction inviting a person to vote is crucial for mobilizing low-propensity people of color to vote. Second, the publishing bias against null results notwithstanding, it is important to share failures in order to allow others to learn from their experiences and not to duplicate lessons learned (Scargle 2000).

Congregation-Led Indirect Contact: Leaflets and Mailings

In the weeks leading up to the June 2006 elections, PICO launched a diverse round of GOTV experiments using indirect methods. PICO was founded in 1972 under the leadership of Father John Baumann. The organization began as a regional training institute to help support neighborhood organizations in California. It developed into a national congregation-based community organization. The organizing model focuses on the relationship between social issues and moral values. PICO is an umbrella organization that includes a variety of congregations; for the CVI project, dozens of California PICO-affiliated congregations engaged in mobilization efforts. They varied significantly in terms of their size, experience, and capacity to undertake mobilization campaigns. Prior to PICO's involvement in the CVI, a number of network affiliates had conducted grassroots voter registration and GOTV campaigns, typically targeting local ballot initiatives concerning education and affordable housing.

PICO's GOTV efforts were meant to mobilize members of PICO-affiliated churches and their surrounding communities, which often included ethnoracial minorities living in low-income neighborhoods. A focus on their congregationally led campaigns is instructive because its religious foundation informs the voter mobilization work with another set of values beyond that of civic duty, namely, moral obligations to God and/or one's religious community. Although there has been a significant body of work on the role of the black church in African American political mobilization, political scientists have been less focused on the role of religion in political mobilization among other voter populations (Wilcox 1990; Wilcox and Gomez 1990; Tate 1993; Dawson 2000; Harris 2001; Harris-Lacewell and Junn 2007). Our analysis here adds to that knowledge. We posit that appeals from pastors or their representatives can be expected to cue targeted voters' social identification as parishioners in addition to their cognitive schemas as voters, potentially making those appeals more effective. Also, the communities surrounding many PICO affiliates were ethnoracially mixed and of low socioeconomic status. Thus, analysis of PICO's varied campaigns shows how religious identification and identification with a marginalized population can intersect with GOTV efforts to influence individual behavior.[5]

The June 2006 experiments conducted by ten local PICO affiliates targeted California communities from the Northern Sacramento Valley to Los Angeles and the Inland Empire (the Riverside–San Bernardino–Ontario metropolitan area, east of Los Angeles). PICO's hypothesis going into this election was that messages identifiably coming from one's local community, and particularly from respected institutions within that community, such as churches, would be effective. Thus, the messages were delivered by neighborhood churches either to residents of the surrounding neighborhood or solely to parishioners.

Two of PICO's California affiliates distributed leaflets to move voters to the polls. The Orange County Congregation Community Organization (OCCCO), PICO's Orange County affiliate, targeted two low-turnout precincts surrounding two of its partner congregations. Volunteers from the two churches, located in Santa Ana and Costa Mesa, hit the streets to drop over 1,000 doorhangers at voters' homes to remind them to vote. The leaflet used a quotation from the U.S. Conference of Catholic Bishops: "Responsible citizenship is a virtue; participation in the political process is a moral obligation. Every voice matters in the public forum. Every vote counts. Every act of responsible citizenship is an exercise of significant individual power." On the back of the leaflets was a map to the individual's polling place. The leaflets raised turnout by 1.1 percentage-points (SE = 1.4), an effect that is almost identical to that found in past published work on similar interventions.

The other leaflet experiment from June 2006 was unexpectedly successful. In mid-May, PICO California's Long Beach affiliate, the Greater Long Beach Interfaith Community Organization (ICO), held a candidates forum in the third city council district with the candidates for city council and mayor. ICO then published the candidates' answers to four community concerns: air quality, youth violence, homelessness, and affordable housing. The answers were distributed to the treatment group on the Saturday before the election on a doorhanger (Figure 2.1).

The result was immense: a 9.2 percentage-point increase in turnout, which is statistically significant at the 0.01 level. We should note, however, that this result is not reflective of a purely indirect campaign. Since the leafleting occurred on a Saturday and canvassers left the leaflets at voters' doors, the distribution of the leaflets was accompanied by a large number of informal face-to-face contacts. Canvassers remember voters

VOTE

TUESDAY, JUNE 6TH

Long Beach
Voter Information

Mayoral Candidates
3rd City Council District Candidates

Candidates' positions on:

- **Air Quality**
- **Youth Violence**
- **Homelessness**
- **Affordable Housing**

Candidates Forum hosted May 11, 2006, by
Greater Long Beach Interfaith Community Organization, ICO.

Greater Long Beach ICO
5600 Linden Ave.
Long Beach, CA 90805
562-984-2727

ICO's mission is to engage, educate, and organize people to act on their faith values.

Greater Long Beach ICO is a member of the PICO National Network. ICO's purpose is to develop an organization based in local congregations that creates a powerful voice for low and moderate income families through leadership training and community organizing. Working through congregations both individually and collectively, ICO is a catalyst for change in Long Beach.

In Long Beach, 10 congregations are members of ICO. These congregations have worked on a variety of issues of local concern, including traffic problems, street lighting, crime, sanitation, and youth activities.

Congregations have also worked together on issues of shared concern including air quality, access to health care, shelter for the homeless, and the need for affordable housing. In the last year ICO leaders have worked with the AQMD to invest fines collected from oil refineries in improving safety and health at local schools.

ICO is a 501(c)(3) and as such does not endorse any candidate. This summary is for voter information only.

Member Congregations

First Congregational, UCC	Holy Innocents Catholic
Lily of the Valley, COGIC	Mt. Carmel Cambodian Center
Second Samoan, UCC	St. Athanasius Catholic
St. Lucy's Catholic	St. Luke's Episcopal
Unitarian Universalist Church	United with Hope, UMC

Figure 2.1. Doorhanger for City Council Election, June 2006
Source: Courtesy of the Greater Long Beach Interfaith Community Organization (ICO).

Summary of ICO Candidates Forum
May 11, 2006

AIR QUALITY

Q What is your position on the proposed inter-modal rail yard next to West Long Beach schools?

Mayoral Candidates

FRANK COLONNA: *Opposed to the proposed inter-modal rail yard. Our* dock rail yards should be used to move containers from the port. Long Beach has done their fair share in moving goods. We need to clean up the port.

BOB FOSTER: Opposed to the proposed inter-modal rail yard. Long Beach is paying the price of cheap goods for the rest of the country with air pollution, health, and safety problems. We need to clean up the port and the 710 Freeway.

3rd City Council District

GARY DELONG: Agrees with his opponent and from all he has heard, the inter-modal rail yard sounds like a bad idea.

STEPHANIE LOFTIN: Opposed to inter-model rail yard. That should be in the desert away from people. We need electric trains on the Alameda Corridor to reduce air pollution. We need to find ways to clean up the port, the air, the water, and the beaches.

YOUTH VIOLENCE

Q If elected, will you increase prevention and intervention programs for Youth? Where will the $ come from?

Mayoral Candidates

FRANK COLONNA: Long Beach spends $4.6 million a year through Parks & Rec on after school programs. Need partnerships with schools for after

REASONABLE RENTS

Q What strategies do you support to increase the supply of housing with reasonable rents? Do you support requiring developers to provide housing for a mix of income levels?

Mayoral Candidates

FRANK COLONNA: We have a problem that happened very quickly. The city has developed 700 units of affordable housing. We need a good, well-thought out Housing Trust Fund to help develop affordable units. We also need to find a way to reduce the costs of developing housing.

BOB FOSTER: Long Beach needs mixed income housing where 20% of the new units are available at below market rates. Long Beach is becoming a city of haves and have-nots. We need affordable housing and better paying jobs.

3rd City Council District

GARY DELONG: Bad public policy is responsible for increasing Long Beach's poverty levels. Strategies to increase the supply of housing with reasonable rents treat symptoms, not the problem. We need better paying jobs. We have been chasing businesses out of town.

Supports encouraging economic development to bring good paying jobs, not supporting this type of housing.

STEPHANIE LOFTIN: We need housing that our workforce can afford. We built all these units around The Pike but the people who work at The Pike can't afford them. When we build new housing some of the units should be made available at an affordable price. These can be the less desirable units in these projects. We also should use 25% of our redevelopment funds for affordable housing.

*****

Each candidate was given the questions and background materials in advance of the forum, and the questions and background materials were presented at the forum. They were each given 2 minutes to respond to the questions. DVD's of the forum are available from the Greater Long Beach Interfaith Community Organization. The answers are given according to office being sought, then alphabetical order.

thanking them for the information and saying how helpful it was. Thus, these face-to-face contacts may have boosted the impact of the campaign.

The unexpected success of this leafleting campaign prompted three follow-up experiments in November 2006. A Fullerton PICO affiliate distributed a one-page flyer in English and Spanish to targeted voters that presented the issue positions and other information about Fullerton city council candidates. In Long Beach, two affiliates distributed leaflets that reminded voters to vote and mentioned local issues of youth violence, affordable housing, air quality, and health care. In North Long Beach, volunteers distributed doorhangers to 840 households in two local precincts (targeting 1,096 registered voters). In West Long Beach, volunteers conducted a similar effort, distributing doorhangers to 557 households (933 voters). In West Long Beach, the leaflets included images of Jesus and the Virgin Mary. This final experiment was expected to be more effective than previous doorhanger efforts because of the images: individuals receiving the leaflet would, it was thought, be more likely to take the time to read the message. Although turnout in the treatment group was slightly higher than in the control group, statistical analysis failed to find a robust effect on participation. The other leafleting efforts by PICO affiliates in November 2006 had similarly weak effects on turnout. Because these November 2006 experiments were unable to replicate the success of the June 2006 ICO leafleting effort, we believe that earlier result was either a statistical anomaly or that the inadvertent personal contacts, rather than the leaflets per se, were responsible for the observed increase in turnout.

In June 2006, PICO affiliates also organized a variety of experiments using direct mail. In Los Angeles, a local congregation organized by LA Voice sent 223 registered voters a personalized letter from the congregation's clergy. Other affiliates sent postcards, often with polling-place information or information about the candidates, along with the quotation about faithful citizenship from the U.S. Conference of Bishops. A meta-analysis of the postcard experiments shows that the standard postcard increased turnout by 0.9 percentage points, and the postcard with polling-place information increased turnout by 2.0 percentage points. These results fall short of statistical significance (one-tailed $p = .16$ and $p = .12$, respectively).

PICO groups also sent mailers to increase voter turnout in the November 2006 election. In San Bernardino, a local group sent mailers that included a brief recapitulation of a voter forum that was held in conjunction with the League of Women Voters, as well as a reminder to vote. In Fresno, a local affiliate sent postcards that emphasized the "sacred duty" to vote and noted that responsible citizenship is a virtue in the Catholic tradition. Similar efforts were made by PICO affiliates in Los Angeles, including mailing postcards emphasizing the Catholic duty to be a responsible citizen. A Visalia affiliate also sent postcards, including not only references to "faithful citizenship" but also stating that concern for the health and safety of the neighborhood was a reason to vote and providing voters with their polling-place information.

Looking at Table 2.1, we see that the pooled results for the PICO mailers and leaflets/doorhangers are smaller than would be expected from an indirect contact, which Green and Gerber (2008) estimate at about a 0.5 percentage point increase in turnout. We also see that the mailers are slightly more effective in the lower-salience June election, a finding

Table 2.1. Meta-analysis of PICO's Indirect Experiments, June and November 2006

	N	Pooled Treatment-on-Treated Effect (SE)
Direct Mail (postcards and letters)		
Pooled: 21 experiments, June and November 2006		−0.07 (0.06)
June only (13 experiments)	14,558	1.1† (0.8)
November only (8 experiments)	12,449	−3.2 (1.0)
Leaflets/Doorhangers		
Pooled: 5 experiments, June and November 2006	10,828	0.9 (0.9)

† $p < .10$, one-tailed

consistent with results from the phone bank and door-to-door campaigns detailed in chapters 3 and 4. In general, our findings indicate that these types of interventions, even when they are congregation based, do not seem to include the sociocultural interaction necessary to move large numbers of voters to the polls.

Asian Americans, Information, and Mobilization: *Easy Voter Guides*

Much of the rationale behind all voter mobilization efforts, using either direct mail or other tactics, is that more individuals will participate if the costs of doing so can be reduced sufficiently (see, e.g., Abramson and Aldrich 1982; Aldrich 1993; Rosenstone and Hansen 1993; Rosenstone and Wolfinger 1978). This rationale has led to various efforts to reduce such institutional constraints on voting as registration laws. Yet Raymond E. Wolfinger and Jonathan Hoffman (2001), in their analysis of the effects of "motor voter" registration laws, found that changes in the cost of registration increased the number of individuals registered but did not have a significant effect on voter turnout. Similarly, Adam Berinsky (2005), in his review of efforts to ease restrictions on voting, including voting by mail, early voting, the relaxing of absentee balloting rules, and Internet voting, found that these efforts had failed to expand the electorate. He concluded: "Political information and interest, not the high tangible costs of the act of voting, are the real barriers to a truly democratic voting public" (473). The true barrier, Berinsky argued, was the *cognitive* cost of participation—the effort needed to formulate political opinions to be communicated at the ballot box.[6]

Berinsky's formulation of the impact of information on cognition is quite different from the one we are advancing in this book. For the sake of clarity, we define what Berinsky calls cognitive costs as voter *capacity* costs. In other words, voter capacity costs constitute the capacity of the individual to assimilate political information and manipulate it in order to develop a set of political opinions. Given that the issue is developing voter capacity, we believe it would be useful to invoke Joseph Kahne, David Crow, and Nam-Jin Lee's (forthcoming) emphasis on the importance of the content of civic education to political outcomes. They find content-centered approaches to civic education, activities or efforts that foster the acquisition of knowledge about a political topic, promote individuals' political interest and efficacy. Thus, information provision that provides this sort of complex, issue-based information should be expected to increase voter capacity and engagement.

Organizers of mobilization campaigns often send mailers to voters, but the information provided in these mailers generally does not address the content-centered costs but instead focuses on procedural information, such as polling-place locations and times. The groups designing these mailers assume that individuals do not need assistance in developing their political opinions, so they provide procedural information meant to facilitate the voting process itself. A direct test of the power of procedural information is provided by Wolfinger, Ben Highton, and M. Mullin (2005), who examined the impact of mailed polling-place information and sample ballots on participation levels across states. They found that turnout was 2.5 percentage points higher in states that mailed polling-place information to registered voters and 2 percentage points higher in states that mailed sample ballots. The effects were even stronger among younger citizens and those with less education. They note: "Providing information matters more for people who are less likely to acquire it elsewhere. Thus, receiving sample ballots in the mail is most consequential for people with less access to information, the least-educated and young registrants, while its effect shrinks to insignificance for college graduates. In addition, these best practices are less valuable to young adults still living with their parents, who can acquire this information more easily from older, more experienced people" (17).

However, as mentioned above, previous studies using field experiments have found mailings to be ineffective in increasing turnout even when they include a voter's polling-place information (Gerber and Green 2000b, 2001; Green and Gerber 2008; Green, Gerber and Nickerson 2003). One possible explanation for this difference is simply methodological. Wolfinger, Highton, and Mullin conducted a quasi-experiment, whereas the other researchers employed randomized field experiments. Another possibility is that these studies did not take into sufficient consideration the type of mailer being used, that is, with procedural information, content-centered information, or both, or the type of voter receiving the information. In today's campaign climate, low-propensity voters are less likely than high-propensity voters to receive any electoral information. It is possible, within that context, that a single mailer could have more of an effect on a low-propensity voter than on a high-propensity voter. Or, if Berinsky's conclusion is correct, it is also possible that mail providing information designed to reduce the content-centered costs of voting, rather than providing procedural information, could have a more positive impact on voter turnout.

Field research by Elizabeth Addonizio and Susan S. Clark provides support for the idea that reducing voters' content-centered information costs will increase their participation. They argue that the true cause of low voter turnout is anxiety about the process and a lack of information about what voters are being asked to decide. Mobilization activities must therefore include not only encouragements to vote but also the cognitive tools to do so, including discussions about issues and candidates. In an experiment spanning elections from November 2002 through the spring of 2004, Addonizio found that providing high school students with detailed information about how to vote and linking the election to issues relevant to young people (e.g., financial aid for college, the military draft, sales taxes) increased participation significantly. Addonizio (2006, 39) concluded that "18-year olds, who are mobilized to vote in a way that incorporates interpersonal, communal, purposive, convivial, and instrumental experiences, turn out to vote at a statistically significantly higher level than those who are not afforded this mobilization. Participating in the First-Time Voter Program increases the probability that an 18-year-old will vote by 19 to 24 percentage points."

Similarly, in 1996, Clark, Mara Wold, and Harriet Mayeri (1997) combined voting workshops with issue discussions and distribution of *Easy Voter Guides* to adult school and community college students aged eighteen to twenty-four. *Easy Voter Guides*, then produced by an organization headed by Clark, continue to be produced each election cycle by the League of Women Voters. They include user-friendly nonpartisan information about ballot items, including pro and con arguments for ballot propositions, and some information about the candidates for office. The guides are designed to provide information that is more accessible than what is normally provided to voters in the state's official sample ballot.

The 1996 effort increased participants' turnout rates from an expected 35–36 percent to more than 70 percent, although we should note that the sample sizes were too small to allow for rigorous statistical analysis.

Even though the small sample sizes and lack of rigorous statistical analysis limit the strength of the conclusions reached by Clark and her colleagues, we believe that the theories underlying that project, combined with the statistically significant results from Addonizio's work, provide support for a hypothesis that providing voters with information that helps them to overcome content-centered barriers to voting can have a positive effect on turnout. The remaining question is whether it was the interactive discussions featured in both of these previous experiments that were crucial to helping move voters to the polls or whether simply providing more information to help voters make political decisions would be sufficient.

To test this hypothesis, we conducted experiments using a direct mailing that was specifically designed to address voters' lack of content-centered information, the *Easy Voter Guide* used by Clark, Wold, and Mayeri (1997). *Easy Voter Guides* are used by a wide variety of groups in California seeking to help educate registered voters about upcoming elections. They are available free of charge in five languages and can also be printed directly off the Internet. Many groups use the guides as a form of direct mail. Thus, *Easy Voter Guides* provide voters with the type of content-centered information that we hypothesize may be more effective in a direct mailing than strictly procedural information. Given Wolfinger, Highton, and Mullin's finding that information was especially effective with low-propensity voters, we tested our hypothesis on a low-propensity voting group in southern California: Asian American voters. We should note that this analysis is not meant to test whether or not the guides serve the purpose of educating voters and ensuring that those voters who do go to the polls are better informed about the process; it is entirely possible that the guides accomplish that goal quite successfully. Here we consider only their effectiveness as a tool to increase voter turnout.

Two CVI groups, APALC and OCAPICA, conducted experiments for the June 2006 and November 2006 elections that allowed us to test the ability of *Easy Voter Guides* to increase voter turnout. APALC sent a standard piece of direct mail to a targeted group of Asian American voters for the June election; both APALC and OCAPICA sent *Easy Voter Guides* to targeted voters for the fall election. This allowed us to test not only the effectiveness of the guides but also their effectiveness as compared to the earlier APALC mailing.

Prior to the efforts described here, scholars had analyzed only three field experiments aimed at increasing Asian American turnout, some of which suggested the possibility that direct mail would be effective with this population. For the November 2002 elections, one effort, by Janelle Wong (2005), used live telephone calls and postcards to mobilize East Asian and South Asian registered voters living in high-density Asian American neighborhoods of Los Angeles County. Although those contacted by phone or receiving a postcard were slightly more likely to vote, the differences were not statistically significant. Another field experiment aimed at South Asian voters (Hindu and Sikh Indian Americans) prior to the November 2004 elections used English-language postcards with varying messages designed to make ethnic or civic identities salient (Trivedi 2005). Again, the difference in turnout between those in the treatment group and those in the control group was not statistically significant. James Gimpel, Wendy Cho, and Daron Shaw (2005) used partisan direct mail (working in cooperation with the Republican incumbent) to try to increase Asian American turnout in a high-profile state legislative election in Texas in 2004. They found that mailers did increase participation, particularly when focused on neighborhood interests, although the statistical power of the effect was limited due to small control groups.

All of this work showed important national-origin differences among the different Asian American groups that were studied. It also suggested that there might be differences in the effectiveness of mobilization strategies for Asian Americans versus non-Latino white voters (Green and Gerber 2008). This is consistent with findings from other studies looking at ethnoracial politics in the United States that have shown that the participation and mobilization models developed to explain turnout among non-Latino whites do not always explain fully what drives turnout among members of different racial minority groups (Fraga et al. 2006; García Bedolla 2005a; Leighley 2001; Lien, Conway, and Wong 2004; Michelson 2005; Tate 1993). It is important, therefore, to test findings across different groups before assuming their generalizability. Asian Americans constitute a growing voting bloc within the state of California, yet at the time of the CVI campaigns little was known about their voting behavior beyond the fact that it often varies by national origin and they have a low propensity to participate in elections (J. Wong, Ramakrishnan, Lee, and Junn 2011). Our hypothesis, based on this past research, was that Asian American voters would be influenced by the provision of information about the election, particularly when that information was content-centered and made even more accessible by providing it in the voter's native language.

One of the important findings from the Wong experiment was that it showed the feasibility of multilanguage efforts, demonstrating that surname lists could be used successfully and cost-effectively to sort Asian registered voters into national-origin subgroups for language-specific targeting. Wong also found that about one-fourth of contacted voters preferred to speak a language other than English, which makes clear the importance of implementing a multilingual campaign when targeting Asian American voters in the United States. These insights were applied when designing the APALC and OCAPICA experiments.

The CVI efforts were multilingual, were based on surname lists of Asian national-origin groups, and used both direct mail and live phone banks. However, these experiments differed from Wong's in two important ways. First, Wong's experiment focused on all Asian American registered voters living in Los Angeles County neighborhoods with a high Asian density. Our experiments were instead limited to low-propensity Asian American voters—defined for the June 2006 election as individuals who had voted in two or fewer of the last four statewide elections, were under age twenty-five, or were newly registered as voters. In November 2006, low-propensity voters were defined as individuals who had voted in three or fewer of the last four statewide elections, were under age twenty-five, or were newly registered. In Los Angeles County, the targeted potential voters included South Asian, Cambodian, Chinese, Filipino (both men and women), Japanese, Korean, and Vietnamese Americans; in Orange County, the effort was limited to Chinese, Korean, and Vietnamese Americans. Second, whereas APALC's effort for the June 2006 election included a relatively simple piece of direct mail, both organizations used English and in-language versions of the information-rich *Easy Voter Guide* for their efforts for the November 2006 election.

In June 2006, APALC ran a campaign consisting of phone calls and direct mail aimed at a variety of Asian national-origin groups. (APALC's phone banking campaign for the June 2006 primary is discussed in detail in chapter 3; here we focus on the mailings.) APALC contacted 1,953 registered voters and sent bilingual mailers to 10,477 registered voters. Groups of registered voters on their list were selected randomly to receive only a phone call, only a mailer, or both. Mailers included basic information about the candidates and measures on the ballot, plus procedural information, including the voter's polling place and the right of decline-to-state voters—those who declined to state a party affiliation—to request partisan ballots.[7] Translation was provided by relevant partner organizations, and the photographs were changed for each mailer to be appropriate to each national-origin group.

Despite the large size of the experiment, the direct mail portion of the campaign had no measurable effect on turnout (although the live phone bank did increase voter turnout, as discussed in chapter 3). Pooling together the four experiments produces an estimated treatment effect of only 0.01 (SE = 0.3) (Table 2.2).[8]

During the November 2006 campaign, APALC called 4,231 registered voters and sent mailers to 10,802 registered voters. In-language mailers were sent to targeted Chinese, Korean, and Vietnamese American voters. In contrast to the June campaign, and to test our hypotheses regarding the effects that content-centered information provision may have on low-propensity voter mobilization, APALC's November mailings consisted of *Easy Voter Guides* that APALC sent either in a native language (for Chinese, Korean, and Vietnamese American voters) or in English. To determine which language materials to send to a voter, APALC used age and place of birth information to make a rough estimate of voters' English proficiency. English versions of the guide went to voters who were either U.S. born or foreign born and thirty-five years old or younger, and translated versions went to Chinese, Korean, or Vietnamese American voters who were foreign born and over thirty-five. Information on nativity was missing for a significant portion of APALC's pool of voters. Language of

Table 2.2. APALC and OCAPICA Direct Mail Experiments, June and November 2006

Organization and Election	N	Pooled Treatment-on-Treated Effect (SE)
APALC, June 2006: 4 experiments	35,066	0.01 (0.3)
APALC, November 2006: 7 experiments	25,335	1.2* (0.5)
OCAPICA, November 2006: 6 experiments	26,763	−0.6 (0.9)

*$p < .05$, one-tailed

outreach to these voters was thus determined by age; the assumption was that older voters were more likely to be foreign born. This determination may have resulted in some voters being contacted in a language they were unable to understand or in which they lacked proficiency, thus reducing the effectiveness of the phone bank and/or mailers. However, since the phone banks used the same guidelines in deciding which language to use in contacting targeted voters and were nevertheless able to significantly increase turnout, we would argue that the mailings' lack of effectiveness cannot be attributed solely to any downward bias caused by inappropriate language of outreach.

APALC sent English versions of the guides to Cambodian, Filipino, Japanese, and South Asian American voters. APALC and its partner organizations prepared bilingual labels that were attached to the front cover of the guides. The labels identified the organizations participating in the project to let voters know who was sending them the guides, listed a phone number to call if the voters had questions, and provided a link to the *Easy Voter Guide* website. The guides were mailed between October 16 and October 23 and arrived between October 20 and October 31, within two weeks of Election Day.

Even though the *Easy Voter Guides* provided qualitatively different information from that in APALC's June 2006 mailing, they had only a small impact on voter turnout (see Table 2.2). Although their impact was greater than expected for a regular piece of direct mail, the actual effect on behavior remained small. Therefore, contrary to our expectations, among low-propensity Asian American voters in Los Angeles County the *Easy Voter Guides*, despite being content-centered and provided in-language, were not significantly more effective in turning out voters than other forms of direct mail. The question then becomes whether the effects would be similar among Asian American voters living in a different geographic context.

Wong's (2005) study found important differences among Asian Americans not only by national origin but also in terms of the geographic context of the turnout effort. She found that those Asian American voters residing in high-density Asian American neighborhoods were more likely to be mobilized when contacted. To test the effects of geographic context and national origin, we also conducted an *Easy Voter Guide* field experiment with OCAPICA, in Orange County. The Asian American community in Orange County varies from that of Los Angeles County in that it is of smaller size and the national-origin distribution is somewhat different. The highest-density Asian American areas in Los Angeles County tend to have residents of Chinese or Korean origin. In Orange County, the highest-density Asian-origin area is mainly Vietnamese. A comparison of the effectiveness of mobilization campaigns in the two areas allows us to explore the effects of both geographic context and national origin on Asian American indirect voter mobilization efforts.

OCAPICA's outreach campaign consisted of mailed *Easy Voter Guides* and/or phone calls from the group's local phone bank. Each ancestry group was divided according to whether a given household was likely to be predominantly English-speaking or not, based on the same criteria used by APALC. OCAPICA contacted 1,917 registered voters and sent *Easy Voter Guides* to 8,700 voters.[9]

The *Easy Voter Guide*s generated results similar to those of other direct mail efforts and weaker than those found for the APALC effort (see Table 2.2). As with experiments looking at the provision of procedural information to voters, the mailings were not effective in increasing turnout. As we found with the PICO efforts, variations in content, political context, and targeted community notwithstanding, the indirect methods mostly had negligible effects on participation; without the narrative sociocultural interaction involved in a door-to-door visit or a live telephone call, such outreach to low-propensity voters was almost always ineffective.

The failure of the *Easy Voter Guide* experiments to have a strong effect on turnout raises the possibility that content-centered information is important but needs to be received in another format (i.e., in person) to have a significant impact on voter behavior. The issue is not the information being provided but its delivery within a narrative format, as part of a sociocultural interaction, so that the information can have a positive impact on the individual's normative understandings of herself or himself as a voter, thus leading to a change in the individual's cognitive schemas. It is only information combined with a sociocultural interaction that can lead to a change in behavior.

This contention is supported by Clark's and Addonizio's work. Clark's study using the *Easy Voter Guide* also included face-to-face discussions of the content of the guides. Addonizio's work, even though it did not use the guides, did include significant interpersonal interaction and discussion of political issues. Their results, combined with our findings, suggest that sending content-centered information to voters, even if of high quality and provided in-language, may not be sufficient to overcome the discomfort that low-propensity voters may feel vis-à-vis the political process. Thus, Berinsky (2005) may be correct in the sense that content-centered information is key. But our work indicates that voters should be given that information in an interactive format, within the context of political discussions, for example, for it to be effective.

Our findings suggest that it is not lack of information that is the most important barrier to participation for low-propensity communities of color. A number of CVI phone bank and door-to-door campaigns were able to have statistically significant effects on voter turnout, as detailed in subsequent chapters. As is true with most successful efforts, these calls did not entail long conversations with contacted voters. Most of the groups' GOTV scripts simply entailed identifying the voters, letting them know about the election, and encouraging them to make their voices heard. In general, we find even brief and relatively uninformative GOTV scripts are nevertheless quite powerful. Door-to-door canvassing efforts, which have been found to be the most effective tactic for turning people out, often do not entail a deep and in-depth conversation with voters; in most cases, a canvasser spends no more than five minutes at the door with the voter. This suggests that it is not necessarily the information conveyed during these contacts that is most important, but rather that the information forms part of a sociocultural interaction. That interaction is what is much more likely to affect an individual's cognition and therefore change that individual's subsequent behavior.

During every election cycle, American political campaigns and interest groups spend millions of dollars on direct mail. Although it is possible that direct mail does influence candidate choice, many of these organizations also send mailings in the hope of turning their supporters out to vote. Direct mail is an appealing option for those candidates and groups because it allows them to contact large numbers of voters without expending the time and resources necessary to implement labor-intensive voter mobilization strategies such as door-to-door canvassing or live phone banking. Yet until recently there have been few rigorous ways to test whether or not the expenditure of those resources is achieving the expected goal. The few tests that had been done indicated that direct mail was not effective in increasing turnout (Green and Gerber 2008). Our findings are consistent with that previous research.

Still, *Easy Voter Guides* or other informational mailers and leaflets may help voters make more informed choices or make them less likely not to vote on offices and initiatives that are placed further down the ballot. Further research is needed to determine how such written materials may help voters overcome those content-based barriers to making informed vote choices, even if the materials do not influence the broader decision of whether or not to vote. What deters individuals from voting is not only a lack of understanding of the candidates or issues but a lack of cognitive identification of themselves with the political process (García Bedolla 2005a). No amount of direct mail, however informative, easy to understand, or user-friendly, can substitute for the personal touch. We shall see in the following chapters that an interactive component is what is necessary to elicit the cognitive shifts necessary to alter an individual's voting behavior.

3

CALLING ALL VOTERS: PHONE BANKS AND GETTING OUT THE VOTE

The room is long and narrow, filled with rows of desks, each topped with a computer monitor and a phone. Empty pizza boxes and soda bottles litter the long tables at the far end of the room. Each phone and computer is manned by a volunteer. The screen displays show whom the volunteers are calling, what language they should use, and what script they should follow during their conversation. Since tonight's phone canvassers speak four different Asian-origin languages, to the observer the room sounds like a modern-day Tower of Babel, where technology has combined with old-fashioned get-out-the-vote personal contact. The organization that put together this phone bank, the Orange County Asian Pacific Islander Community Alliance (OCAPICA), is new to mobilizing voters, but the staff's enthusiasm and organizational skills have enabled them to overcome the many logistical obstacles that might make such a campaign unworkable. The big payoff will come later, when election results confirm that the phone bank made a difference—continued evidence of the effectiveness of GOTV phone banking as a mobilization tactic.

Unlike the indirect methods explored in chapter 2, the live telephone conversations between canvassers and targeted voters used to encourage turnout in the CVI campaigns were generally effective at increasing voter participation. Because the OCAPICA conversations were narrative and interactive, they caused individuals to adopt new cognitive schemas, identifying themselves as voters. A phone call from a live human being, specifically targeting the individual voter, often in the voter's native language, conveyed a message that might have been the same substantively as that was included in the other campaigns' mailers and leaflets, but it was markedly more powerful and transformative because of the manner in which it was delivered—within a narrative sociocultural interaction. As we detail in this chapter, phone banks are a powerful narrative tool that, when used properly, constitute a very effective means of increasing turnout among low-propensity ethnoracial voters such as those included in the California Votes Initiative.

What We Know about Phone Banking

Experimental work has long explored phone banking as a GOTV tactic. The earliest phone bank experiment dates to 1956, when Samuel Eldersveld included live telephone calls as one of the treatment arms in his small GOTV effort in Ann Arbor, Michigan, for the April 5, 1954, local elections. In the two days before the election, thirty-seven "local election apathetics"—those who had voted regularly in prior state and national elections but not in local elections—were targeted to receive a live call encouraging participation; twenty-five targeted voters were successfully contacted, of whom 24 percent voted. The very small sample size for this experiment makes it difficult to generate a robust measure of the impact of the campaign. Another small experiment was conducted by Roy Miller, David Bositis, and Denise Baer in 1980, when some targeted voters were exposed to telephone calls either instead of or in addition to door-to-door canvassing (Miller, Bositis, and Baer 1981). The overall size of this experiment was very small (N = 215); thus, no robust measure of the effect of the calls can be estimated.

A larger early experiment using telephone calls was conducted by William C. Adams and Dennis J. Smith (1980) in May 1979, for the special election called in Washington, D.C., to fill an at-large seat on the city council made vacant by Marion Barry's election as mayor. The experiment included 2,650 randomly selected registered voters in precincts thought to be favorable to John Ray, one of the two candidates vying for the seat, for whom phone numbers could be located in the newly published May 1979 telephone directory. Half were randomly assigned to treatment and control. Calls were made during the two days before the election and on Election Day by professional telephone interviewers from a local opinion research firm. Overall, 950 (72 percent) of targeted voters received a message designed by the Ray campaign endorsing his candidacy. While Adams and Smith commit the methodological error of lumping together their control group with individuals in the treatment group whom they were unable to contact, later correction of their data by Donald Green and Alan Gerber (2008) yields a treatment-on-treated effect of 8.1 percentage points (SE = 2.4).

Several decades later, when Gerber and Green used commercial phone banks to deliver nonpartisan civic duty messages to residents of New Haven (excluding Yale University) and West Haven, Connecticut (Gerber and Green 2000b, 2001), the calls did not increase turnout, but the experiments did launch a wave of replications and extensions that have significantly increased our understanding of how to use phone banks to increase voter participation. Commercial phone banks have been found to be much less effective than phone banks staffed by volunteers (Nickerson 2006; Green and Gerber 2008). An experiment by David Nickerson (2007) in which commercial callers were trained to act more like volunteers (e.g., to speak more slowly) and volunteers to act more like paid canvassers (e.g., to reach a relatively large number of individuals each shift) found that it is the quality of the call, not the status of the caller per se, that drives results.[1] Researchers also have found that the content of the message does not significantly influence phone bank effectiveness, even when comparing partisan and nonpartisan calls (Panagopoulos 2009a).

As with indirect methods, prior to the CVI, few of these phone bank experiments had targeted people of color. To our knowledge there were only three: one targeting African Americans, one targeting Asian Americans, and one targeting Latinos. The National Association for the Advancement of Colored People (NAACP) used commercial phone banks to encourage African American turnout in the November 2000 elections (Green 2004). Targeted voters were from neighborhoods in Florida, Georgia, Michigan, Missouri, New Jersey, New York, Ohio, Pennsylvania, and Virginia with a high density of African Americans. The experimental design called for targeted voters to be called five times (twice in October, twice during the weekend before the election using robocalls, and once more on Election Day). Contact rates were low, and some calls were made to individuals in the control group. Overall, the corrected treatment effect is estimated at 2.3 percentage points (SE = 2.3), indicating no significant increase in turnout.

For the November 2002 elections, Janelle Wong (2005) used live telephone calls made just a few days before Election Day to mobilize East Asian and South Asian registered voters in high-density Asian American ZIP codes in Los Angeles County. Before making the calls, the treatment list was sorted into ethnic-origin groups using surname lists, allowing multilingual calls to be targeted to Chinese, Filipino, Asian Indian, Japanese, and Korean American voters (phone calls were made in English, Korean, Mandarin, Cantonese, Tagalog, Japanese, and Hindi). While the overall treatment effect was not statistically significant (2.3 percentage points, SE = 2.4), the experiment showed the feasibility of multilanguage phone bank efforts and demonstrated that surnames could successfully be used to sort Asian American registered voters into national-origin subgroups for language-specific targeting.

Also for the November 2002 elections, Ricardo Ramírez (2005) worked with the National Association of Latino Elected and Appointed Officials (NALEO) to examine the effect on Latino turnout of live and prerecorded (robocall) phone calls and direct mail. Targeted voters were from precincts where at least 70 percent of voters were Latino and where turnout in November 2000 had been less than 50 percent. This included sites in California, Texas, Colorado, and New Mexico. Only live calls were made in California. Individuals who received a live call either alone or in addition to a robocall or mailer were more likely to vote, by 4.6 percentage points (SE = 1.8); turnout was not affected by the robocalls. Later analysis by Green and Gerber (2008) indicates that the isolated effect of the live calls (calculated by excluding those individuals assigned to also receive robocalls and/or direct mail) was a less definitive 4.5 percentage points (SE = 4.4).[2]

When the CVI was launched in early 2006, there was limited evidence that communities of color could be moved to vote using telephone calls. All three experiments targeting minority groups had failed to find robust statistically significant effects, even with large sample sizes. This chapter offers conclusive evidence not only that such efforts can be successful, but that they are feasible using multiple languages and can produce double-digit increases in turnout. Again, we find that a sociocultural interaction is key to increasing voter turnout. In other words, low-propensity communities of color are quite receptive to messages of inclusion that are delivered by volunteers making live telephone calls.

Phone Banks in the CVI

Many of our organizational collaborators chose to use phone banks almost exclusively. There are many reasons why groups may choose this approach instead of door-to-door canvassing. Even though door-to-door canvassing is known to increase voter turnout significantly, Green and Gerber (2008, 27) note that "mounting a canvassing campaign has its drawbacks." Not only is door-to-door canvassing relatively expensive, producing one additional vote for every $29 spent, it requires a large number of motivated, well-trained canvassers, a target list that is geographically concentrated, and safe access to targeted voters' residences. Phone banking, by contrast, costs approximately $20 per vote, allows each canvasser to make more contacts during each shift, allows groups to more closely supervise their canvassers, can be targeted to voters who are not geographically concentrated or who are difficult to access face-to-face, and does not require volunteers to brave unfamiliar or unsafe neighborhoods or bad weather. While increases in turnout from phone contacts are generally more modest than those from door-to-door efforts, phone campaigns still can have nontrivial effects on voting behavior.

Phone banking is also potentially a more effective tactic for organizing voters who are language minorities. Particularly in the Asian American community, where voter lists can include multiple possible languages, it is nearly impossible to staff a door-to-door canvassing team that can communicate with voters in every potential language. Phone banks, on the other hand, can utilize lists that have been presorted by surname into probable ethnic-origin groups, allowing canvassers with different language abilities to be assigned to appropriate lists, thus increasing the likelihood that contacted voters will be able to have a GOTV conversation in their language of choice.

Given these factors, it is not surprising that our two Asian-serving organizations, the OCAPICA and APALC, used phone banks exclusively.

Two of our Latino-serving organizations, NALEO and the Southwest Voter Registration Education Project (SVREP) also relied heavily on phone banks. In addition, some phone banks were conducted by the PICO (People Improving Communities through Organizing) National Network (PICO). Our analysis in this chapter is derived from eighty-six phone-bank experiments we conducted in collaboration with these organizations: twenty-six experiments by APALC in Asian American communities in Los Angeles, twenty-three experiments by NALEO in Latino communities throughout California, sixteen experiments by OCAPICA in Asian American communities in Orange County, California, twenty experiments in a variety of communities throughout California conducted by PICO affiliates, as well as a one-time phone banking experiment among Latinos in Los Angeles conducted by SVREP.[3]

These experiments include the first GOTV efforts to find statistically significant (and substantively large) effects of phone banks on turnout among Asian American voters, despite the logistical challenge that APALC and OCAPICA faced in organizing and conducting phone banks in up to nine languages—a first, to our knowledge, in voter mobilization work. The phone bank experiment results include the groundbreaking finding that follow-up calls made to individuals that commit to voting in an initial call can lead to double-digit increases in turnout (over 10 percentage points), making live phone banks using this tactic potentially more powerful and cost-effective than door-to-door campaigns. This finding is of great interest to organizations (such as those targeting Asian Americans) wanting to mobilize communities that are geographically dispersed or multilingual. It also may be of interest to community organizations that lack the capacity to field a broad-based door-to-door campaign. We present the results from these phone banks experiments by tactic in order to illustrate the difference in impact between the traditional one-call strategy and a targeted two-call approach.

One-Call Phone Banking Campaigns

At the start of the initiative, many of our participating organizations adopted a traditional one-call strategy to phone banking: by establishing a list of targeted voters and attempting to contact them once by phone to encourage them to vote. Some of the groups also added mailings to their phone-banking efforts, but phone contact remained the centerpiece of each campaign.

Mobilizing Asian Americans: APALC and OCAPICA

One of these groups was APALC. APALC was founded in 1983 and has worked to advance Asian Pacific American civil rights, provide legal services and education, and achieve a more equitable U.S. society. Although APALC is the nation's largest organization to focus on the legal needs of the Asian Pacific American community, it had not conducted a voter mobilization campaign prior to the June 2006 election. APALC's phone bank ran from May 18 to June 5, 2006, from 5:00 to 9:00 p.m. on weekdays and 1:00 to 5:00 p.m. on weekends. Bilingual interviewers allowed for in-language mobilization of the included national-origin groups, including South Asian, Chinese, Filipino, Japanese, Korean, and Vietnamese American voters.[4] In addition to the phone-banking campaign, APALC held a press conference prior to the June 2006 election to explain and publicize the GOTV campaign. The press conference was well attended, particularly by the ethnic media.

APALC's pool of experimental subjects was culled from the Los Angeles County registrar's list of those registered to vote as of April 1, 2006. Asian-origin individuals were identified based on place of birth and full name. APALC used internal Asian-origin surname lists to determine the likely national background of each individual. The file was further culled to include only low-propensity voters, defined as those who had voted in fewer than two of the last four major elections, were younger than twenty-five, or were newly registered to vote. The list of names was then narrowed to include only individuals residing in geographic areas with large numbers of Asian voters. The remaining list of about 110,000 individuals was cleaned by a commercial vendor to include only those with a valid mailing addresses and phone numbers, resulting in a pool of 36,479 registered voters who were then randomly divided into treatment and control groups. Each national-origin group was randomized separately.

Overall, APALC contacted 1,953 registered voters and sent bilingual mailers to 10,477 registered voters. Groups of registered voters on the APALC list were selected randomly to receive a phone call, a mailer, or both. Phone calls were conducted in cooperation with eight other local Asian Pacific Islander organizations. The same GOTV message was used for all ethnic groups: "Voting empowers our communities and is easy." Mailers included general information about the candidates and the measures on the ballot, the voter's polling place, and the right of decline-to-state voters to request partisan ballots. Translations of the mailers were provided by the relevant partner organizations, and the photographs were tailored for each national-origin group.

As we saw in chapter 2, APALC's mailers had weak effects on voter turnout, but its phone-banking efforts were more successful. With the exception of Vietnamese Americans, turnout was higher in the treatment groups than in the control groups. Combining all national-origin groups and doing a 2SLS analysis reveals that turnout among those who received a phone call was 2.7 percentage points higher than in the control group. Given the population's base voting rate of 8.3 percent, this is actually a substantial effect. To raise a group's turnout from 8.3 percent to 11 percent represents a 32 percent relative gain in votes.

Not only is the June 2006 APALC effort notable for its overall success, marking it as the first GOTV campaign targeting Asian Americans to have had a statistically significant effect on turnout, it is also notable for its use of multilingual canvassers. APALC partnered with a number of local organizations serving Asian Americans, giving it access to a cadre of volunteers with a variety of language skills. The phone bank scripts were available in English, Cantonese, Japanese, Korean, Mandarin, Tagalog, and Vietnamese. Each caller received a packet with the English version and a translated copy according to his or her language ability. While Janelle Wong (2005) demonstrated that such a multilingual campaign could be organized, her effort failed to move significant numbers of Asian American voters to the polls. In contrast, we estimate the effect of contact by an APALC canvasser at a statistically significant 2.7 percentage points (SE = 1.5) for the pooled results in June 2006 (Table 3.1).[5] This was the first GOTV campaign to successfully increase turnout while using three or more languages, a feat accomplished by hiring a pool of canvassers with a variety of language abilities, sorting the list of targeted voters by surname to match voters to canvassers, and allowing canvassers to update the database during their shifts to indicate language mismatches. In

Table 3.1. Meta-analysis of APALC's Phone Bank Experiments, June and November 2006

Election	N	Pooled Treatment-on-Treated Effect (SE)[a]
Pooled: 6 experiments, June 2006	36,479	2.7* (1.5)
Pooled: 7 experiments, November 2006	26,305	3.4* (1.7)

Note: Individuals targeted to receive direct mail but no telephone call are excluded; mail experiment results are presented in chapter 2.
[a] Robust cluster standard errors are by household.
* $p < .05$, one-tailed

subsequent iterations, APALC added additional national-origin groups and languages to its campaigns, using similar methodologies.

For the November 2006 election, APALC made several changes to its phone bank campaign. Prior to the November 2006 election, APALC and its partner organizations held seven focus groups to help refine its GOTV messaging. Using this feedback, APALC decided to compare the effects of two messages for each ethnic group (except Japanese and Vietnamese American voters, for whom only the universal message was used).[6] Call scripts featured either the universal message—basically, "Voting empowers our community"—or an alternate message that was specific to each ethnic group. Voters in each ethnic group (except for those of Japanese and Vietnamese origin) were divided into either a universal treatment group or an alternate treatment group, and members of each group were called using the respective script. Callers also informed interested voters about their polling location and gave them other Election Day information, such as polling-place hours and the availability of translated materials. Scripts included national-origin-specific hotline numbers that voters could call for assistance. Additionally, the scripts listed common reasons for not voting that individuals might give (e.g., voting is inconvenient), followed by appropriate caller responses.

The targeted population for the November campaign consisted of registered voters who had Asian surnames, were low-propensity voters, and resided in geographic areas with large numbers of Asian American voters. The resulting subset of the voter registration list of 132,563 voters was sent to a commercial vendor to identify individuals with valid mailing addresses and phone numbers. This procedure yielded 26,305 voters for assignment to treatment and control groups. As in June, targeted voters were selected randomly to receive a phone call, a mailer, or both. National-origin groups again were randomized separately. Phone canvassers made calls in nine languages and dialects, including English, Khmer, Mandarin, Cantonese, Hindi, Tagalog, Japanese, Korean, and Vietnamese. In-language mailers were sent to targeted Chinese, Korean, and Vietnamese American voters. The phone bank ran almost daily from October 18 until November 6, 2006, at APALC's office in downtown Los Angeles. The hours of phone banking were 5:00 to 9:00 p.m. on weekdays and 1:00 to 5:00 p.m. on weekends.

By and large, the effects of the campaign were positive. Pooled results indicate that the phone bank produced a statistically significant increase in turnout of 3.4 percentage points (SE = 1.7), the strongest effect that had been found to date for a single-contact phone-bank effort targeting Asian American voters (see Table 3.1). The mailing of *Easy Voter Guides*, as detailed in chapter 2, did not have a significant effect. Because initial analyses showed the two scripts to be equally effective, here we combine them, making a single treatment group. The results are in keeping with several previous phone banking experiments that have found negligible differences in the effectiveness of ethnic versus universalistic nonpartisan appeals; other script variations have also been found to not produce measurable differences in effectiveness (Michelson, García Bedolla, and Green 2007; Green and Gerber 2008).

Joining the group of organizations participating in CVI experiments for November 2006 was OCAPICA. OCAPICA had worked for more than a decade to improve opportunities and outcomes for low-income Asian and Pacific Americans in Orange County by offering programs on youth development, education, community health, and economic development. Although OCAPICA had long been active in political issues of concern to the Asian Pacific American community, the organization directly mobilized voters for the first time in fall 2006.

In the weeks prior to the November 2006 election, OCAPICA conducted a phone-based voter mobilization campaign designed to encourage participation by members of the Asian American community living in Orange County. Canvassers included eleven Vietnamese Americans, four Chinese Americans (Mandarin speakers), and five Korean Americans, all of whom were fully bilingual. One of the Korean volunteers was a prominent community leader whose voice was often recognized by contacted voters.[7]

The campaign targeted registered voters of Chinese, Korean, or Vietnamese ancestry. The outreach campaign consisted of *Easy Voter Guides* and/or phone calls from the group's local phone bank. For each ancestry group, households were divided between those likely to be predominantly English-speaking and those that were not, using the same criteria that APALC used. This distinction created six ancestry-by-language combinations. Chinese American registered voters were sent *Easy Voter Guides* in either English or Chinese translation and were called in either English or Mandarin. Korean American registered voters were sent *Easy Voter Guides* in either English or Korean translation and called in English or Korean. Vietnamese American registered voters were sent *Easy Voter Guides* in either English or Vietnamese translation and called in English or Vietnamese.

OCAPICA's callers encouraged individuals to take an interest in the issues surrounding the November election, provided polling-place locations and hours, and attempted to reply to common reasons for not voting. Contact rates for the phone-calling campaign varied by national origin and by language within each national-origin group and were generally higher for English-speakers. Overall, the effects of OCAPICA's phone bank campaign were positive. Pooling across all groups generated a statistically significant treatment-on-treated phone contact effect of 2.8 percentage points (SE = 1.9) (Table 3.2), again in line with what would be expected from a good-quality phone-bank campaign.

Latino Phone Bank Mobilization: NALEO

NALEO has worked since 1981 to increase the political empowerment of Latinos in California and nationwide. In the weeks prior to the June 2006 elections, NALEO conducted a phone-based voter mobilization campaign designed to encourage participation by Latino registered voters living in the counties of Fresno, Los Angeles, Orange, Riverside,

Table 3.2. Meta-analysis of OCAPICA's Phone Bank Experiments, November 2006

Election	N	Pooled Treatment-on-Treated Effect (SE)[a]
Pooled: 6 experiments, November 2006	22,771	2.8† (1.9)

Note: Individuals targeted to receive direct mail but no telephone call are excluded; mail experiment results are presented in chapter 2.

[a] Robust cluster standard errors are by household.

† $p < .10$, one-tailed

and San Bernardino. For its phone-banking efforts, NALEO partnered with three local community organizations to contact treatment groups totaling 68,941 individuals. The targeted pool included Latino voters who were young (aged eighteen to twenty-four), had registered to vote since the last major statewide election, or who had participated in only one or none of the previous four statewide elections. Partner organizations included El Consejo de Federaciones Mexicanas en Norte America (in Southeast Los Angeles), El Concilio de Fresno (in Fresno), and Latino Health Access (in Santa Ana, in Orange County). The vast majority of calls to voters in Los Angeles and all calls to the Inland Empire were made from NALEO's home offices in Los Angeles. Phone banking began on Saturday, May 20, and continued through Monday, June 5.[8] Unfortunately, NALEO's contact rates were quite low in this campaign, ranging from a low of 9.2 percent in Fresno County to a high of 12.4 percent in Los Angeles County. The effect of that contact was 2.1 percentage points, but since the standard error was quite high (2.4 percentage points), it is unlikely that this campaign increased turnout (Table 3.3).[9]

NALEO adjusted its approach in November 2006. One of the innovations they instituted in November was cleaning their list to cull nonworking numbers before starting their phone banking. This was accomplished in part through outsourcing to data vendors and updating the organization's lists using outcome information from the June 2006 canvassing effort. Live calls were made to the resulting list of working numbers, making canvassers more efficient in encouraging voter participation. Calls were

Table 3.3. Meta-analysis of NALEO Phone Bank Experiments, June and November 2006

Election	N	Pooled Treatment-on-Treated Effect (SE)[a]
Pooled: 5 experiments, June 2006	68,941	2.1 (2.4)
Pooled: 5 experiments, November 2006	44,406	0.7 (1.5)

[a] None of the TOT estimates reach traditional levels of statistical significance. Robust cluster standard errors are by household.

generated from three different locations. Calls to voters in Fresno were made out of the phone bank operation established by NALEO and managed by El Concilio de Fresno. In Orange County, calls were made from the Latino Health Access (LHA) offices. The remaining targeted counties (Los Angeles, Riverside, and San Bernardino) were contacted from NALEO's centralized phone bank in Los Angeles.[10] Callers included forty volunteers in Los Angeles, ten in Fresno, and fifteen in Santa Ana. Canvassers were trained in Los Angeles by NALEO staff and in the partner organization offices by El Concilio and LHA staff (who had been trained previously by NALEO staff). The phone bank operated from October 20 to November 5.

A total of 8,831 targeted individuals was contacted by phone, representing 27 percent of the treatment group. NALEO's callers reminded voters of the upcoming election and noted the impact of elections on voters and their families, including issues of jobs, education, healthcare, and immigration. Voters were asked to verbally pledge to vote and, regardless of the response, were encouraged to call the group's toll-free number with any questions about voting or the election. The contact rate ranged from 41 percent in Fresno County to 20 percent in San Bernardino; these contact rates are more than double the corresponding rates in June 2006, which we attribute to two changes in NALEO's strategy. First, as noted above, the numbers were screened more carefully prior to launching the phone bank, to reduce the number of nonworking or fax numbers included in the voter lists. Second, contact was attempted twice with targeted voters, rather than only once. The resulting strong increase in contact rates suggests that prescreening is an effective and inexpensive means by which to improve the efficiency of a live phone bank effort. In this case, pooling NALEO's results across five county-level experiments generates an average treatment effect of 0.7 percentage points (SE = 1.5), a negligible impact on turnout.

One hypothesis coming out of our November 2006 analysis of the NALEO campaign was that the scripts they were using were making their phone banks less effective. The scripts were fairly short, consisting of a brief reminder that Election Day was approaching and a request for a commitment from voters to participate. Yet an experiment conducted in November 2004 in North Carolina and Missouri suggested that longer, more interactive scripts might be more effective than the usual shorter scripts (Ha and Karlan 2009). NALEO's March 2007 phone banking campaign was designed to test this hypothesis; the organization conducted a live phone banking campaign for the Los Angeles municipal election with two different scripts. One script, mirroring that used in previous campaigns, was relatively short, reminding voters of the upcoming election and encouraging participation. The second script provided more content, aiming to also educate voters about the candidates and issues on the ballot, and provided for more interaction between the canvasser and the voter. Registered voters in single- and multivoter households were randomized separately, and the treatment groups were further subdivided into two random groups, one for each type of script. Overall, 5,535 voters were assigned for treatment in this campaign.

This experiment by NALEO was markedly more successful than previous experiments. Contact rates were significantly higher: 45.3 percent for the informational message group and 41.0 percent for the basic message group. Unfortunately, these different contact rates (having a difference of 4.3 percentage points) preclude a direct comparison of the effectiveness of the two scripts. The data, however, suggest, if not conclusively, that the longer, more informative scripts worked no better in mobilizing targeted voters: In single-voter households, turnout in the control group was 14.4 percent, compared to 16.6 percent for those targeted to receive the informational message and 16.8 percent for those targeted to receive the basic message. In multivoter households, turnout in the control group was 19.3 percent, compared to 22.5 percent for those targeted to receive the informational message and 20.7 percent for those targeted to receive the basic message.[11] That the different effects generated by the two scripts are not more significant supports our contention that it is not the informational content of GOTV messages that is important but rather the sociocultural and interactive aspects of live conversations with canvassers. Because both simple and informative NALEO scripts in March 2007 were delivered in the same manner, they had similar effects. Whether considered separately or after pooling the two script experiments together, we found that the campaign had no measurable impact on targeted voter turnout.

Overall, these one-call strategies show that traditional live phone banks can effectively mobilize low-propensity voters in communities of color, but are not always effective, given the variation in results we found across organizations and across elections.

Two-Call Campaigns

Latino Voters: SVREP and NALEO

Perhaps the most striking experimental findings to emerge from the November 2006 CVI studies came from SVREP, a group that has mobilized Latino voters in Los Angeles County for decades. Voters in SVREP's pool included Latino-surname voters who had registered after August 1, 2004, or had not voted in any primary or general election since 1998. The study was limited geographically to five city council districts in Los Angeles that were heavily Latino (with average Latino populations of 48 percent). Approximately half of the targeted voters were aged twenty-five or younger.

The GOTV campaign had three components: two mailings introducing targeted voters to the GOTV campaign, calls from a local phone bank, and a small door-to-door canvassing effort.[12] Since phone banking was the campaign's centerpiece, our analysis here focuses on only those precincts where no door-to-door canvassing occurred. The mailings, which were sent approximately three weeks before Election Day and then just before Election Day, included an inspirational message from the head of SVREP, Antonio González, about the salience of the issues on the ballot for Latino voters. After randomization and after excluding the approximately 4 percent of the sample who had moved or dropped off the voter registration lists by the time of voting in 2006, the remaining control group comprised 6,350 individuals, and the treatment group, 19,512.[13] Phone canvassing was conducted in the three weeks prior to the election, with up to six attempts made to contact each individual on the treatment list. The contact rate was 23.5 percent. Callers asked contacted voters whether they intended to vote; those who responded affirmatively were contacted a second time the day before the election and reminded to vote. When possible, SVREP tried to have the same caller who had contacted the voter in the first round make the second contact. As time allowed, some voters were contacted an additional time after the initial and reminder calls.[14]

The effects of this strategy were impressive: the treatment-on-treated effect of phone calls was 9.3 percentage points (SE = 3.2) (Table 3.4). Whether viewed in comparison to the results presented above or in comparison to other recent experimental studies of phone banking, this was the strongest effect found for live phone calls in a study with a large number of observations. Later replications of the tactic by other CVI groups, as detailed below, produced even stronger effects, further endorsing the power of the two-call strategy.

In the February 2008 presidential primary campaign, NALEO conducted phone bank experiments in four counties: Kern, Los Angeles,

Table 3.4. Meta-analysis of SVREP and NALEO Two-Call Phone Bank Experiments, November 2006 and February 2008

Organization and Election	N	Pooled Treatment-on-Treated Effect (SE)[a]
SVREP, November 2006[b]	25,862	9.3** (3.2)
NALEO, pooled: 4 experiments, February 2008	50,750	7.0* (3.6)

[a] Robust cluster standard errors are by household.
[b] SVREP analysis excludes households targeted for its door-to-door canvassing effort.
* $p < .05$, ** $p < .01$, one-tailed

Riverside, and San Bernardino. The phone bank was staffed during the fourteen days before Election Day. NALEO canvassers successfully contacted 10,630 registered voters. As with previous campaigns, NALEO focused its efforts on young voters, newly registered voters, low-propensity voters, and non-voters. In this two-call effort, NALEO called back all voters contacted in the first round, not just "yes" voters (those who said they planned to vote).

In Kern County, NALEO staff trained local affiliates on how to conduct phone bank caller training. In Riverside and San Bernardino Counties, NALEO staff traveled to the offices of local affiliates and conducted the caller training themselves. In Los Angeles, NALEO's home base, NALEO staff not only conducted the same training as in the other counties but also conducted refresher training before each day of canvassing and made on-the-spot suggestions to canvassers as the phone banking was conducted. The quality of the training and supervision was therefore highest for the Los Angeles office. This difference in quality was reflected in the results. Overall, NALEO's efforts in February 2008 increased turnout by 7.0 percentage points (SE = 3.6) (see Table 3.4). In Los Angeles, this figure increased to 12.3 percentage points (SE = 4.7). Effects were smaller in Riverside and San Bernardino and weakest in Kern County (see appendix A). Further discussion of the value of ongoing supervision in phone banks is detailed in chapter 5.

Calling Back Asian American Voters: OCAPICA and APALC

For the June 2008 election, OCAPICA adopted the two-call strategy used by SVREP, targeting voters who self-identified as likely voters during the first call to receive a follow-up call closer to Election Day.[15] The initial pool of 33,405 individuals was randomized to include telephone calls to 6,285 individuals, all of whom also received mailed *Easy Voter Guides*. Later analysis resulted in 399 individuals being dropped from the file because they had of out-of-state addresses or because a telephone number was not available, for a final total pool of 29,763 individuals.[16] Three rounds of calls were made to the initial phone treatment list, resulting in 1,633 contacts with targeted individuals (a contact rate of 26.3 percent). Of those contacted in the first round, 70.4 percent (N = 1,149) said that they planned to vote, and an additional 4 percent said that they had already voted. Only 7 percent of individuals contacted said that they did not plan to vote.[17] After OCAPICA dropped 20 individuals from the "yes" group (those who turned out to be either not eligible voters or not Asian American), a second round of calls was made to the remaining 1,129 self-identified likely voters. Overall, 479 secondary contacts were made with "yes" voters, for a contact rate of 42.4 percent.[18]

Across all the national-origin groups, turnout was higher in the treatment group than in the control group, ranging from a low intent-to-treat effect of 1.9 percentage points for South Asian Americans to a high intent-to-treat effect of 4.4 percentage points for Korean Americans. Pooling across ethnic groups, the effect of treatment was a statistically significant and substantively large 11.1 percentage points (SE = 2.1) (Table 3.5).[19] This pooled result was much stronger than that previously achieved by OCAPICA using a one-call strategy. The jump from a treatment effect of 2.8 percentage points in November 2006 to a treatment effect of 11.1 percentage points in June 2008 strongly suggests that follow-up calls to self-identified likely voters significantly increased the power of the phone bank campaign. Another possibility is that OCAPICA's phone bank calling was qualitatively stronger in the second election, the result perhaps of increased experience. Given the earlier SVREP results, we believe this alternative explanation to be unlikely.

The SVREP, NALEO, and OCAPICA treatment effect estimates are for the overall campaigns; each estimate is best understood as the effect of one or more contacts. Estimating the power of the follow-up calls in particular required a second round of randomization, with only some self-identified likely voters targeted to receive reminder calls. This was

Table 3.5. Meta-analysis of OCAPICA Phone Bank Experiments, June 2008

	N	Pooled Treatment-on-Treated Effect (SE)[a]
Pooled: 5 experiments	29,763	11.1** (2.1)

[a] Robust cluster standard errors are by household.

** $p < .01$

precisely the strategy used by APALC for its June 2008 effort. For the June 2008 campaign, APALC introduced a randomized round of follow-up calls. Individuals who made a commitment to vote during the first contact were either randomly assigned to receive a follow-up call just before Election Day or were assigned to the control group. APALC's June 2008 experiments included six national-origin groups: South Asian, Chinese, Filipino, Japanese, Korean, and Vietnamese Americans. Of the pool of 28,388 individuals, 12,000 were randomly assigned to receive a phone call and a mailed English-language *Easy Voter Guide*. Chinese, Korean, and Vietnamese American voters also received *Easy Voter Guides* in their native languages.

Contact rates for each national-origin group ranged from 17.6 percent to 36.2 percent. When contacted during the first round, individuals were asked whether or not they intended to vote. "Yes" voters were randomly divided into treatment and control groups to be targeted for a second call. Of the 3,758 individuals contacted in the first round, 74 percent (N = 2,777) indicated that they planned to vote, and an additional 2.6 percent said that they had already voted. Only 5.6 percent of individuals said that they did not plan to vote. For the second round of calls, APALC conducted an experiment focused on the 1,901 self-identified likely voters who had indicated that they planned to vote at the polls and not by absentee ballot. The second randomization assigned 1,501 "yes" voters to receive a follow-up call and 400 "yes" voters to be in the control group. Of those assigned to receive a reminder call, 44.3 percent were successfully contacted.

The follow-up calls had a powerful intent-to-treat effect of 5.5 percentage points. A 2SLS analysis generates an estimated treatment-on-treated effect of 13.0 percentage points (SE = 4.9). To parse out which new votes were generated by the first call and which by the second call, we make the following calculations. First, we calculated the net vote gain for the entirety of the calling campaign, which suggested an overall marginal vote gain of 235 votes, with 152 created during the first round and 83 created during the second round.[20] Second, we divided 152 by the number of total contacts in the first round (3,758), generating a first-round effect on those contacted of 4.0 percentage points. This figure is in line with APALC's one-call treatment effects from the 2006 CVI experiments

Table 3.6. Meta-analysis of APALC Phone Bank Experiments, June 2008

	Pooled Treatment-on-Treated Effect, first call	Pooled Treatment-on-Treated Effect, second call (SE)[a]
Pooled: 6 experiments	4.0	13.0* (4.9)

Note: N = 28,388 for first call, N = 1,901 for second call.
[a] Robust cluster standard errors are by household.
* $p < .05$, one-tailed

and well within the expected range for a well-conducted phone bank campaign. The second-round treatment effect of 13.0 percentage points, by comparison, is extremely large and explains why the other two-round calling campaigns (by SVREP, NALEO, and OCAPICA) were so successful (Table 3.6).

The effectiveness of the two-call strategy is an excellent example of how narrative structures, combined with normative understandings of what it means to be a good citizen, combine to influence an individual's cognitive schemas. That so few of these low-propensity voters said they did not plan to vote (8 percent for NALEO, 7 percent for OCAPICA, and fewer than 6 percent for APALC) shows that these voters knew that stating an intention to vote was the socially desirable answer to give. Knowing the answer probably primed these individuals to consider identifying themselves cognitively as voters. The second call served to reinforce this self-understanding, making it much more likely that they would follow through on the initial commitment. Given the experiments involved low-propensity Asian American and Latino voters, it is reasonable to assume that some cognitive movement is necessary for them to reconceptualize themselves as voters. The callback model, because it plays on normative understandings of civic duty within a narrative frame, is effective precisely because of the cognitive impact it has on voters' schemas and resulting self-identifications.

Voter turnout spiked in November 2008 for the historic contest between Democrat Barack Obama and Republican John McCain. While the election was not particularly competitive in California, with Obama ahead by comfortable margins throughout the campaign, turnout was boosted by the desire of voters to be part of the election of the first black president (or, potentially, the first female vice president), and there were several controversial measures on the ballot as well, including an initiative proposing parental notification for abortions for minors and a state constitutional amendment prohibiting gay marriage. Turnout statewide was 59 percent, substantially higher than in the previous elections in which CVI groups conducted GOTV experiments. Given the unique political context of this general election, it is not surprising the CVI results for these campaigns were more modest than in the previous elections.

As a point of comparison, the June 2006 turnout in some of the communities that CVI groups targeted was less than 20 percent; the November 2008 turnout in the same communities ranged from 60 to 90 percent. The high turnout shows that many potential voters, including the low-propensity voters targeted by CVI efforts, were motivated to vote even without contact. Here we see the important role that social context, and particularly electoral context, plays in voter mobilization. Simply put, excitement about the Barack Obama–John McCain contest was so high that "on the cusp" voters— individuals normally moved by these community-based mobilization efforts—were mobilized by that context to vote in the election, whether or not they were assigned to CVI treatment groups. There were simply fewer undecided voters available for these organizations to move to the polls, which muted the variance between control groups and treatment groups. Nevertheless, two phone bank campaigns did produce statistically significant increases in turnout, a testament to the effectiveness of particular strategies for moving low-propensity voters to the polls, even within a historic, extremely high-salience electoral context.

In November 2008, APALC again targeted low-propensity Asian American voters in Los Angeles, including those with South Asian, Chinese, Filipino, Japanese, Korean, and Vietnamese backgrounds. The campaign included phone banking with bilingual canvassers in a variety of languages, as well as mailed English and in-language *Easy Voter Guides.* Contact rates for the first round of calls ranged from a low of 17.2 percent to a high of 31.8 percent. This first round yielded 3,047 self-identified likely ("yes") voters, including 882 absentee voters (28.9 percent) and 2,165 polling-place voters (70.1 percent). As in the June 2008 election, a second round of calls attempted to recontact these "yes" voters; 38.7 percent was successfully contacted among likely absentee voters, 43.5 percent among likely polling-place voters.[21]

Among the six targeted national-origin subgroups, the largest treatment-on-treated estimates were found among South Asian and Chinese Americans. For South Asian Americans, the treatment effect was an astounding 18.9 percentage points (SE = 9.8); the treatment effect for Chinese Americans was 5.5 percentage points (SE = 3.1). The standard errors for the remaining four subgroup experiments were quite high, generating uncertain results. Pooling across all six groups generates a statistically significant treatment effect of 5.3 percentage points (SE = 2.4) (Table 3.7).[22]

Given that the presidential campaign was competitive and highly partisan, we thought it appropriate to examine the role that partisanship might have played in voter responsiveness to the mobilization effort.[23] Further analysis shows that the effect was stronger among permanent absentee voters (PAVs) and among those registered as Democrats and as decline-to-state voters (as opposed to those registered as Republicans). The pooled effect for PAVs is 14.3 percentage points (SE = 4.7); for Democrats, 9.3 percentage points (SE = 4.2); and for decline-to-state voters, 6.4 percentage points (SE = 3.7). All of these effects are statistically significant. The treatment effects for non-PAVs and Republicans are smaller and with higher standard errors. Given the atypical electoral environment created by this historic Obama-McCain contest, APALC's overall effect of 5.3 percentage points speaks to the effectiveness of the two-call strategy for phone banking.

For the November 2008 election, OCAPICA conducted experiments among registered voters of South Asian, Chinese, Filipino, Korean, and

Table 3.7. Meta-analysis of APALC Phone Bank Experiments, November 2008

	N	Pooled Treatment-on-Treated Effect (SE)[a]
Pooled: 6 experiments	26,448	5.3*
		(2.4)

[a] Robust cluster standard errors are by household.

* $p < .05$, one-tailed

Vietnamese ancestry. The experiments mirrored those conducted for the June 2008 election, with the addition of a small text-messaging component. Contact rates varied among national-origin groups from a low of 16.9 percent among Filipino Americans to a high of 33.7 percent among Korean Americans. Follow-up calls and/or text messages were made to 1,202 "yes" voters, including 573 absentee voters (47.7 percent) and 629 polling place voters (52.3 percent). Of "yes" absentee voters, 42.1 percent was successfully contacted with a follow-up call; of "yes" polling-place voters, 38 percent was successfully contacted with a follow-up call. OCAPICA also sent reminder text messages to "yes" voters who agreed to receive such messages. Of twenty text messages sent, eight overlapped with successful follow-up calls.[24]

Looking at OCAPICA's results for November 2008 overall, we see that both the intent-to-treat and treatment-on-treated estimates are negligible across all national-origin groups.[25] We thought that perhaps the electoral context—the experiment was conducted in a strongly Republican area during a presidential campaign which the Democrat was highly likely to win—may have muted the effects of OCAPICA's mobilization work. When we analyze the results by party registration, we find that the mobilization effect was stronger among those registered as decline-to-state voters than among those registered with a political party. Among those registered as decline-to-state, the effect is a statistically significant 7.0 (SE = 4.2); the effects for registered Democrats and Republicans are smaller with higher standard errors, indicating no significant effects. These findings have to be interpreted cautiously, given that we did not randomize the lists by party registration. We found no differences in OCAPICA's effectiveness when looking separately at its campaign's effect on permanent and non-permanent absentee voters. As we found with most groups in November 2008, turnout rates among the control groups were quite high, suggesting a dearth of on-the-cusp voters available for mobilization by OCAPICA.

Latino Voters in November 2008

For the November 2008 election, NALEO conducted experiments in the counties of Kern, Fresno, Riverside, San Bernardino, Orange, and Los Angeles. The experiment in Los Angeles County included

Table 3.8. Meta-analysis of NALEO Phone Bank Experiments, November 2008

	N	Pooled Treatment-on-Treated Effect (SE)[a]
Pooled: 6 experiments	129,306	−1.2 (2.2)

[a] The pooled TOT coefficient does not reach traditional levels of statistical significance. Robust cluster standard errors are by household.

an embedded script experiment that exposed contacted voters to either an "optimistic" script or a "pessimistic" script. Follow-up calls to "yes" voters were made immediately before the election. Contact rates varied from 11.8 to 45.3 percent. The experiments generally generated negligible effects on turnout, with large standard errors, suggesting that overall the campaign failed to move significant numbers of voters to the polls (Table 3.8).

The story is quite different in Fresno County. There, NALEO's campaign generated an intent-to-treat effect of 1.9 percentage points and a statistically significant treatment-on-treated effect of 11.0 percentage points (SE = 5.8). What explains the difference in effectiveness of the Fresno campaign? Because NALEO was delayed in getting the Fresno phone bank operational, the calls were generally made later and thus closer to Election Day; this raises the possibility that timing of contact influenced the results. Because the date of contact was not assigned randomly, we are unable to generate a valid estimate of the effect of contact date as a predictor of turnout. However, the descriptive data is suggestive. In Fresno County, 73.4 percent of first-round contacts were made during the week before the election; in other counties, most first-round contacts were made several weeks earlier. Previous field experiments targeting the general population have shown that contacts made during the last week of a campaign are more effective than those made earlier; the Fresno results are consistent with that general finding and suggest strongly that this may be why the NALEO effort in Fresno was more successful than other efforts (Nickerson 2007; Green and Gerber 2008).

Congregation-Led Organizing and Social Networks: PICO and Its Affiliates

During the weeks leading up to the November 2006 election, PICO affiliates launched a number of local phone banks.[26] Many of these were small in size but well executed, as illustrated by the high contact rates achieved. Contact rates for the phone campaigns ranged from a high of 47.3 percent to a low of 17 percent. In Colusa, Arbuckle, and Williams, three small towns in the northern Sacramento Valley, many of the volunteers were recent graduates of citizenship classes conducted by the local PICO affiliate, the North Valley Sponsoring Committee (NVSC). Callers included seven volunteers in Colusa, six volunteers in Arbuckle, and six volunteers in Williams. Phone banking in the city of Los Angeles was conducted by various Catholic Church affiliates, mostly by bilingual (Spanish and English) youth. The average treatment-on-treated effect of phone calls, pooled across sites, was −1.0 points (SE = 2.7) (Table 3.9).

For the February 2008 election, PICO affiliates conducted a few one-call phone banks. In San Bernardino, youth volunteers from local high schools targeted young voters aged eighteen to twenty-nine in low-propensity neighborhoods. In Stockton, People and Congregations Together (PACT) leaders called Hmong-surname voters, reminding them to vote and inviting them to two voting workshops organized by PACT

Table 3.9. Meta-analysis of PICO Phone Bank Experiments, 2006 and 2008

Election	N	Pooled Treatment-on-Treated Effect (SE)[a]
Pooled: 11 experiments, November 2006	13,926	−1.0 (2.7)
Pooled: 6 experiments, 2008[b]	11,025	−1.9 (3.0)

[a] None of the TOT coefficient estimates reach traditional levels of statistical significance. Robust cluster standard errors are by household.

[b] PICO conducted seven phone bank experiments in 2008; only six are included here. The remaining effort was randomized at the precinct level and thus a reliable TOT estimate cannot be calculated.

and the Hmong Leadership Network. Neither of the two efforts produced measurable impacts on turnout.[27]

PICO affiliates organized two one-call phone banks for the June 2008 election, including one in Orange County that was randomized at the precinct level and one in San Bernardino County that was randomized at the household level. In Orange County, the Orange County Congregation Community Organization (OCCCO) used a phone campaign to target infrequent voters in Santa Ana the weekend before the June election to ask them to vote. In San Bernardino, Inland Congregations United for Change (ICUC) worked with four congregations and eight high schools the two weekends before the election to make calls to infrequent voters. Neither of these efforts yielded measurable increases in voter participation.

PICO conducted three one-call phone bank experiments in November 2008, one targeting Hmong voters in Stockton and two targeting voters in the city of Los Angeles. Overall, these campaigns generated a nonsignificant treatment effect of 6.0 percentage points (SE = 6.7). As was true for many other experiments in the hotly contested November 2008 election, turnout in the control groups was so high that it minimized the ability of even well-conducted campaigns to move more voters to the polls than were already planning to go.

Given that PICO is engaging in live contacts with these phone banks and that PICO affiliates fielded many dedicated and committed canvassers, it may seem odd that the efforts were not more effective. Closer inspection of the details of these campaigns helps to clarify why PICO was unable to match the stronger effect sizes realized by other CVI groups. First, as we mention, the size of these experiments made it difficult for the results to have any statistical power, given the large error terms. Second, few of the PICO affiliates had the resources to conduct their phone banks in one central location, as APALC, NALEO, OCAPICA, and SVREP did. In some cases, calls were made from multiple locations; in other campaigns canvassers were asked to use their cell phones to make calls from their own homes. These structural constraints made it more difficult for PICO organizers to supervise their canvassers, making deviations from the message more likely and potentially decreasing the effectiveness of that sociocultural interaction. With these campaigns, it is possible, too, that PICO was not playing to its main organizational strength: the strong social networks that exist within each of its partner congregations.

In other phone banking experiments, PICO affiliates designed their efforts to take advantage of that organizational strength by testing the role that social networks can play in voter mobilization. In February 2008, a Long Beach affiliate congregation, St. Lucy's, generated a list of potential targeted voters who had voted in fewer than two of the previous statewide primary elections; from that list, volunteer callers identified five friends from the congregation and were assigned also to call five fellow congregants whom they did not know personally and five individuals from the neighborhood who were strangers. The script for the calls was:

> Hello my name is _____. I am a member of St. Lucy's Catholic Church. I am calling you to encourage you to vote on Tuesday Feb. 5th in the presidential primary. After masses on Sunday January 27th and Feb. 3rd the St. Lucy ICO [Interfaith Community Organization] organizing committee will have summaries available on the candidates' positions on housing, environment, immigration, youth and health. These could help you make up your mind on who to support for president. Do you plan to vote in the Presidential primary? Do you want a reminder call? Thanks for your time.

Observed increases in turnout were largest for friends, smaller for fellow congregants, and smaller still for strangers.[28] However, because we do not know the social network status for individuals in the control group (i.e., whether they were friends or fellow congregants of the volunteers), the statistical results are not as robust as we would like.

On the other hand, the results are consistent with those found for the door-to-door SCOPE campaigns we discuss in chapter 4; there, canvassers from the same precinct or ZIP code were more effective in getting out the vote than were individuals from other neighborhoods, suggesting social networks are a powerful GOTV tool. The quality of the sociocultural interaction is likely to be affected by whether the canvasser is part of the targeted voter's social network. When individuals are known to one another, attention to the message is likely to be greater. The canvasser and the target are also more likely to be similarly situated in terms of social position, making them better able to communicate and making the narrative of the conversation more tailored to the participants. And, finally, the cognitive need to follow through on behaving like a "good citizen" is likely to be greater when individuals know that they will probably see the canvasser again and potentially have to report on whether or not they voted.

In June 2008, the Long Beach ICO again conducted a phone canvassing campaign with an embedded social networking experiment. Group leaders were asked to provide lists of twenty friends; these individual lists were then randomized into treatment and control groups. Canvassers encouraged contacted voters to vote and asked if they needed nonpartisan election information; most targeted voters were Latino or Filipino in ethnoracial origin. Canvassers were also assigned to contact other members of the congregation. Targeted members of the same congregation were 0.8 percentage points more likely to vote than were individuals in the control group, while targeted friends were 2.4 percentage points more likely to vote. Though falling short of statistical significance, these results contribute to the growing body of evidence about the power of social networks to increase GOTV treatment effects (see Nickerson 2011).

PICO's phone banking results remind us of the organizational capacity necessary to organize and carry out a large-scale live phone banking campaign. PICO's affiliates varied significantly in terms of the resources and institutional capacity they could commit to this work. As a result, their impact was highly varied as well. The PICO social networking experiments suggest that organizations should design their mobilization strategies with their own organizational strengths in mind. PICO's access to strong social networks within their congregations was an existing resource for their organization, one its affiliates were able to tap into to mobilize voters. By designing its voter work to complement existing organizational resources, these PICO affiliates were able to increase their effectiveness in getting out the vote. The phone banking results from all these organizations show that it is not only the targeted voter who is an important variable in this sociocultural interaction. The institutional and organizational context matters as well. Not all tactics are appropriate for all organizations, just as not all approaches will be well received by all voters. To be most effective, organizations need to tailor their efforts to maximize their existing resources, strengths, and capacities.

Conclusion

We found that the phone bank campaigns conducted under the auspices of the CVI were a powerful tool for moving certain low-propensity voters to the polls. Not only were many of the campaigns remarkably successful, but they also pushed the envelope in terms of what sorts of phone banking efforts are considered possible within ethnoracial immigrant communities, particularly in terms of running a phone bank that includes multiple target languages. While the most powerful single CVI experiment was a door-to-door campaign (that of CCAEJ in June 2006, discussed in chapter 4), we find that phone bank campaigns using the tactic of making follow-up calls to self-identified likely voters were more consistently effective than door-to-door efforts, as well as easier to conduct and more cost-effective. This is illustrated by the results from November 2008, when all but one of the door-to-door experiments failed to show statistically significant impacts on turnout, while two of the two-call phone banks, including the multilingual APALC effort, had strong effects.

The most important and powerful result from the analysis of these phone bank efforts is the power of the two-round phone bank technique and its effectiveness across low-propensity ethnoracial voters from different social groups. During the first round of calls, conducted a few weeks before the election, targeted voters were asked if they intended to vote. Those that said that they planned to participate were targeted to receive a second call just before the election. NALEO, on the other hand, called back all previously contacted voters, regardless of whether that earlier conversation had ended with a commitment to vote. As noted above, the percentage of voters who declined to make such a commitment was very small across all the experiments. Even when that second call did not remind voters of their earlier commitment, our analysis shows that self-identified likely voters still were strongly motivated to go to the polls. The finding is consistent across different types of elections and for both

Latino and Asian American voters, and the estimated effects were much more powerful than those usually generated by a door-to-door campaign. Thus, our results indicate that the conventional wisdom that door-to-door canvassing is the most desirable method of moving voters to the polls does not hold true under all circumstances or for all groups of voters.

We demonstrate in the next chapter that the findings from the CVI phone banks are also much more consistent than those for door-to-door canvassing, both across canvassing organizations and across elections. This relative consistency in result, we argue, is due to their greater consistency in terms of narrative message. In general, the GOTV conversations we report on in this chapter were brief. Even when the scripts for a phone bank did not include what would traditionally be called helpful information—for example, polling-place locations, hours of voting, explanations of ballot measures—contacted individuals were much more likely to vote after speaking with a CVI canvasser than were individuals who were not contacted. In addition, that movement to the polls was consistent within campaigns, even multilingual campaigns. We posit that the consistency in turnout is due to consistency in how the mobilization narrative was delivered. First, because phone banking usually is conducted within one centralized location, the groups conducting the organizing are able to monitor canvassers and to correct those who go off script. In addition, the CVI groups generally were using a computer-based technology for their calling that provided them with the number to call as well as the script on their computer screens in the appropriate language for the targeted voter. That technology helped phone canvassers to remain on message during their GOTV conversations.

A more consistent narrative meant that these efforts had a more reliable impact on the cognitive schemas of targeted voters than did efforts with a less consistent narrative. In addition, the fact that these phone banked calls were not face-to-face contacts minimized the nonverbal cues that could have influenced the impact of the GOTV narrative. The recipient of the call undoubtedly made assumptions about who the caller was, but a phone call is a much less rich sociocultural interaction than a face-to-face contact, thus increasing the likelihood that the GOTV message was the central focus of that contact. Within this context, a live phone campaign using a two-call strategy may be the best choice. On the one hand, it includes the narrative structure and the sociocultural interaction that are key to shifting a person's cognitive schemas in order to move them successfully to the polls. On the other, the ability of the phone banking groups to control the message, together with the phone call's minimization of other social cues informing that broader narrative, makes two-call phone banking a clean approach to voter mobilization. Within the context of the CVI, it showed remarkably consistent and powerful results.

4

KNOCK, KNOCK, WHO'S THERE? DOOR-TO-DOOR CANVASSING AND GETTING OUT THE VOTE

The mercury had already hit eighty degrees Fahrenheit, even though it was not yet nine o'clock in the morning. Marianna and Gianna parked their car on the side of the road and felt the sun beat down on their heads as they made their way down the dusty driveway. Checking their clipboards to make certain they were going to the right house, they did not notice the flock of geese that had been disrupted by their arrival. The sound of flapping wings was the only warning they got before five angry birds were upon them, beaks open and honks blaring. The women beat a hasty retreat to their car and, on their control sheet, marked their inability to canvass at this particular house on their list. Their control sheet did not include an option for "chased by geese," so they listed the result of the attempted contact as "other." Such are the unexpected dangers that volunteers face when attempting to turn out voters in the rural parts of California's Riverside County.

Although most door-to-door canvassing does not end with, literally, a wild goose chase, during every election cycle, organizations and campaigns across the country spend significant time and resources fielding teams of canvassers to knock on doors in order to encourage individuals to vote. This face-to-face canvassing, occurring at targeted voters' homes, is the epitome of the type of narrative-based sociocultural interaction that we believe explains the effectiveness of direct-contact GOTV campaigns. That a stranger has taken the time to come to a voter's door and deliver a personal invitation to join the polity—simply to vote, not to support any particular candidate, party, or ballot initiative—has a powerful effect that goes beyond the actual words of the predetermined script, causing the contacted individual to adopt a new cognitive schema as a voter and, in the long term, enhance community-level social capital. Yet, as we detail in this chapter, we found significant variation in the effectiveness of the California Votes Initiative (CVI) groups' door-to-door efforts, an unavoidable consequence of the richness of the sociocultural interactions that occurred at the targeted voters' doorsteps. Door-to-door campaigning illustrates both the transformative power of GOTV and the considerable challenges entailed in mounting these sorts of efforts.

The Effects of Door-to-Door Canvassing

Although party and community activists have long sworn by the power of grassroots door-to-door efforts, only recently have political scientists begun amassing the empirical evidence to prove their claims. Since the publication of Alan Gerber and Donald Green's (2000b) article on canvassing, hundreds of field experiments have been conducted on the impact of door-to-door canvassing efforts (Green, Gerber, and Nickerson 2003; Michelson 2003, 2005; Nickerson, Friedrichs, and King 2006; Green and Gerber 2008; Green and Michelson 2009). Prior to Gerber and Green's work, conducted in 1998, there were only two published examples of door-to-door GOTV field experiments: one by Samuel Eldersveld and one by Roy Miller, David Bositis, and Denise Baer. Eldersveld (1956) was inspired by Morris Janowitz and Dwaine Marvick's (1956) survey-based research from the 1952 election examining canvassing by party activists, which, they found, increased voter turnout.

In 1953 and 1954, Eldersveld conducted door-to-door canvassing experiments in Ann Arbor, Michigan. The 1953 experiment included an attempt to convince voters to support a proposed revision of the Ann Arbor municipal charter and specifically targeted individuals who lacked information about the proposal or were unfavorable toward the measure; one treatment group was exposed to four waves of mail propaganda, the other to door-to-door canvassing. While only 33 percent of the control group voted (about the same percentage as for the city as a whole), Eldersveld reported that "59 per cent of those who had received our mail voted, and

75 per cent of those who had been personally contacted in the experiment voted" (1956, 156). In April 1954, Eldersveld conducted another experiment, this one focusing on individuals who were "local election apathetics"—those who had voted regularly in prior state and national elections but not in local elections. Some were contacted at their households, some by telephone, and some by mail. The door-to-door canvassing in 1953 had been conducted by Eldersveld's students; in 1954 one treatment group was mobilized by Eldersveld's students while another was contacted by local party canvassers, "to approach more closely a 'reality canvassing situation'" (158).[1] The results confirmed for Eldersveld the benefit of door-to-door efforts: in the "residual" (control) group, turnout was only 6 percent, compared to 10 percent in the mail group and 25 percent among those contacted personally. Eldersveld (155) concluded:

> This analysis revealed that canvassing efforts were closely related to voter activation and, to a certain extent, were also linked to a larger vote for the party canvassing, although a "boomerang effect" was also detected. More important were the findings of differential effects for predispositional types, with "apathetic" persons staying home more than "effective citizens," despite party canvassing. These investigators also found a contrast in the effectiveness of canvassing those under concerted primary group pressure for a candidate and those in a "conflict" or neutral primary group situation. There was only limited effectiveness as a result of canvassing those already under concerted pro-Eisenhower or pro-Stevenson primary group pressure, but individuals in a conflict or neutral primary group situation had less tendency to stay home if they were canvassed. These findings indicate, therefore, certain conditions under which personalized voter activation appeals can succeed.

Interestingly, Eldersveld's conclusions support our decision to emphasize cognitive differences among individuals and the resulting differences in responsiveness to GOTV appeals. Overall, his study found that turnout increased 25 percent among those contacted at their homes by students, 29 percent among those contacted by their homes by party canvassers, and 24 percent among those contacted by telephone.

As noted by Green and Gerber (2008) and as mentioned here earlier, the Eldersveld studies had serious methodological flaws. Those in the treatment group who were not contacted were lumped together with those in the control groups, and the sample sizes were very small.[2] In the 1953 experiment, for example, the turnout rate of 75 percent for the contacted group refers to turnout by fifteen of twenty individuals; in 1954, only sixty-four individuals were contacted through door-to-door canvassing (forty by students, twenty-four by party canvassers). Thus, the standard errors generated by a more robust analysis of his data make it difficult to determine the true impact of the experiments. Still, the experiments were remarkable for their innovation, and it is surprising that no other researchers turned to such studies for several decades.

Roy Miller, David Bositis, and Denise Baer (1981)—also discussed here earlier—were the next to use field experiments to study the power of door-to-door GOTV; they examined the effect of contact by a precinct committeeman on turnout in the 1980 Illinois primary election in the seventh precinct of Carbondale, Illinois. Comparing home visits to telephone calls and mailings, the authors found that letters were most effective for voters aged twenty-one to thirty and phone calls for those aged thirty-one to fifty-nine; none of the three tactics was effective for voters aged sixty or older. Not surprisingly, given the small scope of the experiment (215 individuals including the control group), the number of individuals in each treatment arm for each age group was quite small, and the findings did not reach statistical significance. In fact, the experiment had nine treatment groups, in addition to the control group, for the authors also explored the power of contact timing and multiple contacts. The researchers compounded this lack of statistical power by repeating the error made by Eldersveld of putting those for whom contact was attempted but not completed into the control group, rather than addressing the failure-to-treat problem.

Despite the intriguing findings that came out of these early efforts, field experiments generally fell out of favor with political scientists for another two decades, until the work by Gerber and Green (2000b), conducted in 1998. In their New Haven experiment, Gerber and Green cooperated with the League of Women Voters to create a nonpartisan campaign called Vote '98. More than 1,600 individuals were contacted at their homes, 4,800 registered voters were reached by a commercial phone bank, and more than 11,000 households were targeted by direct mail. The estimated treatment effects were 8.4 percentage points for door-to-door contact, and 0.51 percentage points for direct mail, while the calls from the commercial phone bank were not found to increase turnout.[3] Subsequent experimental studies have confirmed Gerber and Green's (2000b) results in terms of the power of door-to-door canvassing as a GOTV strategy. Of the forty-five door-to-door experiments reviewed by Green and Gerber (2008), thirty-six successfully increased turnout, with an average of one additional vote produced for every fourteen contacts, although the yield was smaller for low-propensity voters. In addition, door-to-door canvassing has been shown to increase turnout among other registered voters in a household where one individual is contacted, with a spillover effect onto other household members of about 60 percent (Nickerson 2008).

The forty-five door-to-door canvassing experiments reviewed by Green and Gerber (2008) tended to be conducted with general populations, with little attention paid to the low-propensity communities of color that were the focus of the CVI. While it may be tempting to assume that findings with general populations can be generalized to ethnic communities, research has shown that behavioral models developed using samples that are largely non-Latino white do not always explain fully African American, Latino, or Asian American political behavior (Tate 1993; Verba, Schlozman, and Brady 1995; Dawson 2000; García Bedolla 2005a; J. Wong et al. 2011). In addition, Robert Putnam's exploration of the relationship between social capital and interpersonal networks has been supplemented by other research suggesting that these dynamics may also operate differently within ethnoracial communities (Putnam 1995, 2000; García Bedolla 2005b; Harris 1999; Hero 2003; Chávez, Wampler, and Burkhart 2006).

Thus, it is important that GOTV analyses include experiments carried out within communities of color. Prior to the launch of the CVI in 2006, only a very small number of door-to-door voter mobilization field experiments had been conducted within black and Latino communities; none had been carried out targeting Asian Americans. In November 2001 and November 2003, the Association of Community Organizations for Reform Now (ACORN) organized three door-to-door canvassing efforts targeting African American registered voters (Green and Michelson 2009). The three campaigns all focused on areas with a majority of African American voters; they included an effort in Bridgeport, Connecticut, that aimed to raise support for a living wage ordinance; a campaign in Detroit, Michigan, designed to increase turnout in the city's closely contested mayoral race; and a campaign in Kansas City, Missouri, intended to support a proposed increase in the city sales tax. Results varied across locations, but these experiments all had large and statistically significant impacts on turnout. In Bridgeport, turnout was increased 14.4 percentage points among those contacted; the effects in Detroit and Kansas City were 7.8 percentage points and 7.0 percentage points, respectively.

Pre-CVI door-to-door field experiments had also examined the impact of door-to-door GOTV tactics on Latino voter turnout. In 2001, a nonpartisan door-to-door canvassing experiment was designed to increase turnout in a school-board election in the majority-Latino rural town of Dos Palos, California (Michelson 2003). Although both Latinos and non-Latinos of all party affiliations were targeted, turnout increased only among Latino Democrats, suggesting that the ethnicity and the partisanship of the canvassers (all of whom were Latino Democrats) may have had an impact on the campaign's effectiveness. A similar 2002 experiment in Fresno, California, expanded on these findings by using canvassers of all races and ethnicities in an attempt to increase Latino youth participation in the state's gubernatorial election. This effort found that Latino canvassers were more successful at reaching Latino voters than were non-Latino canvassers, but that all canvassers were equally effective at mobilizing contacted voters (Michelson 2006). A door-to-door campaign in Maricopa County, Arizona, conducted by ACORN in November 2003, encouraged Latino voters to vote to maintain the county hospital. Those who indicated in an initial round that they intended to vote yes were targeted to receive a second contact from canvassers. This campaign had a large and statistically significant impact, increasing turnout by 12 percentage points among contacted voters in one-voter households and 17.6 percentage points in two-voter households (Green and Michelson 2009).

In sum, at the launch of the CVI in 2006, most research on GOTV had focused on white, regular voters. The few campaigns that had looked at the effects of door-to-door canvassing among African American and Latino voters had found this approach to be effective in turning out these voters. Yet these campaigns had been conducted either by one community organization—ACORN—or by an academic (and her students) with no organizational or community ties. Although these previous studies suggested that substantively large and statistically significant impacts on turnout could be generated using face-to-face visits, the experiments were of limited generalizability.

The CVI campaigns, by comparison, involved an academic analysis of real-world campaigns carried out by established community-based organizations using their staff and volunteers. We turn now to a description of the CVI experiments, focusing on each partnering community organization in turn: the Central American Resource Center (CARECEN), Strategic Concepts in Organizing and Policy Education (SCOPE), the Center for Community Action and Environmental Justice (CCAEJ), African American Churches United (AACU), and the PICO (People Improving Communities through Organizing) National Network (PICO).[4] Our analysis is based on data from 117 door-to-door canvassing experiments conducted by participating CVI groups from June 2006 through November 2008, including six efforts by CARECEN among Latinos in Los Angeles, four experiments by SCOPE in the mixed-race community of South Los Angeles, seven experiments in mixed-ethnoracial communities by CCAEJ in Riverside and San Bernardino Counties, California, four experiments by AACU, and ninety-six experiments conducted by various PICO affiliates throughout the state.

The Logistics of Door-to-Door Canvassing

Door-to-door canvassing is considered the most effective GOTV tactic, producing the largest increases in turnout among individuals successfully contacted. However, it is also the most logistically complex, requiring the repeated preparation of maps, walk lists (lists of voters to contact with codes for canvassers to record the outcome of each attempt), and other materials for canvassers, who will be left on their own for several hours, often in neighborhoods with which they are unfamiliar. Canvassing door-to-door is also somewhat inefficient, in that repeatedly returning to a house to reach a targeted voter who in earlier attempts was not found at home requires considerably more effort than making a second or third attempt to contact an individual by phone. Door-to-door campaigns also require attention to the personal safety of canvassers, which generally means sending volunteers out in teams rather than individually and limiting canvassing to daylight hours. For fall campaigns, this can leave a small window of opportunity between when targeted voters return home from work (and therefore are available to be contacted) and when it will be too dark to safely send canvassers into the field. In some communities, particularly in rural areas, canvassers must return to their automobiles frequently, for the distance between targeted households is too great to be covered efficiently on foot. All these logistical difficulties must be taken into consideration when evaluating the impact of the door-to-door campaigns.

Canvassing Urban Poor Latinos: CARECEN

CARECEN has been active since 1983 in the Pico-Union/Westlake community of Los Angeles, an area heavily populated by recent immigrants from Mexico and Central America, particularly Guatemala and El Salvador. CARECEN was created to help Central American political refugees regularize their migration status in the United States and has been very successful in providing legal services to the local community, including assistance with immigration cases, labor violations, and housing. CARECEN also provides educational programming, such as citizenship classes. They only recently began working directly to promote voter mobilization. Prior to the randomized experiments described here, CARECEN had worked to increase local voter turnout in the March and May 2005 mayoral contests in Los Angeles.

The targeted area for all CARECEN efforts, Pico Union/Westlake, is located just west of downtown Los Angeles. The area is bounded on the east by the 110 Freeway (Interstate and California Route 110), on the south by the 10 Freeway (Interstate 10), on the west by Normandie Avenue, and on the north by Beverly Boulevard. The area presents several barriers to voter education and outreach. It has a reputation as a transitional newcomer area with many undocumented and noncitizen residents, which keeps it off the radar of traditional political parties and campaigns. The population generally has limited facility with the English language. Voters often live in high-density apartment complexes that are difficult to access. The gang activity in the area makes residents highly suspicious of strangers and unwilling to open their doors to them. And finally, given the large number of undocumented residents and the large number of area residents who fled repressive regimes, individuals in this area are generally wary of "official" visitors.

For the June 2006 election, CARECEN targeted neighborhood voters who were Latino and who either had registered since the last statewide election or had voted in three or fewer of the last four statewide elections. The mobilization effort began several months before the election, in early April. The canvassing team was composed of forty-three community members, mostly Latino, and included thirteen individuals who had worked on previous CARECEN GOTV efforts.[5] The canvassers ranged in age from fifteen to sixty, and most (thirty-one) were women. The canvassers each attended one training session, as well as weekly orientations covering weekly goals and reminders about reporting and the campaign message. Canvassing was conducted four times each week, from 5:00 p.m. to 8:00 p.m. on weekdays and from 4:00 p.m. to 7:00 p.m. on weekends. Most precincts were walked at least three times, and considerable time was spent by canvassers waiting in front of locked gates, hoping someone would provide them with entry to the apartment complex and thus access to targeted voters.

Contacted individuals were invited to vote, asked what they thought were the most important issues facing the neighborhood, and introduced to CARECEN as an organization, including an inquiry as to whether or not they wanted to receive further literature or contact from CARECEN. Despite the difficulties that canvassers faced in accessing voters, CARECEN's contact rates were more than respectable. Overall, 36.4 percent of individuals without known phone numbers were successfully contacted by the door-to-door canvassers, as were 45.8 percent of those with phone numbers.[6] Owing to some errors in recordkeeping, some individuals were contacted more than once. CARECEN used primarily monolingual Spanish-speaking canvassers to conduct the campaign; as a result, canvassers were not able to communicate well with individuals in the treatment group who were monolingual English speakers. The extent to which this affected the mobilization effort is unknown.[7]

Comparing turnout rates among those in the treatment groups to the rates in the control groups reveals that the CARECEN mobilization effort was not very successful in terms of increasing turnout. 2SLS analysis finds that door-to-door canvassing increased turnout by an estimated 2.2 percentage points (SE = 1.8). The effect clearly falls short of the expected mobilization effect of a door-to-door campaign, and the high standard error makes the results subject to a high degree of uncertainty.

One possible explanation for the small impact of CARECEN's efforts in the June 2006 election is that the organization's early presence in the field gave contacted voters time to forget that they had been contacted. Fully 48 percent of individuals targeted for door-to-door visits were contacted before May 1; 72 percent were contacted more than three weeks prior to Election Day.

For the November 2006 campaign, CARECEN shifted its strategy to involve repeated contacts for a smaller treatment group over a shorter period of time in the field. CARECEN targeted over 3,000 occasional and new Latino voters, defining "occasional" voters as those who had voted between one and three times in the previous five statewide elections, and "new" voters as those who registered after September 2005. The November effort focused on door-to-door canvassing and added Election Day telephone reminders.

The canvassing script mirrored that from the June 2006 campaign, including encouragements to vote, a brief survey, and information about services provided by CARECEN. In addition, canvassers provided contacted individuals with *Easy Voter Guides* to educate them about the election and spoke to them about the campaign and the importance of voting.[8] In comparison to the June 2006 GOTV effort, the targeted population was reduced from 6,000 to 3,000 in order to allow canvassers to spend more time talking to voters and to increase contact rates. In addition, the campaign began only five and a half weeks before Election Day, rather than eight weeks before, as it had in June. The canvassing team included thirty-five individuals, half of whom were bilingual in English and Spanish, a change made in order to avoid the problem encountered during the June campaign, when monolingual Spanish-speaking canvassers were unable to communicate with monolingual English-speaking voters. Canvasser training was also changed, focusing more on election and ballot initiative information than on local issues or other CARECEN services. Canvassing was conducted up to five days each week, including evening hours on weekdays and from 4:00 p.m. to 8:00 p.m. on weekends. First contacts were made from the last week of September through the third week of October 2006. Second contacts followed from the third week of October to the first week of November 2006. A round of follow-up calls was made on Election Day.[9]

A few weeks into the campaign, canvassers began asking contacted voters to sign pledge cards committing themselves to vote. Contacted voters were asked to write their name and address on a postcard; after polling-place information was added to the reverse side, these postcards were mailed back to voters a week before Election Day. During their Election Day poll monitoring, CARECEN workers reported seeing these postcards left on pollworker tables—an indication that the voters had received the postcards and carried them to the polling place. Election Day reminders were made by phone, and canvassers also delivered doorhangers to the homes of previously contacted voters. Overall, CARECEN's contact rate for the campaign was a strong 52.9 percent.

Comparing turnout in the treatment and control groups reveals that the mobilization effort was again only marginally successful in increasing turnout. Turnout in the control group was 52.5 percent, slightly higher than the 52.2 percent turnout rate for the treatment group. Applying 2SLS analysis to the results generates a treatment-on-treated effect of −0.5 percentage points (SE = 2.9). Again, the high standard error makes the results subject to a high degree of uncertainty.

These disappointing results were again possibly due to the early start to the campaign or perhaps to the canvassing script not being sufficiently focused on a GOTV message; instead, much of the information provided by canvassers referred to other services provided by the organization. Thus, rather than taking away from the conversations the message that they were being invited into the polity, those contacted may have instead focused on CARECEN's offers of legal assistance, their educational programs, and their day laborer center. Another possibility is that the impact of the mobilization campaign was diminished because the pool of voters targeted by CARECEN included a significant number of "habitual non-voters," who may have been difficult to mobilize.

For the February 2008 election, CARECEN's door-to-door canvassing began only four weeks prior to Election Day, with shifts six days each week from 6:00 p.m. to 8:00 p.m. on weekdays and from 4:00 p.m. to 7:00 p.m. on weekends. The teams of volunteers were specifically assigned to canvass their own neighborhoods, a change made in light of findings from the SCOPE efforts in 2006 (discussed below) that suggested that neighbor-on-neighbor contacts were more effective than non-neighbor contacts. CARECEN's script included a shorter message more focused on the election specifically than in the 2006 campaign, and the organization provided canvassers with blue CARECEN vests so that they would be more easily identifiable to neighborhood residents and therefore have easier access to voter's homes. In the training of canvassers, CARECEN increased the amount of role play that took place prior to sending volunteers into the field. Increased quality control was also implemented, including managing cases, monitoring canvassers in the field, calling voters to confirm contact, and monitoring canvasser reporting more closely than before.

CARECEN had a strong contact rate (49.8 percent) and was able to contact 1,788 voters. The strength of this contact rate is especially notable given the staff turnover during this campaign (the organization lost its director of civic participation just weeks before the election), as well as significant stormy weather, which caused some residents to lose electricity and made it difficult to canvass. Follow-up was less thorough than in November 2006; fewer than 100 individuals were sent reminders on Election Day. Turnout was 54.1 percent in the control group and 54.6 percent in the treatment group, a difference of only 0.5 percentage points. 2SLS generates a nonsignificant treatment estimate of 0.9 percentage points (SE = 3.2).

For the June 2008 election, CARECEN incorporated a more systematic second-contact strategy than before, going back to visit targeted voters that had already committed to voting and delivering a reminder card indicating a voter's polling place. The first round of contacts generated a strong contact rate (48.0 percent), reflecting successful contacts with 2,000 targeted voters, of whom 96 percent (N = 1,919) said that they planned to vote.[10] These self-identified likely voters were re-contacted in some fashion during Election Day weekend or on Election Day; overall, almost 70 percent (N = 1,339) were successfully contacted during this second round.[11] Despite this change in strategy, CARECEN was again unable to move significant numbers of targeted voters to the polls. Turnout in the control group was 20.4 percent, compared to 22.3 percent in the treatment group, for an intent-to-treat effect of 1.9 percentage points. 2SLS analysis generates a treatment-on-treated effect of 4.0 percentage points (SE=2.6).

For the November 2008 election, CARECEN implemented a competitive process for hiring canvassers, selecting those seen as most effective and reliable in training sessions to canvass during the actual campaign. Some returning canvassers were assigned group leader roles and were distributed geographically around the targeted neighborhood to provide ongoing supervision and support for canvassers in the field. Overall, CARECEN walkers contacted 23 percent of their treatment group, for a total of 998 individuals. Turnout in the treatment group was 65.0 percent, compared to 64.9 in the control group, an intent-to-treat effect of 0.1 percentage points. The treatment-on-treated effect estimate is 0.7 percentage points (SE = 6.0).

None of the five door-to-door experiments conducted by CARECEN from June 2006 through November 2008 was particularly effective at increasing turnout, and there are high standard errors associated with each effort (Table 4.1). While all of the CARECEN turnout effects fell short of what we would expect from a door-to-door campaign, the findings are valuable as part of our overall investigation into how best to increase turnout among low-propensity voters. As detailed above, CARECEN targeted a difficult-to-contact population with a very low propensity to vote. In addition, the canvassers were working in dangerous neighborhoods under difficult circumstances. Thus, the amount of sociocultural interaction necessary to move the voters to adopt a voter schema was likely greater than for voters from the communities targeted by other CVI groups. This was illustrated in the historic and high-turnout November 2008 presidential election, in which the treatment and control groups in Pico Union both voted at a rate of about 65 percent—much lower than that of other communities in that election—as well as by CARECEN's low contact rate for the November 2008 election, only 23 percent.

Table 4.1. CARECEN Door-to-Door Experiments, 2006–2008

Election	N	Treatment-on-Treated Effect (SE)[a]
June 2006, pooled[b]		2.2 (1.8)
No phone number	1,631	0.6 (3.9)
With phone number	5,415	2.6 (2.0)
November 2006	6,148	−0.5 (2.9)
February 2008	5,180	0.9 (3.2)
June 2008	5,995	4.0 (2.6)
November 2008	6,205	0.7 (6.0)

[a] None of the TOT coefficient estimates reach traditional levels of statistical significance. Robust cluster standard errors are by household.
[b] The June 2006 experiment was randomized separately for households with and without valid telephone numbers in the voter file.

Still, we believe CARECEN's campaigns were not as effective as others for several other reasons. CARECEN's training focused little on the actual GOTV conversation. Training sessions also tended to be more frequent and in-depth at the beginning of the campaign and tended not to be continued throughout the campaign. That meant that canvassers who missed a training session or who joined the campaign after the beginning of the campaign had limited opportunity to gain the knowledge or experience later. As a result, many canvassers went into the field with little or no training. CARECEN also sent canvassers out by themselves. Although canvassers traveled in teams of two, they were instructed to canvass opposite sides of the street. This kept experienced canvassers from helping new ones and also, as our observers reported, resulted in significantly more variability in terms of what was actually said by canvassers on the doorstep. Finally, CARECEN's canvassing efforts were more focused on informing the community about their services and less centered on getting out the vote. Thus, the canvassing narrative included multiple messages for the voter. Although the visits may have made the targeted voters feel more included and attached to their broader community, the sociocultural interactions were not able to change their cognition sufficiently to make them see themselves as voters. Thus, they were not moved to go to the polls. (A more detailed analysis of why we believe CARECEN's campaigns were not as effective as others may be found in chapter 5.)

Multiracial Organizing in a Rapidly Changing Urban Community: SCOPE

SCOPE has worked since 1993 to reduce structural barriers to social and economic opportunities for the poor and working-class mixed African American and Latino community of South Los Angeles. For many years, the organization has also striven to increase civic engagement and voter turnout in this area. To accomplish its goals, SCOPE has spent years recruiting volunteers from South Los Angeles who are committed to canvass precincts prior to an election. Walkers are often residents of the areas slated for mobilization.

For the June 2006 election, SCOPE targeted all voters living within twenty-six selected precincts in South Los Angeles where the organization has worked for several election cycles to mobilize voters, randomly assigning households to the treatment or control groups. The door-to-door campaign was conducted by two kinds of canvassers: volunteers working on Saturdays (called Neighborhood Education Teams) and paid street teams working throughout the week (called Street Action Teams).[12] The campaign started in mid-May, about four weeks before Election Day, but SCOPE made the bulk of its contacts during the last four days of the campaign. During the weekend before Election Day, SCOPE canvassers also attempted to speak again with voters contacted earlier.

Overall, canvassers contacted 1,916 targeted voters, for an overall contact rate of 34.7 percent. 2SLS analysis generates a treatment-on-treated effect of 2.6 percentage points (SE = 3.3) (Table 4.2). Although many

Table 4.2. SCOPE Door-to-Door Experiments, 2006–2008

Election	N	Treatment-on-Treated Effect (SE)[a]
June 2006	7,345	2.6 (3.3)
November 2006	15,367	6.6** (2.1)
February 2008	8,973	3.4 (2.3)
November 2008	17,036	0.5 (1.1)

[a] Robust cluster standard errors are by household.
** $p < .01$, one-tailed

canvassers were residents of the targeted precincts, only 168 of the contacts were between neighbors, defined as individuals living in the same precinct. Nevertheless, the results suggest a slight neighbor effect, in that those contacted by their neighbors were more likely to vote than were those contacted by individuals from the larger South Los Angeles community or beyond. Unfortunately, the small number of neighbor-to-neighbor contacts in this campaign left the social networking results open to a fair amount of statistical uncertainty.

The effect of neighbor-on-neighbor canvassing was tested further with SCOPE's campaign for the November 2006 election (Sinclair, McConnell, and Michelson, forthcoming). The campaign began on October 7, 2006, and continued daily through Election Day. While the June 2006 campaign had targeted all registered voters in SCOPE's precincts of interest, the November 2006 effort was limited to low-propensity voters, including individuals who had voted only occasionally in the past or who were newly registered. The canvassing script was based on a community-oriented mobilization approach; it included the line "We're out today talking to our neighbors about the upcoming elections." Although canvasser assignments to walk lists were haphazard and not entirely random, they were not based on any area characteristics, allowing us to compare the results of neighbor-to-neighbor and non-neighbor contacts. Here we defined neighbor-to-neighbor contacts as those between canvassers and targeted voters living within the same ZIP code.

Canvassers included 147 South Los Angeles residents; 63 were black, 77 were Latino, and 7 were white. Most (101) were women. Trainings were held with fifty leaders and canvassers twice before the program was launched in September; in addition, training sessions, role plays, and evaluations were held daily with the Street Action Team and each Saturday with the Neighborhood Education Teams. The canvassing message included two basic parts: first, a brief survey in which voters were asked to identify the most motivating message for or against Proposition 87 (the Clean Energy Initiative) and, second, an invitation to vote.[13] The campaign targeted 11,789 registered voters in fifty precincts in South Los Angeles. Overall, 5,341 individuals were successfully contacted, for a contact rate of 45.3 percent. The intent-to-treat effect was 3.0 percentage points; the treatment-on-treated effect was a significant 6.6 percentage points (SE = 2.1).

Examining the effect of contact separately for those canvassing their local neighbors and those canvassing non-locals, we find that neighbors increased turnout by 8.5 percentage points (SE = 3.0), while non-locals increased turnout by 5.2 percentage points (SE = 2.9). In other words, while door-to-door canvassing in general had a powerful effect in this campaign, canvassing by individuals working their home ZIP codes had an even more powerful effect, suggesting that this is an important way to capitalize upon existing social networks within communities. Further analysis of these results indicates that increasing the number of neighbor-on-neighbor contacts by 10 percentage points will garner an increased treatment-on-treated effect of 3.8 percentage points.[14]

For the February 2008 presidential primary election, SCOPE conducted a door-to-door canvassing campaign during the three weeks leading up to Election Day. In addition to encouraging voters to participate, canvassers conducted a survey related to its 2008 focus on Green Jobs.[15] Voters were asked whether they thought South Los Angeles would benefit from Green Jobs and whether they wanted to see more solar panels in the neighborhood. The experiment included 8,973 voters, about two-thirds of whom (N=5,994, or 66.8 percent) were randomly assigned to the treatment group. Overall, 50.4 percent were successfully contacted, and those contacted were 3.4 percentage points more likely to vote (SE = 2.3). That these effects were smaller than those previously achieved by SCOPE is probably because of the high level of turnout in the control group; the control group voted at a rate of 58 percent, and the treatment group at a rate of 59.7 percent. Looking at subgroups, we find that the effect of canvassing is almost completely limited to young voters, who were probably excited by the Obama candidacy and thus more open to being mobilized to turn out in this presidential primary election. Within the pool of 1,699 voters under thirty years of age, canvassing increased turnout by a significant 8.8 percentage-points (SE = 4.8) among those contacted, whereas among those thirty or over, the campaign's effect was 1.1 percentage-points (SE = 2.2).

The November 2008 SCOPE campaign mirrored in many respects the February 2008 campaign, including the context of a high-salience election for this heavily African American community. This campaign also included a Green Jobs survey; contacted individuals were asked the following questions before they were asked to commit to voting: "1) What is the most important way renewable energy can benefit South LA and the City of LA: jobs for poor and working families, reduction in air pollution, or cleaner communities with more parks? 2) Do you think that City government should . . . be a leader in funding programs to reduce air pollution? 3) . . . be a leader in creating jobs for poor and working families? 4) . . . be a leader in funding programs to attract Green Manufacturing Businesses to LA?"

As was the case in February 2008, the campaign was extremely successful at contacting targeted voters, with a contact rate of 59 percent for its pool of 13,881 registered voters. In the earlier 2008 campaign, SCOPE had some trouble recruiting volunteer canvassers, leading it to reduce the number of Saturday walks from four to two. For the November election, SCOPE reached out to local high schools and colleges to recruit new, younger canvassers and completed the usual four full Saturdays of precinct-walking before the election, with an average of twenty-seven walkers working every day. Turnout in SCOPE's control group for this election was remarkable: 88.2 percent. Although turnout was slightly higher (88.5 percent) in the treatment group, this high base turnout rate clearly reflects the salience of the election to this community of voters and the lack of on-the-cusp voters available to be mobilized by SCOPE's campaign. Our estimate of the treatment effect in November 2008 is therefore negligible.

SCOPE'S campaigns are examples of well-organized mobilization efforts carried out by an experienced staff using a large pool of experienced and motivated community organizers. Yet, we still find variation in their effectiveness across elections and among different types of voters. It is not surprising that their mobilization effort had a limited impact in the November 2008 presidential race, in which nearly all eligible voters in this heavily African American neighborhood turned out to vote for the nation's first African American president. In their script ("rap"), SCOPE always asked the canvassers to connect local issues—green jobs, pollution, and clean energy—to the importance of voting. In addition, they told targeted voters how few eligible voters were voting in their neighborhood before SCOPE's GOTV efforts started and how those numbers had changed as a result of their work. This is a narrative of empowerment, one that tells the voter that "people like them" vote, that voting has a concrete impact on their neighborhood's well-being, and that therefore they should vote also. Our analysis suggests that even a narrative as powerful as this one was not always successful at moving targeted voters to the polls.

Targeting Mixed-Ethnoracial Rural Communities in California's Inland Empire: CCAEJ

The Center for Community Action and Environmental Justice (CCAEJ) was founded in 1978 to battle toxic waste in Glen Avon. For more than three decades, CCAEJ has been working on environmental justice issues in Mira Loma and Glen Avon, two unincorporated rural communities in the northwest corner of Riverside County, California.[16] The goal of the organization is to empower low-income ethnic communities in Riverside and San Bernardino Counties—counties in southern California's Inland Empire—to fight for environmental health and justice.

Before June 2006, CCAEJ had never conducted a voter mobilization effort, instead focusing on community organization and policy advocacy. Their existing Salud Ambiental, Latinas Tomando Acción (SALSA)—Environmental Health, Latinas Taking Action—program coordinated local residents, particularly Latinas, to connect health and quality of life issues with the need for civic involvement to effect public policy reform. These activities were non-electoral, focusing on bringing people together for education and conversations with policymakers. In joining the CVI, CCAEJ took the next logical step, using voter mobilization to increase the political power of local residents to achieve local policy changes.

For the June 2006 election, CCAEJ targeted five precincts in their core neighborhood in Glen Avon. Because of the low concentration of registered voters in this largely Latino and African American area, CCAEJ cast the net widely: the pool of registered voters in the experiment included all new registrants and all voters who had voted in at least one of the previous five major elections.

During the week before the election, canvassers went door to door to encourage individuals in the treatment group to vote. All of the canvassers were residents of the five targeted precincts. Canvassers encountered numerous challenges in their attempts to reach voters because of gated communities, guard dogs, livestock, and a general lack of sidewalks in the targeted areas. In addition, because many houses in the neighborhood did not include targeted voters, there was often a considerable distance to walk between contact attempts. Nevertheless, one-fifth (19.7 percent) of those assigned to the treatment group were contacted successfully. There was a clear learning curve, with many walkers doubling and tripling their number of contacts per shift after the first attempt, when they were more experienced with the precinct terrain (and also when temperatures were considerably lower). Overall, walkers went out on four consecutive Saturdays (May 13, 20, 27, and June 3) and on Sunday, June 4. The twenty-six canvassers included twenty women and six men, aged fourteen to sixty-six; eighteen were Latinos, and eight were white.

Contacted individuals were asked to sign a pledge card promising participation in the upcoming election. The card reminded individuals of the importance of their vote to the community, the country, and the future and asked individuals if they wanted to volunteer in the GOTV effort. They were also asked to complete a short survey, including questions about their level of satisfaction with elected officials and their opinion of the most important public issue in their community. Voters were given packets from the canvassers that reinforced the GOTV message. One included numerous photographs and graphics and read in large letters (in English in one side, in Spanish on the reverse): "Local Voices! Local Votes—Count! Campaign. Vote June 6! We vote at the polls and we vote in the streets!" The CCAEJ logo and a contact telephone number were included. Canvassers also distributed a trifold leaflet that explained why voting was important and provided helpful information—for example, that first-time voters should bring a photo ID to the polls and that voters are allowed to bring sample ballots and other materials into the voting booths.

At 5:00 a.m. on Election Day, volunteers began distributing doorhangers at the residences of all successfully contacted voters, reminding them to vote and repeating the helpful information noted above, as well as each individual's polling-place location. This resulted in some secondary face-to-face contacts when residents encountered the volunteers at their doorsteps; however, the number of such contacts was not recorded. CCAEJ also monitored the polls during the day. Not only did this allow them to document the lack of bilingual poll workers at some locations, but it also meant that they were able to provide translation for those mobilized voters who encountered them at the polls and asked for help.

In the five targeted precincts, turnout among those randomly assigned to the control group was 11.1 percent, compared to 19.6 percent among those randomly assigned to the treatment group. This 8.5 percentage-point difference (the intent-to-treat effect) is both substantively large and statistically significant. 2SLS analysis provides an estimate of the effect of actual face-to-face contact of 43.1 percentage points (SE = 12.5) (Table 4.3). In other words, when CCAEJ canvassers actually contacted a person on the target list, they increased his or her probability of voting from 11.1 percent to 54.2 percent—the largest estimated treatment effect to emerge from a voter mobilization field experiment.[17]

For the November 2006 election, CCAEJ's targeted voter pool was expanded significantly to include thirty precincts: the same five Riverside County precincts as in the June 2006 campaign, plus twenty-five additional precincts in San Bernardino County. Perhaps not surprisingly, given the strong connection made with the voters contacted in the June election, CCAEJ requested that these individuals not be included in the

Table 4.3. CCAEJ Door-to-Door Experiments, 2006–2008

Site and Election	N	Treatment-on-Treated Effect (SE)[a]
Riverside County		
June 2006	1,781	43.1** (12.5)
November 2006	2,458	0.4 (15.7)
June 2008	5,970	15.7** (5.6)
November 2008	7,300	−3.4 (5.7)
San Bernardino County		
November 2006	7,128	5.1 (6.4)
June 2008	4,444	0.1 (3.2)
November 2008	7,496	6.3 (7.3)

[a] Robust cluster standard errors are by household.
** $p < .01$, one-tailed

experiment and instead be automatically assigned to the treatment group, allowing the organization to maintain communication with them for this next election round. This highlights one of the complications of real-world experiments conducted with community organizations. Academics and community activists can have different goals, and this is a perfect example of that type of conflict. While we hoped to randomly assign the 215 individuals to treatment and control for the November election GOTV effort in order to test for habit formation effects, CCAEJ leaders were concerned that doing so might mean that individuals with whom a strong connection was made in the spring would not be contacted again, leaving them wondering just how committed CCAEJ was to their individual voting rights and their community.[18]

For the November GOTV effort, CCAEJ's pool of 9,586 registered voters included 4,874 Latinos (51 percent), 3,132 African Americans (33 percent), and 1,580 "others." After randomization, the treatment group included 3,668 Latinos, 2,338 African Americans, and 1,203 "others."[19] The door-to-door campaign began on October 7 and lasted through Election Day, including six Saturday walks and one Sunday walk. Precinct captains also walked on weekdays and did some weekday phone banking. Because CCAEJ did not record the manner of contact for voters, we cannot separate out the door-to-door contacts from the phone bank contacts.[20] Many of the canvassers for the November effort had relationships with precinct residents: all thirty Riverside County canvassers and 84 percent of the San Bernardino canvassers were residents of the targeted precincts; the remainder were from other areas of San Bernardino. With the exception of non-local volunteers, walkers were assigned, when possible, to the precincts in which they lived. Of the Riverside canvassers, twenty-six were women and four were men; overall, forty-nine canvassers were Latino, seventeen were African American, five were white, and two were Asian American.

Contacted voters were provided with a voter information card delineating their voting rights and the voter guide provided by the secretary of state's office. Canvassers asked voters to sign pledge cards promising to vote and asked them to identify the political issues they were most concerned about. CCAEJ canvassers conducted an extensive follow-up during the weekend before Election Day and on Election Day itself. During the weekend follow-up, they provided voters with flyers reminding them to vote and specifying their polling place. On Election Day they placed doorhangers with this information on each voter's door during the morning and canvassed throughout the day.

Overall, canvassers successfully contacted 19.5 percent of those assigned to the treatment group in Riverside County and 25.5 percent of those assigned the treatment group in San Bernardino; again, these are healthy contact rates given the nature of the targeted population and its geographic dispersion. Turnout in Riverside was 53.4 percent in the control group and 53.5 percent in the treatment group, for an intent-to-treat effect of only 0.1 percentage points and a treatment-on-treated effect of 0.4 percentage points (SE = 15.7). In San Bernardino, turnout in the control group was 45 percent, and turnout in the treatment group was 46.3 percent, resulting in an intent-to-treat effect of 1.3 percentage points; the treatment effect for San Bernardino was a not statistically significant 5.1 percentage points (SE = 6.4). In sum, CCAEJ did not replicate its outstanding results from June 2006.

We have speculated that the inability of CCAEJ to duplicate the success it had in its earlier campaign reflected the operational challenge the organization faced by scaling up its canvassing efforts to a substantially larger geographic area. CCAEJ contacted more than six times as many voters in November 2006 than they had in June of that year—a significant increase in the size and scope of their campaign. Yet they were conducting the November mobilization effort in areas, particularly in San Bernardino, where CCAEJ was not as established as an organization and where CCAEJ lacked a well-developed volunteer network. This may have made their work less effective. The lack of impact in Riverside County, in particular, may also be related to the dilution of organizational focus that derived from the expansion of the mobilization effort in both places. In addition, the removal from the experiment of the 215 voters successfully mobilized in the spring—the targeted voters it was easiest to contact and who were the easiest to move to the polls—meant that CCAEJ was left with a pool of more-difficult-to-contact voters to mobilize in November.

CCAEJ worked again to increase turnout in Riverside and San Bernardino Counties in the weeks prior to the June 2008 primary election. The campaign mirrored that of November 2006 in many respects. A team of forty canvassers worked five weekends and four weekdays from May 3 to May 31, 2008. Canvassers distributed voter guides and urged individuals to vote while also introducing them to CCAEJ or providing updates about CCAEJ's work. Targeted communities included Mira Loma and Glen Avon, as in 2006, as well as Pedley and Sky Country, all in the same northwest corner of Riverside County, and the city of San Bernardino's Westside neighborhood. All canvassers were Latino, and most were women and local residents of the targeted communities (85 percent overall). All local canvassers were assigned to walk their own neighborhoods.

This time the Riverside County effort was successful but the San Bernardino effort was not. Turnout increased by 15.7 percentage points (SE = 5.6) in Riverside County. Yet the campaign had negligible estimated effects in San Bernardino County. Hoping to gain further insight into why CCAEJ was unable in November 2006 to duplicate the June 2006 effect, we employed a team of three student observers to take field notes during CCAEJ canvasser training and canvassing sessions for the June 2008 campaign. In other words, we investigated whether or not quality of canvassing was an issue.

Although CCAEJ staff meant to run identical campaigns in the two geographic areas, analysis of the field notes indicates that the campaigns were quite different. First, each office used scripts for the canvassers that were different in the emphasis on community power. The Riverside scripts reference local power in both versions:

> My name is ____ and I'm a volunteer with the Center for Community Action and Environmental Justice. We are fighting to improve the quality of life for local residents. (Riverside, June 2006)

> My name is ____ and I'm with CCAEJ. We're a community organization that builds power in our community by encouraging people to vote. This is a historic election. It is the first step in determining who will lead our country. There are many important issues on the ballot. Riverside voters need to show their voting power in this election. (Riverside, June 2008)

The San Bernardino script, on the other hand, encouraged voting without connecting voting to personal or community empowerment. These are small differences, but one can imagine how the Riverside CCAEJ scripts could lead to very different conversations and therefore lead to sociocultural interactions that could have a strongly positive effect on voters' cognition.

In addition to the scripts, both training and staff-canvasser camaraderie varied between the two offices, probably because the Riverside office was more established. The Riverside training sessions were reported to be more interactive than those in San Bernardino, and the office seemed better able to establish feelings of community and mutual accountability between staff and canvassers. The Riverside canvassers tended to be more experienced overall and had had longer relationships with CCAEJ. Canvassers in San Bernardino were less able to make efficient use of their walk lists and maps. They were more likely to be unable to correctly identify the group for which they were canvassing or to define the group's acronym (CCAEJ) for contacted voters. Finally, San Bernardino canvassers were mobilizing voters in very poor and challenging parts of the city. Our observers reported canvassers encountering large numbers of abandoned and foreclosed homes, hostile dogs, and dangerous situations much more often in San Bernardino than in Riverside.[21] As we saw with CARECEN, this must have made their already difficult work even more challenging.

A final round of CCAEJ experiments was conducted for the November 2008 election, including treatment groups of 5,010 individuals in Riverside County and 5,986 individuals in San Bernardino County. As in June 2008, four Riverside neighborhoods and one in San Bernardino were targeted; four weekend walks and six weekday walks were conducted between late September and early November. Canvassers included ninety-five volunteers from the local communities, mostly women, including fifty in Riverside and forty-five in San Bernardino. In both counties, despite healthy contact rates (24.1 percent in Riverside and 23.7 percent in San Bernardino), effects on turnout were negligible, with large standard errors.

Overall, for the efforts in Riverside County, where CCAEJ is based and where canvassers were more experienced, the group was able to increase turnout significantly in the June primaries but had little effect in the fall elections. In San Bernardino, all three campaigns had negligible effects.

An analysis of CCAEJ's organizational structure may help explain some of the inconsistencies in CCAEJ's results. As part of the CVI, the organization developed a flow chart showing how they saw their voter work aligning with their other programs. The chart showed how CCAEJ conceived of GOTV work as part of its overall mission of community empowerment. Although the title of the mobilization campaign was "Local Voices, Local Votes, Count!" the descriptors they used did not relate to voting specifically. Instead, they used these labels: citizenship classes, platform development, initiative analysis, and precinct leader recruitment. The campaign was conceptualized as being about developing CCAEJ's issue platform and was much more clearly related to its policy initiatives. Prior to joining the CVI, CCAEJ had long been involved in community organizing and in building support for its policy programs; the group had in fact had been quite successful at both. Yet those enterprises are quite different from turning individuals out to vote. It is possible that this ambivalence was present in their campaign organization and messaging, making their results inconsistent. It is highly probable that CCAEJ's door-to-door efforts did broaden its activist network; what the organization did not broaden as consistently was the electorate.

Organizing Urban Congregations: AACU

AACU is a congregation-based organization serving African Americans in Los Angeles County. Although the organization had been active for some time on various public issues of interest to its constituents, its participation in the CVI marked its first attempt to engage in voter mobilization activities. This effort was conducted with sister networks in Riverside and San Bernardino Counties, with a focus on low-income, older African American populations. In the weeks leading up to the November 2006 elections, the organization conducted a door-to-door voter mobilization campaign designed to encourage members of AACU church congregations and voters living in a one-mile radius of each AACU church in those three counties to participate.

Canvassing was conducted between October 21, 2006, and Election Day, resulting in contacts with 87 voters in Los Angeles County, 197 voters in Riverside County, and 231 voters in San Bernardino County, across thirty-six precincts. Canvassers talked with voters about the election, provided them with educational materials, asked them to sign a pledge card, and conducted a short survey asking voters their opinions about whether they thought it was a good idea for churches to be involved in political education. Participating congregations also distributed voter education materials. Their pastors talked in their sermons about the importance of voting and urged their congregants to vote.

The proportion of people assigned to the treatment groups who were actually contacted was on the lower side: 13.3 percent in Los Angeles, 23.8 percent in Riverside, and 22.5 percent in San Bernardino. Although the total number of voters contacted in this first GOTV effort by AACU was almost identical to the total number of contacts by CCAEJ in its first attempt, the contacts represented a much smaller proportion of the targeted pool. Because of the relatively low contact rates and fairly small targeted groups, the results are subject to a fair amount of statistical uncertainty. This reflects the challenges faced by the organization in its first GOTV campaign and the fact that the neighborhoods they targeted were generally considered difficult to canvass.

In Los Angeles County, the estimated treatment-on-treated effect is 14.4 percentage points (SE = 25.4). In Riverside County, the estimated effect is −8.2 percentage points (SE = 14.5). In San Bernardino County, the estimated effect is −4.0 percentage points (SE = 10.6). Pooling these results generates a treatment effect of −3.4 percentage points (SE = 8.1) (Table 4.4).[22] While none of the treatment-on-treated estimates reach traditional levels of statistical significance, the effort in Los Angeles county was more successful than those in the Inland Empire. There are several possible explanations for this. First, the proportion of African

Table 4.4. AACU Door-to-Door Experiments, November 2006 and March 2007

Site and Election	N	Treatment-on-Treated Effect (SE)[a]
November 2006		
Los Angeles County	12,608	14.4 (25.4)
Riverside County	11,171	−8.2 (14.5)
San Bernardino County	10,416	−4.0 (10.6)
Pooled	34,195	−3.4 (8.1)
March 2007		
Los Angeles	10,393	−1.4 (2.0)

[a] Robust cluster standard errors are by household. None of the TOT coefficient estimates reach traditional levels of statistical significance.

Americans in the treatment group in Los Angeles County was higher than in the Inland Empire counties. Since the campaign was designed as a way to mobilize African Americans, the group's message probably resonated more with that population than with others. Second, the communities in San Bernardino and Riverside are much more spread out and tend to be less established. The organization's model was based on mobilizing the area around the church; it to some extent rested on the assumption that the church serves as an anchor for the community and helps to define a particular neighborhood. Given the higher levels of residential mobility in California's Inland Empire, a church is less likely to play this role in San Bernardino and Riverside counties than in Los Angeles. In sum, it was harder to contact people in the Inland Empire (owing to geographic dispersion of the population), and those contacted probably had weaker links to local congregations, probably reducing the effectiveness of the canvassers' message.

The organization again worked to mobilize voters for the March 2007 municipal election in the city of Los Angeles. During the November 2006 campaign, canvassers had noticed that despite the intended focus on older African American registered voters, many individuals on the treatment lists were not African American.[23] This may have reduced the effectiveness of the campaign in that canvassers enthusiastic about mobilizing African Americans may have been less convincing in their communications with non-blacks. To increase the proportion of African Americans targeted in the March 2007 campaign, initial lists of low-propensity voters in targeted precincts in Los Angeles were first culled to remove individuals with Latino surnames. The organization was significantly more effective at contacting targeted individuals in this second effort: it contacted 35 percent of those in the treatment group (N = 1,819).

Despite the stronger contact rate, this second GOTV campaign was still ineffective at moving targeted voters to the polls. Turnout in the treatment group was 11.2 percent, 0.5 percentage points lower than turnout for individuals in the control group. The difference is not statistically significant; that is, having been contacted by the group's volunteers in March 2007 had no measurable impact on a voter's turnout. There is some suggestion, however, that AACU's efforts were more effective for African American voters, its preferred targeted group. The turnout rates were 11.7 percent for those in the control group, 9.6 percent for those in the treatment group who were not contacted, 8.6 percent for those who were contacted but who were not black, and 15.9 percent for contacted blacks. It is possible that had AACU been better able to narrow its target list to the population it wanted to contact, or had perhaps changed its mobilization narrative to appeal to a larger range of voters, it would have been more successful. Following the March 2007 election, however, AACU did not engage in any additional GOTV efforts as part of the CVI.

Organizing Statewide Congregations: PICO

PICO is a national network of faith-based community organizations. The network was founded in California in 1972 and works to train local community and congregation members in ways to improve the quality of life in low-income and immigrant communities through policy initiatives. Prior to PICO's involvement in the CVI, a number of network affiliates had conducted grassroots voter registration and GOTV campaigns, typically targeting local ballot initiatives concerning education and affordable housing. During the weeks leading up to the November 2006 election, four PICO affiliates took part in door-to-door canvassing experiments, all of which also included distribution of *Easy Voter Guides* to targeted voters.

PICO had its biggest mobilization effect in November 2006 in Colusa, a small community in the northern Sacramento Valley. Canvassing in Colusa was conducted by three recent graduates of the local PICO affiliate's citizenship classes. While *Easy Voter Guides* were distributed in both English and Spanish, both the canvassers and the targeted voters were Spanish-dominant speakers. Of the four PICO door-to-door experiments conducted for the November 2006 election, the one in Colusa was by far the most successful, generating a contact rate of 66.8 percent, an intent-to-treat effect of 6.4 percentage points, and a statistically significant treatment effect of 9.6 percentage points (SE = 5.5). Organizers were also pleased to see that the effort had a beneficial effect on the three canvassers, who overcame their fear of public speaking and concerns about language barriers in order to encourage others to vote. It is possible that the mobilization message was particularly effective given that the messengers were new citizens; future research randomizing the nativity of canvassers would help clarify how their status contributed to the group's success in Colusa.

The other three PICO efforts in November 2006 did not have statistically significant impacts on voter turnout. In Sacramento, canvassing was conducted by eight volunteers and four staff members from a local church-based group; they focused on voters who had participated in four or fewer of the past six elections. The contact rate was relatively good, 32.9 percent. *Easy Voter Guides* and handwritten notes were left for people not at home. Almost all of the volunteers who participated in the door-to-door outreach were bilingual in Spanish or Hmong, and the targeted neighborhood surrounded a PICO-affiliated church with a Spanish-speaking congregation. Four of the eight volunteers were eighteen years old or under. Turnout was higher in the treatment group than in the control group by 4.4 percentage points, but the high standard error generated by this relatively small effort means we cannot be certain of the treatment effect.

In Fullerton, a community in Orange County, door-to-door canvassers distributed *Easy Voter Guides* as well as homemade nonpartisan guides to city council candidates. Materials were left at households when people were not at home, and 47.6 percent of targeted voters were successfully contacted. Some monolingual Spanish-speaking canvassers experienced language barriers when trying to communicate with voters, which may help explain why the effort had no measurable impact on turnout. Another less successful PICO effort was in Bakersfield, where canvassers delivered *Easy Voter Guides* and also conducted short interviews to determine priority issues among residents. Only 22.4 percent of targeted voters were successfully contacted; voters not at home were left handwritten notes. This effort also failed to measurably affect turnout.

Pooling across sites, the four November 2006 PICO experiments increased turnout by 3.1 percentage points among those whom the canvassers contacted, but that impact did not reach statistical significance (SE = 3.9) (Table 4.5).[24]

In the February 2008 election, PICO affiliates conducted twenty-one door-to-door experiments and one mixed door-to-door and phone bank campaign. As with the November 2006 campaigns, the PICO experi-

Table 4.5: PICO Door-to-Door Experiments, 2006–2008

Election	N	Pooled Treatment-on-Treated Effect (SE)[a]
Pooled: 4 experiments, November 2006	4,289	3.1 (3.9)
Pooled: 20 experiments, February 2008[b]	10,356	9.5** (3.0)
Pooled: 4 precinct-level randomization experiments (16 precincts total), June 2008	14,180	0.9 (13.9)
Pooled: 15 experiments, June 2008	13,774	1.0 (1.3)
Pooled: 4 precinct-level randomization experiments (16 precincts total), November 2008	9,349	21.2 (25.8)
Pooled: 30 experiments, November 2008	17,418	1.1 (1.7)

[a] Robust cluster standard errors are by household. They are by precinct for precinct-level randomization experiments.
[b] Two experiments are not included: one experiment randomized by precinct and one for which reliable standard errors cannot be calculated.
** $p < .01$, one-tailed

ments in February 2008 tended to be small, making the results again subject to a fair amount of statistical uncertainty. A notable exception was the mixed-method campaign conducted in Winters, a small town in the northern Sacramento Valley (in Yolo County), where the contact rate was an impressive 90.5 percent and the treatment effect among those contacted was 12.9 percentage points (SE = 6.6). This is a very strong effect, and the size of the impact on turnout is particularly impressive given the relatively small size of the experiment (N = 287).

The next most successful PICO door-to-door experiment in February 2008 was carried out by PICO affiliate LA Voice. LA Voice's voter development campaign focused on door-to-door canvassing targeting 1,005

Latino infrequent voters. The effort was led by seventy-five volunteer leaders involved with LA Voice's organizing campaign, which combines citizenship classes with leadership development and training in community organizing. Volunteer leaders from local congregations canvassed the neighborhoods for three weekends (Saturdays and Sundays) in a row, as well as during the week just prior to Election Day. The campaign's contact rate was 36.6 percent, and the treatment effect was a statistically significant 10.4 percentage points (SE = 5.6). Many LA Voice volunteers were new citizens and voting for the first time; others were in the process of getting their citizenship. The unstated message conveyed by these canvassers—urging others to do what they did not yet have the legal standing to do and thus emphasizing the value of voting—may underlie their success in moving targeted voters to the polls.

The twenty other experiments PICO ran in February 2008 did not have statistically significant results. Half of these remaining experiments were conducted by PICO's Sacramento Area Congregations Together (ACT), which targeted a treatment pool of 1,008 voters across Sacramento for mobilization. ACT engaged a number of volunteer leaders, including many youth leaders, who walked precincts during the two Saturdays prior to the election. In addition to infrequent voters in eighteen low-turnout precincts, ACT also targeted Hmong-surname voters in eight precincts in Sacramento with high concentrations of Hmong residents. ACT volunteer leaders were prepared to carry out these efforts through a number of training sessions provided by ACT staff. These key leaders in turn provided training to new volunteers in their respective communities.

PICO's Relational Culture Institute (RCI) affiliate, located in the Bakersfield area, coordinated three door-to-door experiments in February 2008 focused in precincts surrounding member congregations located in low-income communities with many African American and immigrant families, as well as a fourth effort in a low-income area of East Bakersfield. RCI employed what it called a "place-based mobilization strategy" to complement the door-to-door GOTV campaign. This included a Martin Luther King, Jr. birthday celebration and barbeque at Mt. Zion Church on January 5, 2008. All targeted voters were invited to attend a free barbeque and a short program. During the event, RCI volunteer leaders interacted with targeted voters, engaging in informal conversations around the group's purpose and goals. RCI's door-to-door campaign took place during the two Saturdays preceding the February 5 election. In addition to promoting voter participation, RCI used the February 2008 voter development campaign as an opportunity to initiate dialogue with neighborhood residents about concerns in their communities.

Two of the larger-scale campaigns that PICO mounted in February 2008, each targeting over 1,000 voters, were carried out by Inland Congregations United for Change (ICUC) in Riverside and San Bernardino Counties and Faith in Community (FIC) in Fresno. In the Inland Empire, ICUC conducted the largest door-to-door effort for PICO in February 2008, engaging 100 volunteer leaders, including sixty-five youth leaders from local high schools, to walk low-income areas of San Bernardino and Coachella Valley that had high concentrations of immigrant residents. In San Bernardino they carried out their work in cooperation with CCAEJ. In their large-scale effort, FIC targeted two precincts surrounding affiliated Catholic churches located in low-income communities with large numbers of immigrant families. The volunteer FIC leaders involved in this effort had previously been part of a yearlong citizenship class that included training in the PICO model of community organizing and civic participation.

Three smaller campaigns rounded out PICO's February 2008 efforts. In Stockton, People and Congregations Together (PACT) engaged volunteer leaders from a diverse array of congregations and community organizations to encourage local Latino and Southeast Asian American voters to participate. In Modesto, Congregations Building Community (CBC) conducted its door-to-door campaign in an ethnoracially diverse low-income community. Nine volunteer leaders with the congregation were trained by CBC staff to canvass the area around the congregation on the two Saturdays prior to the February election. Finally, the Orange County Congregation Community Organization (OCCCO) targeted largely Latino communities surrounding local affiliate churches.

Looking at the pooled door-to-door experiments (not including Winters), we find a statistically significant effect among those contacted of 8.6 percentage points (SE = 3.4). Including the mixed-method Winters campaign in our calculations raises this estimate to 9.5 percentage points (SE = 3.0). In other words, despite their individual variability, as a whole the February 2008 PICO door-to-door experiments generated a very healthy increase in voter turnout, well within the range we would expect from a well-conducted door-to-door canvassing campaign.

Buoyed by their success in February 2008, PICO affiliates continued to focus on door-to-door efforts for the June 2008 primary election. In Bakersfield, Faith in Action (FIA) used door-to-door canvassing to encourage turnout but also to develop relationships between leaders and neighborhood residents. Voters contacted were first engaged in a conversation about their concerns for the neighborhood and then asked to vote as a way of having their voices heard. In addition, FIA held a mayoral forum in Bakersfield attended by 244 residents that focused on community concerns, including public transportation, the inequity of parks and recreation in low-income areas, and youth violence.

The North Valley Sponsoring Committee (NVSC) affiliate coordinated efforts in the Sacramento Valley. NVSC volunteer leaders in the small farming town of Maxwell and the cities of Anderson and Sacramento canvassed the neighborhoods surrounding their congregations, mostly located in low-income and immigrant communities. Volunteer leaders in Maxwell and Anderson canvassed precincts during the Saturday before the election and canvassed the Sacramento precincts over the two Saturdays prior to the election. Bilingual youth leaders who canvassed with NVSC also volunteered at polling places on Election Day to help with translation.

In Sacramento, ACT canvassed precincts around member congregations and also hosted a mayoral candidates forum in May that was attended by more than 1,100 people. Four of the five mayoral candidates participated in the forum, which was organized by ACT youth leaders and focused on youth issues. After the forum, the mayoral candidates were invited to submit written statements of their youth agenda to ACT; these statements were compiled and distributed during the June 2008 GOTV campaign. In Stockton, PACT worked with dozens of volunteer leaders from two congregations to canvass low-propensity voters and hosted a mayoral candidates forum attended by more than 300 Stockton residents. As in Sacramento, statements were taken from the candidates at the forum and given to canvassed voters.

In Modesto, CBC and youth from eight local high schools and organizations knocked on the doors of infrequent voters in four Modesto precincts during the two weekends before the June primary election. Voters were asked to vote and given polling-place information. CBC canvassers also engaged voters in conversations about the issues and changes they would like to see in their neighborhood and community and were invited to future CBC meetings to further discuss those issues. In Fresno, Faith in Community (FIC) and dozens of volunteers from FIC member congregations, neighboring schools, and community organizations knocked on doors the two Saturdays before the June primary. FIC also held several candidates forums, including a mayoral forum to discuss local concerns. In San Bernardino, ICUC worked with four congregations and eight schools to canvass low-propensity precincts during the two weekends before Election Day.

Many of these experiments generated impressive contact rates, including 79.4 percent for one precinct in Fresno and 80.0 and 89.2 percent for two experiments conducted in Stockton. Other contact rates achieved by various PICO affiliates were also quite healthy, even when they did not reach these high levels. For this election PICO requested that many experiments be randomized at the precinct level, rather than at the household level, in order to streamline logistics. Yet experiments randomized at the precinct level (rather than at the household level) generate larger clustered standard errors, making achieving statistical significance more difficult even when similar experiments are pooled. For the door-to-door June 2008 campaigns randomized at the precinct level, pooling generates a treatment-on-treated effect of 0.9 percentage points (SE = 13.9). Pooling the fifteen door-to-door experiments that were randomized at the household level generates a treatment-on-treated effect of 1.0 percentage point (SE = 1.3). We should note that these results need to be interpreted with caution. Unlike in earlier rounds, the data collected by PICO affiliates for the June 2008 experiments were plagued by measurement error, with multiple instances of incorrect coding for the outcome of contact attempts. In other words, for this set of experiments we do not have reliable data for individual contacts, so we may have inaccurate estimates of the impacts of these campaigns.

For the November 2008 election, PICO affiliates conducted fifty-one door-to-door experiments. Four of those were randomized at the precinct level and forty-seven at the household level. One of these campaigns reached statistical significance—ACT's effort among Hmong American voters in North Sacramento. It was the only November 2008 CVI door-to-door campaign that had a statistically significant effect on voter turnout. ACT ran similar campaigns in North and South Sacramento, both targeting low-propensity Hmong American voters and providing in-language materials focusing on Hmong community concerns. Yet the effort in North Sacramento achieved a much higher contact rate (47.1 percent), suggesting a higher-quality campaign. While other CVI campaigns for this election also achieved high contact rates, this level of saturation in a small community that is not usually on party and candidate radar screens may account for this unique outcome. Many Asian American communities are excluded from mainstream GOTV efforts, but this is even more true for the Hmong community because of the low socioeconomic status and low levels of participation of Hmong American voters.[25]

By far the largest of PICO's November 2008 efforts was undertaken by ICUC in San Bernardino (N = 4,569). Leading up to the November election, ICUC engaged more than 120 volunteer leaders from two member congregations and youth leaders from local organizing committees to canvass infrequent voters in two wards in San Bernardino. ICUC conducted GOTV training over a two-day period in conjunction with CCAEJ; additional training was conducted on the day of canvass.

The next two largest campaigns, each targeting more than 1,000 voters, were carried out by CBC in Modesto and FIC in Fresno. In Modesto, more than 100 CBC volunteer leaders from eight congregations and community organizations canvassed neighborhoods surrounding member organizations in Modesto during the two weekends before the election. CBC also held a voter education workshop at which participants received training in how to properly fill out ballots and were given polling-place information. Additionally, CBC held a voter education forum with the mayor of Modesto, a county supervisor, the Modesto city school-board president, representatives from the Congress member's office, and city and county officials. More than 300 residents attended the forum. In Fresno, FIC worked with more than 100 volunteer leaders from seven member congregations and community organizations to reach infrequent voters. FIC held four citywide training sessions and two orientations to prepare for its GOTV campaign; sessions were offered in Spanish, Hmong, and English. Additionally, FIC held a candidates forum for local races. FIC's GOTV work attracted considerable media attention from local news television stations, particularly its campaign in the low-income community of Pinedale.

In addition to conducting a number of larger campaigns, PICO also expanded its experimental repertoire in November 2008. PICO's LA Voice experimented with a mobilization campaign using neighborhood lists generated by canvassers to include residents of their neighborhood. Volunteer leaders were recruited from member congregations to be precinct captains for their home neighborhoods and given short lists of names of low-propensity voters in their neighborhoods (generally just the few city blocks adjacent to their own homes) to contact through door-to-door canvassing. Even though these experiments with the precinct captains were quite small, the vast majority of those for whom contact information was provided—in eleven of the sixteen individual experiments—had a positive effect on turnout. Again we see the power of social networks in voter mobilization.

LA Voice also engaged in more traditional door-to-door canvassing in November 2008. Approximately seventy-five LA Voice leaders from all across the city of Los Angeles participated in LA Voice's November GOTV campaign. Leaders each conducted door-to-door outreach efforts in their local neighborhoods, which ranged from East Los Angeles to Santa Monica, South Los Angeles, Hollywood, and Mid-City. LA Voice conducted one to two training sessions at all participating congregations during monthly organizing committee meetings and hosted a one-day training session at the LA Voice office in mid-October 2008. Leaders and organizers trained the participants in how to answer questions about local propositions and initiatives and role-played canvassing situations with leaders.

FIA engaged in ten door-to-door campaigns in November 2008 targeting voters in a variety of congregations and locations in the city of Bakersfield. They canvassed targeted voters on the three Saturdays leading up to the election and on Election Day and trained canvassers at the beginning of each Saturday. In the Stockton area, PACT engaged sixty-eight local leaders, including forty youth, to contact infrequent voters around six member congregations and community organizations. PACT also held two candidate forums—one on state issues and one on the local school-board race. More than 100 people attended each forum. Additionally, PACT compiled and distributed to voters a booklet on responses received from mayoral and city council candidates. PACT's GOTV work was featured on the front page of Stockton's local newspaper, the *Stockton Record*, and PACT was featured on the local Univisión affiliate.

Overall, the coefficient estimates for PICO's November 2008 door-to-door campaigns are generally weaker than those from previous election campaigns, reflecting the high level of base (control group) turnout for this historic presidential election. For the four precinct-level experiments (three by ACT and one by ICO), the pooled treatment-on-treated effect is 14.6 percentage points (SE = 21.4). Despite the one PICO campaign with a statistically significant impact—ACT in North Sacramento—our pooled analysis of the experiments randomized by household (not including the LA Voice social networking campaigns) produces a nonsignificant treatment effect of 1.1 percentage points (SE = 1.7). This suggests that most PICO canvassers, like their counterparts in the other November 2008 CVI campaigns, had few voter targets available to them to move to vote in this exceptionally high-turnout electoral environment.

When considering the results from all the CVI door-to-door campaigns, we find evidence that the messenger matters. This conclusion varies from that of Sidney Verba, Kay Lehman Schlozman, and Henry E. Brady (1995, 154), who found that "respondents, once asked, are not systematically more likely to accede to requests from those who share their race or ethnicity or their gender than to requests from outsiders." Even though we were not looking at messenger differences by race and gender per se, our findings suggest the mobilization message is more effective if it is delivered by someone who could be defined by the targeted voter as a neighborhood or community insider. Experiments by SCOPE and PICO indicate that immediate neighbors and fellow members of congregations were more influential than non-neighbors and non-congregants in moving voters to participate. Given that SCOPE canvassers were multiracial and that they were organizing in a multiracial neighborhood, it seems that shared neighborhood was an important factor for targeted voters. Similarly, PICO canvassers were able to mobilize their neighbors successfully even for the highly salient November 2008 election. Within these contexts, these canvassers may have been working to create a new type of "linked fate," one based on shared neighborhood circumstances rather than simply ethnoracial identity (Dawson 1994). At the very least, we see that these sociocultural interactions were significant and powerful enough to change the behavior of targeted voters.

Yet even when the canvasser was a stranger, not a neighbor, our results show that a simple request to participate remained a powerful motivator to turn out. In these undermobilized, low-propensity communities, invitations to join the polity were widely accepted and acted upon, with significant and robust increases in participation in a variety of electoral and community contexts, for a variety of ethnoracial groups located across the state of California, from the northern counties above Sacramento to the Inland Empire and South Los Angeles. Turnout in the control groups ranged from the single digits—for example, 5.4 percent in Riverside in the June 2008 CCAEJ campaign—to highs reaching saturation, such as the 88.2 percent rate for SCOPE's control group in November 2008. Yet personal invitations to vote emphasized and underlined by the appearance of a volunteer canvasser on one's doorstep generated significant increases in targeted voter turnout.

Our analysis of these 117 door-to-door canvassing experiments, conducted by the same groups across multiple electoral cycles, in high-salience and low-salience elections, in different geographic and local contexts, and with appeals to a diverse set of voters, shows that door-to-door campaigns are effective in getting low-propensity voters from communities of color out to vote. The results suggest that well-run campaigns fielded by organizations with strong reputations and strong institutional capacity are able to have significant positive effects among these voters. We also found that canvassing that takes advantage of existing social networks can be more effective than campaigns using non-local walkers. It is that sociocultural interaction on the doorstep—the personal invitation into the polity—that makes this strategy so powerful and effective.

Yet our findings also inject a note of caution into the generally positive frame surrounding the effects of door-to-door canvassing. Most published studies have reported on successful door-to-door campaigns. Our work with these organizations shows that not all campaigns are effective, even when carried out by the same group. Some of this variation is owing to the electoral context, some to staffing changes or alterations in the organization's approach to the work. We are not the first experimenters to find that sometimes door-to-door campaigns do not work, but stories of failure have more difficulty getting published in academic journals (Gerber, Green, and Nickerson 2001). However, these findings might be more instructive for groups attempting this work than those showing unqualified campaign success. For that reason, we go into greater depth about the strengths and weaknesses of these campaigns, and possible explanations for this variation, in chapter 5.

The Variability and Power of Door-to-Door Canvassing

The dyadic sociocultural interaction between canvasser and voter, and how it varies, is a large part of the reason why we see such variation in results across door-to-door campaigns. Every dyadic sociocultural interaction is situated within a different neighborhood and electoral context, with varied nonverbal cues, resulting in unique sociocultural interactions each time one takes place. In our observation of campaign training, we saw significant variability in how some of the organizations approached this work, especially among those who experienced staff turnover in the midst of the electoral season, like CARECEN and CCAEJ. In contrast, SCOPE, because that organization has long-term experience with this work, was the most consistent in this regard. To make up for differences in individual background, often groups will assign more experienced canvassers to partner with newer ones, but this is not always possible. Many canvassers are sent into the field with little training and limited supervision. As a result, we found much more variability in the delivery of the message at the doorstep than we did with the delivery of the message on the phone. Some canvassers made up their own scripts, changed some parts of the script, or delivered the script differently each time they talked to a voter. In addition, *how* they delivered the script varied considerably across canvassers, in terms of eye contact, tone of voice, posture, and the seriousness with which they took the work. These nonverbal cues are an important part of a sociocultural interaction and inform the narrative dyad.

Thus, although door-to-door is perhaps the most powerful tactic for getting out the vote, it is also the most variable. This is because the sociocultural interactions in these conversations on the doorstep are richer in context and interaction than are those that occur on the phone. In just one minute of face-to-face contact, humans interpret a wide range of information, much of it outside the verbal communication taking place; they respond to appearance, facial expressions, posture, et cetera. In addition, many of our participating organizations used the mobilization conversations to engage in organization building. Almost all told voters about what their organizations do, many had issue surveys as part of the canvassing script, and all invited voters to participate in organizational activities. Therefore, it is entirely possible that the efforts were quite successful in building a reputation for the organizations and fomenting support for their issue-based work. Perhaps it is the combination of these goals that, at times, diluted the GOTV message. It may be best to conceptualize phone banking as a less complicated form of personal contact—one that, because it lacks nonverbal cues, is more able to remain focused solely on the voting message. Door-to-door canvassing, because it includes these additional cues, may in fact be doing important political work by building social capital above and beyond voter turnout. However, these impacts fall beyond the scope of our statistical analysis.

This discussion is not meant to minimize how important and effective door-to-door canvassing is for increasing voter turnout. The significant effects generated by many of these campaigns are testament to that fact. But we believe that researchers and organizers should also consider what additional kinds of civic engagement are likely to result from canvassing conversations. In these campaigns, voters from marginal communities had individuals come to their homes, not to sell them anything, but just to deliver the message that their vote and voice mattered. The campaigns also taught voters that there were community organizations in their neighborhoods engaging in efforts to improve the community's overall well being. We know that this kind of personal invitation and this kind of collective engagement are rare in American politics. Because they are even rarer in high-immigrant, low-income ethnoracial communities, they increased not only voter turnout but also community-level social capital. That impact on the American polity must be taken into consideration when assessing the power of door-to-door campaigns.

5

NOTES FROM THE FIELD: RUNNING AN EFFECTIVE MOBILIZATION CAMPAIGN

Lucas and Jackson, aged fourteen and seventeen, felt out of place in this neighborhood. Even though it was located only a few blocks from their school, it was over a mile from where they lived, and the area felt completely unfamiliar. The lawns were fenced and gated, with large, fierce-looking dogs patrolling the small patch of land in front of each house. Recruited by their local church, the boys had volunteered to help motivate individuals to vote. For every hour they worked, a club at their high school would receive a donation. Yet, when they found themselves in the field, they began to feel nervous about what was expected of them. They had received little training from church organizers about how to talk to voters and had little political experience themselves. They found it daunting to imagine knocking on strangers' doors to talk to them about voting. To make matters worse, one of the first houses they visited was home to two unfriendly pit bulls that took issue with being woken from their nap by strangers wanting to visit their owner's house. Being chased by the dogs made them even more wary about the work they had agreed to do. The resident voter, needless to say, did not receive a door-to-door canvassing visit that day.

Unleashed aggressive dogs, wild geese, and hostile targeted voters were just a few of the unexpected challenges that CVI canvassers faced as they worked to mobilize low-propensity voters across the state of California. These are some of the many contextual factors that affect campaigns but rarely get mentioned in the voter mobilization literature. Yet they do have an impact on canvasser morale and therefore on overall campaign effectiveness. After our evaluations of the CVI campaigns during the 2006 elections, we found that there was a great deal of variability in how effective these efforts were. Campaigns that looked very similar on paper—implemented by established organizations with similar levels of capacity, motivated volunteers, and experience in voter mobilization—nevertheless had strikingly different results. The anecdotal information from the field during the 2006 elections suggested to us that organizational and contextual factors might help to explain that variability.

When we looked to the literature to provide us with guidance about what factors might be at play, we found that published experimental work on face-to-face canvassing almost always showed the campaigns to be effective. The studies described door-to-door canvassing as effective in mobilizing a variety of populations, including youth, Latinos, and African Americans (Green and Gerber 2008; Michelson 2003, 2005, 2006; Green and Michelson 2009). Published reports seemed to suggest that door-to-door canvassing *always* worked, regardless of the quality of the campaign. Yet Donald Green and Alan Gerber's (2008) brief summary of the dozens of door-to-door campaigns that have been conducted since their path-breaking work in 1998 (Gerber and Green 2000b) includes references to several (largely unpublished) campaigns that failed to move voters to the polls. The problem, then, is that almost all published reports—possibly owing to the bias against publishing null results—suggest that door-to-door canvassing is universally successful, whereas a more thorough examination of known experiments reveals that door-to-door canvassing sometimes produces results that are weak or inconclusive (Sterling, Rosenbaum, and Weinkam 1995).

Some studies have considered the question of quality in mobilization campaigns, at least in terms of phone banking. David W. Nickerson (2007, 271) notes that phone banking volunteers have tended to be more successful than paid callers in encouraging voters to participate because "conversations with volunteers appear genuine and organic to voters." Their genuineness overcomes the seeming advantage of professionals, who are "better trained and possess more experience." His research separates ideological commitment from good preparation for phone banking: training professional canvassers to be more conversational and compelling volunteer canvassers to sound more scripted. The results show clearly that quality of phone bank conversation, not ideological commitment, explains variations in phone bank effects. Quality phone banking relies on a conversational tone, on allowing canvassers to establish rapport with voters (Nickerson 2006). We posited that the same issues of quality control might also help explain variations we found in the effectiveness of the CVI GOTV campaigns. But this was pure speculation on our parts. On a practical level, the existing literature left us with little guidance about how to conceptualize and identify the factors that are necessary, if not sufficient, for campaign effectiveness.

During the February, June, and November 2008 election cycles we sought guidance by employing dozens of multilingual field observers to monitor organizational training and canvassing efforts.[1] To our knowledge, this is the first time that large-scale field experiments have been combined with in-depth qualitative observational data. We believe that our analysis of the over 1,000 field reports we received across the three 2008 election cycles, reflecting more than 3,000 hours of field observations, provides a unique insider's view of the nuts and bolts of running campaigns, the idiosyncratic nature of their implementation, and, therefore, a better understanding of how organizational capacity, priorities, and tactics intersect to influence campaign effectiveness. From a theoretical standpoint, we are opening up the black box of the canvassing operation and considering how canvassers and the organizational infrastructure in which they are embedded influence the quality and impact of the mobilization conversation. In doing so, our goals are to suggest that researchers consider how to incorporate these issues into field experiment design and to provide a primer for organizations interested in embarking on this sort of organizing effort.

Methodology

To carry out the qualitative portion of our evaluation, we recruited a multilingual research team made up mostly of graduate students and some undergraduates. Our field team participated in one day of training in observation before each electoral campaign; we discussed the purposes of the research, the principles and ethics of field observation, and the documentation we were asking them to provide after each observation session. Most of our observers worked for us for more than one campaign cycle. Each time they observed a GOTV training or canvassing session, they were asked to fill out a standard form about each canvasser they observed, to record the time spent observing, and to rate how conversational the canvasser was, how long the interaction took, and what portion of time during the conversation was spent specifically on the GOTV message (all reporting forms may be found in appendix B). They also were asked to provide a brief narrative outlining the strengths and weaknesses of each canvasser and to record any issues of note within that observational session.

During the training sessions, we showed films of mock canvasser training sessions and mock canvassing interactions, in addition to engaging in repeated role plays, in order to calibrate the team's understanding of what constituted a conversational interaction. To ensure the internal validity of their evaluations, we made certain when scheduling the observers to rotate them across shifts and canvassers so that individual campaigns were rated by a variety of observers. This was especially challenging with our Asian-language observers, since it required that we have at least two observers for each language and for each Asian-serving organization (APALC's and OCAPICA's geographic distance from one another made using the same observers for both groups not always feasible). During each electoral cycle, we continually fielded comments and feedback from our research team; we used that information to adjust and enhance our observation plan. The result was a voluminous amount of material about all the 2008 campaigns, with a focus on the best and worst of the canvassing efforts.

Ensuring Campaign Quality

We want to begin this discussion by emphasizing how challenging canvassing work is, whether on the phone or door-to-door. Most people are not comfortable talking to strangers, much less contacting strangers to tell them how they should behave (and, by implication, when talking to low-propensity voters, suggesting that their previous behavior—not voting—was not how they should have behaved). Our observer reports repeatedly reflected the difficulty of sustaining canvasser morale in the face of the many obstacles that canvassers encountered while engaging in these efforts. Here are just two examples:

> The three canvassers were enthusiastic at the outset and at times very conversational. They all spoke at least some Spanish and this was particularly crucial as this was a very poor, and almost entirely Latino neighborhood. [The canvassers need] more rehearsal time spent dedicated to what to do when you know someone is present in the house, but they don't acknowledge you. There were many refusals on the part of the contacts. [The canvassers] failed several times to ask for other contacts that were registered at the same address. This again speaks to the lack of rehearsal time spent during training . . . Safety was a bit of a concern on the part of the canvassers as the neighborhood was abundant with unleashed dogs . . . A journalist covering the GOTV campaign was bitten. Enthusiasm on the part of the canvassers faded after many refusals as well as having the few contacts that were made turn out to be quick exchanges where the contacts most often had already voted. (PICO Burbank, June 2008)[2]

> On several occasions, when a contact actually did arrive at the door the canvassers stood in silence, uncertain of what to say or which one of them was going to say it. Again, perhaps this speaks to a need for more extensive rehearsals [role plays] during the training session. (ICUC San Bernardino, June 2008)

Thus, the discussion that follows must be understood within the context of community organizations with limited resources fielding teams of mostly volunteers to engage in very challenging political work. The CVI canvassers continued to go into the field and face these obstacles because they believed in the importance of what they were doing. Maintaining their canvassers' motivation and their belief in the cause and ensuring that canvassers are representing their sponsoring organization appropriately are the major challenges that any organization faces when engaging in this work. All of the CVI organizations did exceptionally well given their many operational constraints. In the analysis that follows we can learn from their work; the analysis should not be considered an indictment of any particular organization, its staff, or its activities.

Recruitment

Given how demanding canvassing is, it is not surprising that the most overarching finding from our in-depth analysis of the 2008 campaigns is how difficult it is for community organizations to recruit, train, and motivate high-quality canvassers. This was true in every electoral cycle. Especially with regard to a door-to-door campaign, recruiting volunteers, ensuring that they are well trained and comfortable with the script, and making sure they arrive on time, leave when they are supposed to, and reach their target number of contacts each shift are huge challenges for organizational supervisors. All of our groups used a large proportion of paid canvassers, although the hourly rate tended to be quite low. Some organizations instituted remuneration systems that rewarded returning canvassers. Others created higher-paid "group leader" positions to reward and keep experienced volunteers. Yet all the organizations were aware that it was not the money that kept canvassers engaged in this challenging work but their commitment to the overall cause. As SCOPE pointed out in its final report, being one of their neighborhood education team (NET) leaders required a "deep level of organizational commitment, investment, and political will." The organizations that were best able to foster and nurture that organizational commitment and political will were better able to recruit and keep talented and experienced canvassers to conduct their mobilization work.

SCOPE, for example, was skilled in fostering an esprit de corps among its volunteer canvassers and paid street teams. To be hired as a paid canvasser by SCOPE, an individual had to fill out an application and sign a "doctrinal commitment" to SCOPE's organizing philosophy. Thus, at the most basic level, those involved in a paid capacity in the campaign had to have a level of buy-in beyond their pay. In organizational meetings and training sessions, SCOPE continually stressed the ways their voter mobilization effort was part of an Integrated Voter Engagement (IVE) program that linked voter outreach with SCOPE's policy work promoting the development of Green Jobs in South Los Angeles. Trainers and SCOPE staff, therefore, continually made connections between each individual's vote and the voter's ability to address the community's pressing economic needs. In addition, SCOPE held training sessions for its canvassers before each walk, reinforcing the nuts and bolts of how they should do their work and also inspiring them about what they were about to do and making clear that they were part of a larger collective effort to create social change in their community. That sense of purpose was reinforced at the end of each canvassing day when canvassers came together to discuss what they had accomplished with their day's work. Thus, canvassers' feelings of mutual accountability and broader purpose got carried into the field, helping SCOPE in its mobilization efforts. It also helped SCOPE to recruit and retain highly motivated and effective canvassers.

Other groups, such as CCAEJ in Riverside and the PICO National Network's Congregations Building Community (CBC) in Modesto, also worked to foster a positive sense of community, collective responsibility, and mutual purpose across their canvassing teams. CCAEJ's Riverside office created an intimate atmosphere to strengthen the ties between the canvassers and the CCAEJ staff. For example, the group shared homemade meals provided at the end of each canvassing day. PICO's CBC Modesto workers also shared provided meals. Canvassers met in a park at the end of the day and were offered pizza. As the canvassers were eating, they were encouraged to share their stories about the day, both the good and the bad. For both of these groups, sharing a meal at the end of the day while discussing and laughing over collective successes and failures helped to develop a sense of community and camaraderie among canvassers and staff.

Groups also made important accommodations for canvassers, including providing activities for canvassers' children and multilingual training for the canvassers. Because a large proportion of the Riverside CCAEJ canvassers were mothers, the staff provided canvassers' children with two large tubs—one filled with toys and the other with crayons and coloring books—so the children had something to do while the women were in the office. The simple accommodation to the women's need for child care strengthened the ties among canvassers, their families, and the CCAEJ staff. Even though other organizations allowed canvassers to bring their children to walks and training sessions, few had a plan for keeping the children occupied so their mothers could focus on their canvassing work.

CVI organizations also provided important language accommodations to their canvassers during training. Both SCOPE and PICO's LA Voice conducted their training in English and Spanish, providing simultaneous translations to Spanish-speaking canvassers, either using headsets or translators. Although there sometimes were technical glitches, this accommodation made Spanish-speaking canvassers feel like a part of the team and ensured that they were much better prepared to go into the field than they would have been had the training been conducted only in English. These supports and accommodations helped these groups to build team spirit and also to recruit and retain experienced, committed canvassers.

Another innovation with the canvasser training at CCAEJ Riverside was the use of a unique ice breaker: a ball game. The canvassers would stand in a circle and toss a beach ball back and forth. The segments of the ball were labeled with different numbers. Whatever number the canvasser catching the ball's thumb landed on, she or he had to answer the associated question. The questions included various facts about canvassing that the organizers were expected to be familiar with, such as their responsibility to remain nonpartisan, to mark the walk lists in a certain way, and to know what the acronym CCAEJ stood for. Through this game, CCAEJ Riverside found a simple way to conduct refresher training while getting canvassers' blood moving and building team morale before they went out into the streets. Our observers noted that as a result, "all of the organizers appeared to be very close to most of the canvassers and communicated with them in a very casual and intimate manner. Canvassers were always assigned to the same precinct areas. Canvassers were very familiar with the canvassing lists" (CCAEJ Riverside, June 2008).

Other recruitment efforts employed by our groups seemed less effective. Because the November 2008 presidential campaign drew so much attention and created such a high level of excitement within the California electorate, the CVI organizations found themselves competing with partisan campaigns to secure volunteers. In the end, many of the CVI groups turned to alternative sources of volunteer talent, particularly high school students. A number of PICO affiliates throughout California used high school students for their November 2008 campaigns.[3] Through their volunteer efforts some of these students were earning money for their favorite high school organizations. Although many of these youth were committed and effective in their work, our observer reports suggest that some of them may have had a lower level of commitment and professionalism than other canvassers. Observers reported these students leaning on doorjambs when talking to voters instead of standing up straight, delivering the mobilization message inconsistently, and evincing a lack of conviction in their voices:

> The canvassers did not read [the] script or deliver the message of voting to the voters. Canvassers were not conversational. They didn't take their job seriously. For example, when they arrived to a home they would giggle. Susana was shy and only spoke with one voter. As for Andrea she did most of the talking with voters. When the voters would ask questions the canvassers were confused and not well prepared. (PICO, Long Beach ICO, November 2008)

Some of this lack of professionalism may simply be because canvassing is difficult, and even more so when a teenager is being asked to knock on an adult's door to tell the adult how to behave. Some of the PICO affiliates made a point of sending out adults with the students, which seems to have lessened the problem. These observations reflect how challenging the role of canvasser may be for adolescents. But they do raise the point that organizations need a clear strategy for recruiting volunteers, a sense of the potential strengths and weaknesses of the recruits, and plans for addressing those strengths and weaknesses.

Similarly, some of our phone banking campaigns also had difficulty fielding strong volunteers during the November 2008 presidential election. OCAPICA, in particular, seemed to be negatively affected in Republican Orange County given the expectation that the Democratic presidential candidate was going to win. Observers described November 2008 OCAPICA volunteers as "not very excited about the campaign" during training. There were also many more reports in November of callers chatting with one another and of many more canvassers who were described as "first time" (and nervous) callers. OCAPICA staff spent time walking around the phone banking room to try to make those nervous callers feel comfortable and confident in their work:

> The supervisor [Aala] asked if the canvasser needed help when she seemed flustered. Aala spent a lot of time to thoroughly answer questions to make sure the canvasser was clear. OCAPICA staff generally walked around to answer questions, or be available to them. They passed out water to callers . . . [As a result], the canvasser felt comfortable asking Aala questions, and spoke with her about various things three times. Ty and Liz, the other staff members, were also present and circulating to help answer questions. At about 7:30 pm, Ty announced to everyone that they should also tell voters about a voter hotline phone number, and gave that number out. (OCAPICA, November 2008)

APALC also seemed to have more new canvassers in November 2008, and they also were reported as being less motivated than callers in previous campaigns:

> He was making personal calls at the start of the phone canvassing session with his cell phone. It seemed like he was not eager to start his work . . . He barely followed the script and called in a way you would call an acquaintance. For example, the conversation would start like "Hello, I am calling on behalf of the Asian American Project as a student volunteer. Is ______ home?" In some instances, he would say "Hello?" and the person receiving the call would just hang up on him. To me, it lacked professionalism and the rest of the conversation was not quite on track with the script and did not follow the right steps and expressions. (APALC, November 2008)

In addition, our observers pointed out that many of the new callers signed up for shifts with their friends, and they often sat next to one another in the phone banks. This proximity had the negative consequence of leading these phone canvassers to begin racing to see who could reach their contact quotas first. Because these canvassers were working in a centralized phone banking office rather than walking door-to-door independently, OCAPICA and APALC supervisors were able to catch and address these problems. We saw these sorts of lapses in all the 2008 campaigns. But, the fact that reports of such behavior were much more common in the November 2008 campaign shows how the ongoing challenge of volunteer recruitment can become even more intense during high-salience elections.

Training and Feedback

As we saw above, the training process is related to recruitment insofar as groups are able to use their training sessions to foster feelings of mutual commitment and accountability among their canvassing staff. Overall, we found that training that was interactive, especially programs that included opportunities for realistic role-playing before sending canvassers out into the field, were especially effective not only at preparing canvassers to deliver the script but also in building their confidence and their feelings of ownership of the campaign they were involved in. In particular, organizations that solicited canvasser feedback and had systems in place for integrating that feedback into a campaign as it progressed were able to field more effective campaigns than those that did not. Effectiveness increased for two reasons. (1) Canvassers who felt heard also felt important and felt that their experiences mattered, which helped to maintain their commitment to the mobilization effort and to the organization itself. As a result, they tended to be more effective at mobilizing voters. (2) Canvassers are an organization's eyes and ears. All the organizations that participated in the CVI were working with limited resources. If they listened to canvassers regarding what parts of the script were most effective, what neighborhoods or groups of voters seemed more responsive to mobilization, and what aspects of the logistics worked best, they were better able to target their resources in ways that were likely to have the greatest impact.

Many organizations did an excellent job of soliciting and incorporating canvasser feedback into their campaigns. The most common way of doing this was to bring all the canvassers back to the main office at the end of the day to debrief and talk about what went well and what needed improvement. Groups like CCAEJ Riverside and PICO's CBC Modesto that provided food at these debriefing sessions were successful at creating a relaxed atmosphere where canvassers felt heard and supported. In addition, given that their canvassers often had just walked in 100-degree heat for six hours, providing them with a solid meal was critical to keeping up their morale as well as their blood sugar. Other organizations, such as PICO's Sacramento Area Congregations Together, used this sort of feedback to motivate new canvassers. In one debriefing session, a group leader shared her experience of having an elderly woman she contacted begin to cry because in her thirty years as a voter, no one had ever come to her door to invite her to vote. These sorts of stories reminded canvassers of why the work they were doing was important and worthwhile despite all the difficulties they may have faced, and would continue to face, in the field.

Other, more irregular approaches to soliciting feedback were less effective. For example, CARECEN's canvassers often did not have their own transportation and were dispersed over relatively long distances to do their canvassing. Many of them had to get rides from fellow canvassers or take the bus to get to their targeted precincts. As a result, "There is also a lack of interaction amongst all the canvassers. They leave without talking to each other and do the same when they get back. There is no exchange of ideas or tips" (CARECEN, February 2008). To spare them the time and effort it would take to return to the central office (and then make the long trip home), in June 2008 CARECEN staff tried holding once-a-week feedback sessions on Saturdays where canvassers could share their experiences and ask questions of the larger group. Yet these sessions were voluntary, so no session included a majority of canvassers. In November 2008, again in an attempt to balance opportunities for feedback with their canvassers' transportation and time constraints, CARECEN implemented a group-level feedback system. Group leaders would meet with their canvassers at the end of the day near the targeted precincts to get feedback that they would then relay to the central office. This allowed canvassers to go straight home from their canvassing areas. CARECEN implemented this policy to streamline their demands on canvasser time while still collecting important feedback.

Yet, since CARECEN did not have daily training sessions before canvassing started, as SCOPE did, nor any other sort of collective orientation during the canvassing sessions, its walkers lacked a sense of connection with the larger collective and a sense of common purpose. In addition, its canvassers could not share their wisdom with the larger group, nor learn from others; they had no opportunity to develop a more extensive repertoire of potential approaches to their canvassing work. This group-based approach also placed the group leader in a much clearer position as supervisor to the canvassers, thus creating a feeling of hierarchy that had not been present in previous campaigns. By inserting the group leaders as the liaisons between the CARECEN staff and the canvassers, CARECEN inadvertently made canvassers feel more like employees than community activists working together for a cause.[4] Our observers reported numerous comments from canvassers expressing unease with this new hierarchy. Some of this unease could have been a reflection of animosity arising from the fact that the group leaders earned more than the other canvassers. But some unease also seemed rooted in resentment about having to speak through the group leaders, which seemed to have led to an overall sense that their feedback was not being heard by CARECEN staff.

More punitive approaches to training canvassers did not seem to be effective either. Two CVI organizations decided to randomly call voters marked as contacted on the walk sheets in order to check up on their canvassers' reporting. In both cases, supervisory staff let canvassers know that they were going to follow up in this way. One supervisor went so far as to tell his canvassers that if he found "canvasser fraud," he would shut down the campaign. From our observations, canvassers who were told that their supervisors would verify their work did not behave any differently; canvassers continued doing their work in much the same way as before, without any significant increases in quality. Both these organizations, it so happened, were organizing in dangerous and challenging neighborhoods. One can imagine that a canvasser working for free or for very little money, who was spending hours knocking on strangers' doors in inclement weather and, at times, in dangerous situations, would not respond well to being told they were not trusted to have accomplished what they said they had accomplished. Less punitive approaches that focused on establishing feelings of trust and accountability would probably have been more effective in achieving the organizations' GOTV goals.

The more effective GOTV groups that we observed were able to produce feelings of mutual accountability by establishing direct feedback loops, developing what are known in the organizational behavior literature as "flat" hierarchies (van Alstyne 1997; Borgatti and Foster 2003; Cummings and Cross 2003; Harris and Raviv 2002). In a flat hierarchy, individuals across all levels of an organization are able to have contact with one another, which increases their impact on decision making. In an analysis of the effect of hierarchical design on work group performance, Jonathan N. Cummings and Rob Cross (2003, 208) find that high-performing groups tend to have "sufficient ties among members to facilitate information flow, without over-reliance on one member." Their findings, they conclude, "suggest an important link between structural properties of work groups and performance . . . [It may be] effective to engage in processes that help to promote lateral connectivity so that groups can leverage their collective intellect" (208). They suggest that their analysis be extended to informal organizations, such as those in the CVI study. Although our observational analysis of these groups' efforts is by no means definitive, it does suggest that those groups best able to integrate their canvassers into the feedback loop, thereby leveraging their "collective intellect," seemed to be more effective overall.

Supervision

Given the high level of turnover in canvassers between one campaign and the next, and even during campaigns, most canvassers had limited GOTV experience; many had never engaged in an activity that required them to initiate scripted discussions with strangers. Therefore it was important for organizations to develop effective systems for canvasser supervision. The organizations that engaged in ongoing training and supervision had more consistency in the quality of their campaigns than did the others. Supervision covered a number of aspects of the campaign, including controlling the message and gathering and managing data.

CONTROLLING THE MESSAGE Getting canvassers to stay on script was by far the most common challenge faced by all the CVI organizations. Especially in the case of door-to-door canvassing, our observers found a wide range of variability in terms of the degree to which canvassers delivered the message and even knew what organization they were representing. The CVI organizations attempted a wide variety of messages during the course of the CVI electoral campaigns. With each analysis, we began by determining what seemed to work best at getting out the vote in terms of messages and what did not. In addition to comparing the effectiveness of messages across the CVI groups, we analyzed a number of experiments comparing the effects of different messages delivered by the same group. An embedded script experiment with APALC in which we compared an "ethnic duty" message with a "civic duty" message found no statistically significant difference in their impact on turnout; similarly, a NALEO November 2008 embedded script experiment in Los Angeles found no difference between an "optimistic" script and a "pessimistic" script. Our analysis of a March 2007 message experiment with NALEO suggested that a more information-rich message was no more effective than one that just cued the importance of voting. In general, organizations like SCOPE and CCAEJ Riverside used scripts that cued collective needs and how they related to voting. For example, SCOPE's script said:

> Hi, I'm your neighbor ______. I'm also a volunteer with AGENDA,[5] we're a social justice organization here in south LA. Did you know that in the past two elections south LA has turned out more voters than the other areas of the county? Normally, south LA votes at least 10–15 percent below the rest of the city. That is why we've been ignored and neglected by politicians for decades. Now we have a progressive mayor that's saying we need to create jobs and that south LA deserves to get those jobs. And we need to make sure he delivers on this promise. One way is to make sure we keep voting. (SCOPE, June 2006)

We can see in this script that SCOPE is cueing a geographically based collective identity. It is defining that identity as a voter identity—"people in south LA have been turning out to vote." Therefore, were the targeted low-propensity voters to vote, they would be acting like their neighbors in South Los Angeles. SCOPE is also signaling their organizational impact. The script credits the turnout in the past two elections to SCOPE's mobilization efforts in South Los Angeles. They are inviting voters to join a successful cause. It is clear how this script cues a sense of mutual accountability, collectivity, and political efficacy on the part of targeted voters.

Scripts that connected voting to something concrete, and in particular scripts that spoke to issues of collective empowerment, seemed to be more effective than others. In addition, messages that were clearly focused on voting also seemed to be more effective. For example, CCAEJ Riverside's voter surveys were significantly shorter than those from San Bernardino, making more of the conversation about turning out to vote. SCOPE also was more effective in those campaigns where it fielded a shorter voter survey. At first we believed that the effectiveness was due to the fact that the message to vote was not diluted with other cues. We still believe that to be accurate, but our observations suggest another factor: shorter scripts more focused on voting were less likely to be subject to canvasser improvisation in the field. In other words, a simpler, more direct voting message made it easier for canvassers to remain on script. Our observers noted that deviating from the script was, indeed, a chronic problem.

Some canvassers, because they were inexperienced and perhaps lacked confidence in their public speaking, did not deliver the entire script. When faced with a targeted voter, they said only, "I'm here to tell you to vote," or "I'm here to let you know that there is an election coming up on _____." Others simply asked, "Do you plan to vote in the coming election?" and then said, "Thank you," and left, regardless of the answer. This report from Long Beach is typical:

> The canvassers had very little knowledge about the voting procedure and frequently asked questions. I'm not sure they were instructed with additional information that people may frequently ask since all the time they would turn to me [the observer] for advice. The main purpose of their visits seemed like finding each household and checking if they were going to vote or not. A typical canvassing would go like "Hi, I'm _____ from ICO. We just wanted to know if you're going to vote for the Nov. 4th election. Okay. Thank you." There were never any questions on whether voters had any questions regarding the election, GOTV or the importance of getting people who would not vote engaged. (PICO, Long Beach ICO, November 2008)

Other canvassers, because they had had limited experience with the organization they were working for, could not identify it correctly or answer questions about its mission. Some of PICO's high school canvassers, for example, chose in their canvassing conversations to identify with their school rather than with PICO.

At the other end of the conversational spectrum, some canvassers were very effective communicators, entering into lengthy conversations on the doorstep with targeted voters or sometimes their family members and discussing politics and neighborhood issues at length but rarely talking about voting in the targeted way that the organizations had asked them to. For example, in June 2008, CCAEJ Riverside had a canvassing team that was very good at conversing with voters but not as effective in terms of asking them to vote:

> The group seemed very experienced. They had already familiarized themselves with the neighborhood and its citizens, so they quickly went through their precinct area without any trouble. They were confident with every contact and never once referred to the script (although they did briefly recite a few memorized sections). They were very conversational in their approach. The canvassers would go out in pairs and in my particular pair, Juana and Gema, they decided to take turns speaking. This seemed to keep the flow of conversation organized and uninterrupted when making contact. Six out of seven of the contacts spoke predominantly or only Spanish, so it helped that Juana and Gema's primary language was Spanish . . . [Yet] what I noticed right away with this pair was that they spent no, or very little, time encouraging the GOTV message. For the most part, they only spoke about the local issues and upcoming events (i.e., trying to get streetlights in this neighborhood that had none, a town meeting concerning local issues, and the voting process for those issues, and the grand opening of a community water park). (CCAEJ Riverside, June 2008)

The observer goes on to note that the pair often got into long conversations with voters about different topics. In one instance, Gema knew one of the contacts personally, and they began talking about their mutual families. When the voter's daughter came into the living room, Gema commented on how fat the girl had become, and admonished the mother (who also happened to be the targeted voter) to put the child on a diet. This experience suggests the wide range of possible of messages that canvassers could be delivering to targeted voters during a door-to-door campaign.

Two examples from PICO's Faith in Action affiliate in Bakersfield also show the variability in how a group's message got translated in the field by different canvassers:

> [The canvasser] interacted by simply making that one to one contact and having what sounded like a casual conversation . . . she would mention the voting percentage rates of wealthier areas in Bakersfield and compare it with the percentage rates of the area in which the citizen was located. She rationalized this by suggesting that the citizen compare this with the more readily available resources that the other side of town had. She would then show the citizen a map covered with dots that specified the areas in which the infrequent voters were located. (PICO, Faith in Action, June 2008)

> The group of canvassers was very young and they did no role playing in the training session. When they went out into the field, the girls canvassing were unprepared. They had not reviewed the scripts and acted shy when they were going to knock at someone's house. One of the girls went off script and did not follow the directions that were given to her. These girls were very unprepared . . . they did not know what questions [from the voter] they could and could not answer . . . they were not engaging with voters, not conversational at all . . . [At one doorstep] the infrequent voter they approached refused the literature the girls wanted to hand out. The girls . . . felt really intimidated by this situation. During the canvasser training not a lot of time went into explaining what to do when approached by an angry voter or what to do when there is more than one voter in a household that needs to be contacted. The girls would not ask for any additional voters, and then only when they checked their sheets after leaving the house did they realize they should have contacted two people instead of one. (PICO, Faith in Action, June 2008)

These canvassers are working for the same organization, ostensibly delivering the same message, but we can see that the first canvasser supplemented her script with a great deal of useful and probably persuasive information. The information had been provided in the group training session, and the canvasser had put it to good use. Those in the second group, no doubt because of their youth and lack of experience, were less able to utilize the information given at their training sessions and therefore may have been less able to move voters to the polls.

Similarly, SCOPE, despite the high quality of its training and high organizational capacity, also showed significant variability in terms of canvasser effectiveness:

> Canvasser introduces herself appropriately, even shakes voters hands. Fantastic communication skills. Vocal tone of voice was normal and realistic. Great Spanish translation. Wonderful job in engaging with voters. Canvasser had great responses regarding voters' questions. Outstanding job in delivering script to voters. She appropriately informed voters about the proposition packet. Over all, she did a terrific job. (SCOPE, November 2008)

> Canvasser was not conversational at all. Did not read script. Canvasser did not read survey questions to voters. For example, when canvasser would get to a voters house, she would only say "Hi my name is Juana Muñoz and I am walking the block to ask people if they're going to vote." After the voters said yes to the canvasser, then Juana would respond "thank you for your time." (SCOPE, November 2008)

Our observations from CARECEN in June 2008 show similar variability. Miguel, a recent immigrant who had been in the United States for only seven months, was described as tentative in his conversations at the door: "Whenever he asked for people and recited the script, he would look down at his notes. He rarely emphasized the GOTV message." In contrast, another team of CARECEN canvassers is described as having a very different approach:

> The group had three canvassers and each person had a designated job. One woman would speak about the importance of voting and use as examples the current issues directly affecting the local neighborhoods (i.e., the lack of street lights). The next

> girl would follow up with a survey in which each citizen would rate an issue on a scale of 1–4. The third person was in charge of noting each contact's response and also keeping track of where each house was located and filling in the precinct chart. Both speakers were very articulate and effective communicators; they briefly and clearly covered all the necessary points—making good use of the little time they had with each contact. (CARECEN June 2008)

Other CARECEN canvassers were found to be quite skilled, too:

> I followed Osmi and she was a very experienced canvasser. She is one of the most efficient canvassers I have ever observed. She knocks on the door three times only so she doesn't waste any time waiting for someone to answer that's not home. Osmi also has personalized her message. It goes something like, "Hello my name is Osmi and I am here looking for _______ to encourage you/them to vote on November 4th. [Once the voter comes to the door] Have you made up your mind on whether you'll vote or not on November 4th? Oh, you will/won't? Fantastic or I'm sorry to hear that. Let me also invite you to join CARECEN at its informational forum on November 1st to help you make the best decision for you. Thank you for your time." This was her standard approach and it was so effective, efficient, and amiable. She knew her way around the neighborhood, knew what she could and could not say. She also knew which apartment buildings she should wait for someone to let her enter and which she could hold off until Saturday when she had more time. Lastly, at one apartment building as we were on the elevator a person asked what we were doing. Osmi told him and he was a voter on her list. She spoke with him in the elevator so that saved her some time. She was able to do this because she was so comfortable with her role as a canvasser. She was a great person to follow and learn from. (CARECEN, November 2008)
>
> I observed a very experienced canvasser. She was enthusiastic, knowledgeable (she was able to answer every question asked of

> her), and she had a great and effective strategy for canvassing the neighborhood. She was able to adapt her message to young voters and older adult voters. She emphasized the importance of voting and repeated the hours of the voting booths and the various voting stations located around the neighborhood. She was very personable and friendly. Even when people did not want to talk or open the door, she kept asking them short questions to get them to interact with her. The people who had short conversations with her was because they were rude/rushed, not because she wasn't great at getting people to listen to her message. It was a joy to watch her interact with various people. (CARECEN, February 2008)

One CARECEN canvasser seems to have used his noncitizen status as an advantage in convincing targeted voters to turn out and vote:

> Because this particular canvasser could not vote, he felt very passionate about his job. There were several instances where people did not sound convinced about their commitment to voting and José would motivate them by telling them it was their duty since there were people living in this country who were ineligible to vote. The canvasser knew his precinct well and could point out which houses he had visited on which day. The canvasser always left by saying, "Remember, February 5th—is the day to vote." (CARECEN, February 2008)

Other groups, such as CCAEJ, also had effective canvassers:

> Sofia is the strength. As a seasoned veteran and someone who connects extremely well with everyone she contacts, Sofia demonstrated the way a canvass should be done. Her strong presence, verbal skills (both English and Spanish) and ability to make personal connections made all the difference. Although she was very familiar with the script and could have done the canvass completely unscripted, she still used the form as a guide to ensure she didn't miss anything, that she delivered her message, and that she asked her questions in a uniform manner throughout. (CCAEJ San Bernardino, June 2008)

Another CCAEJ San Bernardino canvasser is described as less effective:

> The biggest weakness was the difficulty the canvasser had in conveying the reason for his visit. The message was very general about elections on June 3rd and some voters were quickly confused and asked if they were presidential elections. The canvasser then said no, but had difficulty articulating what kind of elections they were. Instead he handed a pamphlet as a way to inform the voter. I think a few more training sessions would be helpful in preparing canvassers. (CCAEJ San Bernardino, June 2008)

The CVI organizations varied significantly in terms of their levels of experience with canvassing work, the quality, frequency, and content of their training, and the amount of experience their canvassers had. Yet our observers found excellent and not-as-effective canvassers working for every one of these groups. Since it is impossible for organization staff to accompany every canvasser at all times, this variation is inevitable and typically goes unobserved. Individuals come to door-to-door canvassing with varied levels of natural ability and differences in terms of their willingness to follow directions. Training is important, but even excellent, ongoing training cannot completely erase this human-level variation. That variability in the quality and content of the sociocultural interaction on the doorstep goes a long way toward explaining why our door-to-door results are less consistent than results from the phone bank campaigns.

In a phone-banking effort, the same human tendencies to improvise are present, but the centralized structure of the phone bank makes it easier for organizational supervisors to remind callers of the script and to intervene when they fail to follow it. For example, both APALC and OCAPICA put up signs all around their phone bank rooms, in large letters so that callers could see them, reminding canvassers of the hotline numbers, their targeted contact goals for each category of voter, and other information they might need to share with voters during their calls. The organizations put together half-page cheat sheets for callers that they taped to each of the computer monitors. Beyond the supervisors' efforts to provide easily accessible information, being on the phone allows canvassers to reference their scripts more easily than is possible when speaking to someone (and trying to maintain eye contact) in a door-to-door interaction. Our observers noted that before calls, APALC and OCAPICA canvassers often referenced their materials:

> [She] reads over her materials diligently to prepare herself better. She has the script out ready to look over and has some key factors highlighted. (APALC, June 2008)

In many of the OCAPICA and APALC reports, observers mention that callers referenced the script or that they used notes to remind themselves of the message while on the phone. This type of referencing and reminder is not as easy to achieve when walking door to door.[6]

Not surprisingly, our observers' reports on the phone bank callers were more consistently positive for different callers than were their reports on the door-to-door canvassers:

> [The caller] is trilingual. Very hard working. She is very good at trying to convince voters to vote. Moderate calling speed. She is polite and friendly and helps voters find their nearest polling place. She encourages voters to take advantage of their voting rights . . . Good positive energy, vibe, and attitude. (APALC, June 2008)

> Caller very fluent and very professional when speaking to voters. Good use of vocabulary in carrying message across.[7] She is very fast. Good energy and vibe in effort of encouraging voters to vote. Saying things like, "it's a good opportunity for Asians to cast their votes." It was almost like a commercial or some sort of campaign movement. (APALC, June 2008)

> She was very conversational in Mandarin, Cantonese, and English and very good at engaging in unscripted conversation and answering very nuanced questions about the June and November elections, registering as a decline to state voter, and the Asian American Voter Project, especially for younger voters. She also used the *nin* (very formal) form of address with elderly voters. (APALC, June 2008)

> Good positive attitude when hung up on by voters. Hard working. She follows the script. She is very polite and energetic. She

> seems very excited to phone bank and nicely greets voters "good night" at the end of the call. (OCAPICA, June 2008)

> The caller came in today with an upbeat attitude. She is extremely formal, and friendly. She speaks exceedingly proper. Her vocal tone is very clear. She is respectful, and courteous to callers. Does extremely well in answering all of voter's questions. Makes sure voter received all necessary materials. Obtains voter's method in voting [absentee vs. at the polls]. Great job in asking to speak with other voters in the same household. Overall, she did extremely well. (OCAPICA, November 2008)

Overall, our reports from the phone banks showed much more consistency in the sociocultural interactions than we saw in the door-to-door campaigns.

But even with the reminders and cheat sheets, callers sometimes went off script.

> The canvasser did not follow the script word-for-word and, while at times this enables a more casual conversation, it also discourages the voter to stay on the phone. For example, the canvasser often omitted from which organization the canvasser is calling. As a result, a significant number of voters hung up before the canvasser delivered the GOTV message. The canvasser expressed that the script is difficult to follow because the translation uses too many "jargons" familiar to only politically engaged people (i.e., the translation of "Asian American Voter Project" in Vietnamese is awkward, not casual). (OCAPICA, June 2008)

> The canvasser did not follow script (i.e. referred to herself as calling from "OCAPICA" and did not explain what it is). The canvasser was unprepared—she lost a lot of time reading and rereading the script several times. The canvasser was not fluent in Vietnamese (pronounced many names incorrectly, stuttered in Vietnamese). Added to this was her nervousness and her unpreparedness. (OCAPICA, November 2008)

Yet the close supervision that canvassers had during phone banks, with callers usually being located in one room with one or two staff present at all times, meant that lapses were almost always caught and addressed quickly. In the previous example, the caller's concerns about the translation were taken into consideration and adjustments were made to the script. Another OCAPICA story is representative of these types of interventions:

> This caller identified his name first and then explained about the [Asian Pacific Islander Vote Project] and the reason for phone banking very clearly. Therefore, voters tended to stay longer instead of hanging up at the beginning of the call. But, at the very beginning of his phone banking he did not follow the script (in English), so a supervisor directed him to follow these steps as his script: introduction, make sure they've received the important voting materials, and then a focus on the GOTV message, and last provide additional information such as hot line number and polling places. He followed these steps for the rest of his phone banking and his phone banking went well and was fairly conversational. (OCAPICA, June 2008)

Here a new phone canvasser was not following the script, yet the supervisor was able to intervene almost immediately, before he had completed even one shift. This type of real-time intervention is almost impossible in a door-to-door campaign.

We had reports of these sorts of real-time interventions across our phone banking organizations. At NALEO, for example,

> at some point, Miguel [the supervisor] did have to tell some of the younger phone bankers not to mess around (they were chatting, laughing). It was really simple though, and didn't come off as oppressive, but was firm. (NALEO, Los Angeles, November 2008)

Our APALC observations also reflected the staff's continual engagements and interventions to ensure that the phone banks continued to run smoothly. The observations from November 2008 were typical of all their campaigns:

> Today was the 1st day, it took about 15–20 minutes for APALC to set everybody up . . . Pink papers of the five points to hit dur-

ing a phone call were posted in every canvassing room, which was very helpful.

Before they started canvassing Eric went around the room to make people comfortable in their seats by helping adjust the [computer] monitor, phone or keyboards.

Before the start of the session Donna gave a brief notice to everyone in the room about follow up calls. That the canvassers will be calling those who said they would be voting by either mail or at the poll. Afterwards, she went on about how they shouldn't be talking about unnecessary things when they were calling to save time. Also, she told the canvassers to try and do the introduction part just like the way the script is prepared since many were neglecting to do so, as well as always mentioning the hotline information at the end.

Some people were new to the follow-up calls since they were to fill out [paper] sheets rather than computer screens. Donna and Eric were busy at the start of the session to instruct new canvassers on the follow-up calls and checking the computers. It took up quite some time, about 10 minutes so some were not starting to canvass at the dot of 6 o'clock.

Donna was going around the room hearing how the people were canvassing. It seemed helpful to first encourage the canvasser [about] what they did well and then point out some matters that they were doing wrong. In most cases, it helped the canvassers do better.

For a few times, this man kept leaving messages on answering machines that contained a briefing of an introduction, voting materials, the ballot, whether they knew if they were supposed to vote by mail or at the poll and if they needed any assistance, they should call the hotline number. After Eric found out [the man not actually talking with prospective voters], he stopped doing so.

As we saw with OCAPICA, APALC staff were continually engaged in monitoring and improving their phone canvassing work. The structure of a phone bank made it possible for them to give new instructions, as we see above, at the start of each session. Or they could instruct canvassers to alter strategy mid-session. And finally, the proximity of the canvassers to the supervisors meant that the supervisors could intervene and correct canvassers on the spot, ensuring that the overall GOTV message was delivered in a more consistent fashion than we saw in the door-to-door efforts.

Our analysis shows there was much more variability across canvassers and more variability in the nature of the sociocultural interaction on the doorstep than on the phone. This variation, in conjunction with differences in the cues within the scripts and in the way organizations conducted training, is what we believe explains the higher levels of variability we found in the results of the door-to-door campaigns.

The ability of CVI organizations to supervise phone banking more closely not only helped the groups keep their canvassers on message but also helped them to develop the important feedback loops that we mentioned above and to foster the esprit de corps that is critical for a successful mobilization effort. First, having the supervisor present made it possible for canvassers to ask questions in the midst of their phone calling, giving them immediate feedback and also creating a supportive atmosphere. These observations from APALC and OCAPICA are typical:

> The Project Manager came in to check on us from time to time. [There was] a friendly, welcoming environment (laughter, sharing of experiences, etc.). [The] supervisor is alert, ready to answer questions. He walks around the room from time to time, cheerful and friendly. (APALC, June 2008)

> All callers were in one room so the atmosphere was easy for asking questions (and peer callers chimed in, etc.). (OCAPICA June 2008)

OCAPICA also brought in a Vietnamese-language coordinator (since neither of the staff supervisors spoke Vietnamese) to "act as a personal aid to Vietnamese callers." The goal was to provide extra help, and the callers had this assistance available to them during each phone banking shift that included outreach to Vietnamese voters. Finally, both OCAPICA and APALC scheduled breaks in the middle of their phone banking shifts, usually with food provided, where callers could sit with supervisors to talk about how things were going and strategize about how to make their calls more effective. These forms of additional support served the dual function of maintaining campaign quality by making the calls more consistent and making callers feel heard and invested in the mobilization process.

Another issue relating to the GOTV scripts and canvasser supervision was the inclusion of short surveys by a number of the organizations in their canvassing scripts. For some, the survey was intended to serve as the foundation for a public announcement about community support for a particular set of issues. For others, the surveys were for internal use; they were meant to gauge support for the group's services and/or programs. As with the GOTV message, our observers found that the implementation of the surveys varied significantly.

One issue was the length of the instrument. Most targeted voters were not willing to sit through being asked a long series of questions on their doorstep. This meant that canvassers often became unwilling to go through the entire instrument, filling in answers on their own or simply skipping whole sets of questions. For example, in CCAEJ San Bernardino, a mother-and-daughter team were effective canvassers, but they were inconsistent in soliciting survey responses across targeted voters from different ethnoracial groups:

> The mother-daughter team worked well, probably better than the average Spanish-English team. In any case, it was convenient to have one speaker of each language since the neighborhood was mixed Hispanic and African American . . . [Yet] when administering the survey to target voters, the follow-up question: "Do you have any concerns or complaints about your community? What are your concerns?" was given mostly to the *Mexicanos* and not so much to the African-American contacts—it was a comfort with making conversation issue. (CCAEJ San Bernardino, June 2008).

Other observers found variability in the degree to which CCAEJ Riverside canvassers successfully completed their surveys versus canvassers from San Bernardino:

> Among the Riverside canvassers, there is more of an insistence on the part of the Riverside canvassers to get every single field on the canvassing lists filled. That is, they insist on asking and getting answers to the GOTV and CCAEJ-specific questions. Not once, on a Riverside observation did I see reluctance or hesitation (even in the face of rude or unfriendly contacts) to ask the handful of questions on the script. (CCAEJ Riverside, November 2008)

One can imagine that the quality of the information received varied across canvassers from the two offices, as did the effect of the administration of the survey on GOTV conversations.

Finally, long or short, the surveys seemed to complicate the canvassing process, giving canvassers another thing to keep track of. For inexperienced or nervous canvassers, this could be especially burdensome.

> The canvassers were carrying too many things. They had a survey and a pledge for the voter and sometimes they forgot to do one or the other. Plus, I think that it also overwhelmed the voter. (PICO, Faith in Action, Bakersfield, November 2008)

It is not clear, then, how effective the organizational surveys were in advancing these groups' mobilization goals.

Our two organizations serving Asian Americans, APALC and OCAPICA, utilized surveys differently. To find out what community members thought were the most important issues facing them, both organizations held a number of focus groups prior to each campaign in order to solicit feedback about different political questions. They used that feedback to frame their mobilization message and the structure of their GOTV campaigns. APALC and OCAPICA did include questions for voters in the phone bank script itself, but those questions were related to whether the voter had received in-language voting materials from their county registrar. If the voter had not, the caller provided them with a contact number to request the materials. These questions served an organizational purpose, since APALC and OCAPICA had long worked to ensure the provision of in-language voting materials to language-minority voters, as required by law. They used their phone banking to gauge how many voters, and of what national origins, had not received materials. But their questions were directly related to voter needs and voter access, and they were able to provide helpful information to voters on the spot. Their survey, then, was clearly related to the GOTV message and served as another way to make the targeted voters feel important and empowered within the electoral arena.

Overall, our observers found that what the CVI groups wanted their canvassers to say and what was actually said in the field varied dramatically. This is understandable. Canvassers enter into this work with varied levels of experience and ability, and knocking on a stranger's door or cold-calling a home to tell a stranger to vote is a difficult thing to do. There were a few ways, however, that CVI groups were able to minimize this variability in the delivery of the script. First, groups who conducted phone banking in a central location were much better able to monitor what their canvassers were saying and to intervene when problems arose. Those phone bank campaigns that relied on individuals using their cell phones to call voters from remote locations ran into many of the same problems that we saw with door-to-door canvassing.

Second, campaigns that sent out door-to-door canvassers in pairs were better able to maintain consistency in what occurred on the doorstep than those that sent out single canvassers. SCOPE tended to pair new canvassers with more experienced canvassers. This provided the new canvassers with another training opportunity, as they often deferred to the more experienced canvasser on the doorstep until they felt comfortable with the script. Thus the new canvassers could hear responses and approaches to voter resistance and voter questions before they took the lead themselves. More generally, our observers found that canvassers who had partners were less likely to go off script—perhaps because they knew that a second person was watching.[8] Yet many of our CVI organizations, because of a lack of volunteers, sent canvassers out alone, or sent them out in pairs but had them canvass opposite sides of the street. Canvassing alone seemed to have a negative impact on overall quality, as reflected in the degree to which those solo canvassers were able to remain on script.

We also think it important not to send canvassers out alone for safety reasons. Over 80 percent of the canvassers for these CVI campaigns were women, and we have no reason to believe this percentage is an anomaly.

These women were walking in dangerous neighborhoods and knocking on strangers' doors. CARECEN canvasser reports mentioned that women regularly heard catcalls from men, came across drug deals during their walks, and had to walk in buildings with dimly lit corridors populated with "dangerous-looking" men.

> Lastly, the canvassing is done from 4–8 PM and a few times she [the canvasser] seemed a little concerned for her safety because it was dark and there were groups of men outside in the street which would at times "cat-call" to her and I. I can see how this time in the evening would cause one to be intimidated. (CARECEN, February 2008)

Other canvassers had to work in similarly challenging areas:

> The area canvassed today included a number of foreclosure/abandoned/for sale homes, apartment buildings with restricted access (a main entrance key was needed to get access to the apartment, and a number of names that corresponded to businesses, warehouses or to nonexistent addresses). Elaine, who is from the general area (about half a mile from where we were canvassing) often mentioned that she knew people who used to live in this house or that house, reflecting the transient nature of the neighborhood. (CCAEJ San Bernardino, November 2008)

> We were in a very rough neighborhood with many abandoned or foreclosed homes, front yard dogs, houses with addresses removed or obscured, and with several people who simply refused to answer the door. The women rushed through the list and did not stop to take a break or engage in conversation. (CCAEJ San Bernardino, November 2008)

Given the dangers present in these neighborhoods and the canvassers' lack of familiarity with the areas, it is not entirely surprisingly that two canvassers were robbed in San Bernardino:

> Two boys went to a rough part of San Bernardino and got robbed at knife point for their iPods and skateboards. Everyone should be advised to keep all their personal belongings at a safe place

and not take them out with them when canvassing. (ICUC San Bernardino, November 2008)

Because of these challenges, as part of the task of supervising campaigns, organizations need to make every effort to make the canvassing work as safe as possible. This includes having canvassers knock on doors in (at least) pairs, providing them with shirts or vests that identify them as part of the organization, providing them with flashlights, particularly on dark nights or if they are canvassing in dimly lit apartment buildings, and, finally, making certain that every pair has a working cell phone with them and an emergency contact number (in addition to 911) that they can call to get picked up immediately should something go wrong. Unfortunately, in the chaotic atmosphere that is often characteristic of campaigns, these safety precautions sometimes get overlooked, or shortcuts get taken, because organizations feel shorthanded or pressed for time. But safety must form part of any well-designed canvassing effort.

GATHERING AND MANAGING DATA The CVI was unique in that community organizations were being asked to collect data for a third party, who would conduct an evaluation of their work. But many of the lessons we learned about data management are applicable in more typical campaigns, in which organizations engage in their own internal evaluations. The CVI organizations saw their voter mobilization work as interfacing with their organizational goals in different ways. Some saw it as a way to build their membership base, others as a way to inform the community about their social service programs, and yet others as a way to deepen and develop their volunteer activist networks. All these goals required that the organizations maintain an accurate tally of whom they had contacted, in what fashion, and how each person responded. The consistent and accurate gathering of that data by canvassers and its effective collection and use by the organization was another significant challenge faced by the CVI groups.

Our phone banking organizations conducted their work using a cutting-edge new technology, developed by NALEO, that allowed their voter lists to be uploaded into a web-based interface. The callers sat in front of computer monitors, and information about their next targeted voter—name, phone number, in-language script, and pertinent contact information—appeared on the screen. The canvasser input information about each call directly into the computer interface, and that information was appended and recorded in the central database.

Though an elegant system in theory, there were some difficulties in practice, as with all technology. The system required that organizations purchase and clean their lists before loading them into the interface. In the case of our Asian American organizations, those lists had to be broken down by national-origin group, and then each voter had to be assigned a language to be called in.[9] This was a complicated process. In an ideal world, the preparation would guarantee that each caller would call only the appropriate targeted voters in the appropriate language. Vietnamese-language callers would only have Vietnamese voters come up on their screens with either Vietnamese or English scripts. The system worked remarkably well, but there were some glitches. On more than one occasion the computers went down, meaning the callers had to input their calls and results using pen and paper. The paper lists were often incomplete or sometimes had duplicate numbers. In other instances the callers exhausted a particular list but could not continue calling until more targeted voters of that national origin were loaded into the system. Thus, although the computer interface did simplify data collection in some respects, it also required a nontrivial amount of data savvy on the part of the organizations that used this technology.

Volunteers had to be trained to use the computer interface. Not surprisingly, they came to this work with varied computer skills and differing degrees of comfort with computers. The organizations had to organize training sessions that would be effective with volunteers who had very different skill sets. The difficulty of accomplishing that is reflected in an observer's report of NALEO's experience:

> One of the things that stood out to me most as a weakness was the presentation about running and using the phone bank and using the computer interface. The presenter brought up a lot of information that was not needed and that confused the attendees. The main trainer, Ethan, would have to keep interrupting to let everyone know that nobody actually had to do or worry about the things she [the presenter] was bringing up. Many of the attendees voiced their confusion numerous times. The person

> making this presentation did data entry so her tutorial used a lot of technical terms that attendees were unfamiliar with. With all this said, however, once the group was taken into a computer room where everybody actually got to look at the program for themselves and use it, a lot of confusion was cleared from the air. (NALEO, Los Angeles, November 2008)

Where the canvassers were multilingual, groups like OCAPICA and APALC also had to be able to communicate the important aspects of the computer interface in multiple languages:

> Older canvassers need to know how to use a computer interface when calling voters. Language trainers should be able to find appropriate individuals who speak the language to explain the computer interface to the volunteers. This gentleman also spent a great deal of time asking and studying about the computer interface. (OCAPICA, November 2008)

The canvassers' differing levels of comfort with the interface also led to quality-control problems in terms of coding call outcomes:

> I notice that she is not being careful when clicking the response buttons on the computer screen (i.e. at one point says the conversation she had was in Spanish, when it was in English). (NALEO, Los Angeles, November 2008)

Thus, although this computer technology simplified many aspects of implementing the multilingual phone banks, it also presented some challenges in terms of training and execution.

The door-to-door campaigns also faced data collection and management issues. In preparing for the door-to-door canvassing campaigns, the participating organizations had to create walk lists: sheets of paper that include the names of the targeted voters, their addresses, and some pertinent information (often age and gender) that may help in correctly identifying targeted individuals. These lists also typically include a set of codes—information the canvasser must fill in (often by checking boxes or circling words) to show what happened with each contact. The codes often cover such details as whether the specific individuals were contacted, whether they planned to vote, whether they were not at home, whether a message was left with a family member, whether a targeted voter was no longer at the address, whether the targeted voter was deceased, and so on. Because the walk lists have a limited amount of space, these codes are often given in shorthand—for example, "not home" becomes NH, and "will vote" becomes YV. If the campaign is bilingual, the codes and shorthand must be translated into another language as well. Confusion about the codes often can lead to errors, as we found in our observations.[10]

> The control sheets were later dealt with haphazardly [by the training staff] right before they [the canvassers] left to canvass, so it was not presented [n]or [were they] instructed properly. Later, the canvassers did not seem to care much about the accuracy of the sheets and had no idea how to categorize certain situations. Such as if someone in the house said they would vote or not vote, the canvassers would put the same mark for all the people in that household without asking them. (PICO Long Beach ICO, November 2008)

> There were incidents when the canvassers would pass by the house and found pickets like "postal workers back Obama" and would assume that these people in the household were going to vote, checking "vote" on the control sheets. Moreover, if there were several people in a household they had to talk to separately, the canvassers were not aware of doing so and would mark the same answer of what one person had said. That is, if one person said they'd vote, the rest of the people in the house were automatically checked as voting . . . After following them for the whole canvassing session, I realized they desperately needed more professional training and education about the election. From my perspective, the control sheets they filled out are highly unreliable since most were not home, moved away or checked by what one person in the house had said. (PICO, Long Beach ICO, November 2008)

> The young men were happy to be working and believed in the importance of getting out the GOTV message. They were enthusiastic. They ended both with extra emphasis on the GOTV message. The canvassers were very familiar with the neighborhood,

> however were not properly trained with the logistics of their job. It seemed like they did not role play prior to being let loose in the neighborhood. They were not familiar with the forms they had to fill out either. (CARECEN February 2008)

In addition to finding that canvassers had difficulty using the codes listed on the control sheet, we also found that some canvassers made up their own coding system to use instead:

> I noticed that the canvassers would use personal codes on the precinct lists in order to identify the homes that they already contacted and those that they had not. Even though this option is printed on the lists, I have typically seen a few of the canvassers using their own symbols, such as stars, hearts and checks. (CCAEJ San Bernardino, November 2008)

This is part of the reason why many organizations hold a short training session before each walk: to try to ensure that the data are as accurate as possible. One of the central goals of those refresher training sessions is to go over and explain the control sheets. Our observations indicate that those organizations that send canvassers into the field without an explanation of the codes or without periodic refreshers end up with inaccurate data from their canvassers, more so than do organizations that take steps to systemize the collection and inputting of data.

Along with the walk lists, organizations conducting door-to-door campaigns have to produce maps for their walkers to help them orient themselves on their walks. It is important that the maps be easy to read and accurate. In addition, our observations show that organizations cannot assume that canvassers can read the maps without proper training. Canvassers with all the participating organizations continually got lost or ended up on the wrong side of the street, or even sometimes on the wrong side of town.

> The canvassers were entirely inept at reading the map given to indicate where to go. As a result, they started nearly 45 minutes after leaving the office despite only traveling a couple miles at most. This continued with their inability to get a sense of where

> the houses were in relation to the map. (CCAEJ Riverside, November 2008)
>
> The canvassers' ability to read and interpret a map needs serious improvement. We wasted a lot of time walking back and forth on the same streets. (CCAEJ San Bernardino, November 2008)

Getting lost or having to walk great distances between houses not only decreased the time available for canvassing but also left canvassers frustrated and frazzled when they finally arrived at voters' doors. As we saw in chapter 4, our experiments found that canvassers were more effective the closer they were to their homes. We posited initially that this was because they were more comfortable being in their own neighborhoods and because they were able to establish feelings of commonality and trust with targeted voters by letting them know that they themselves lived close by. Given the degree of difficulty that canvassers had with map reading, we believe that the effectiveness of canvassing neighbors may also stem from their ability to find the right house, providing them with another level of comfort as they engaged in their GOTV work. The following assessment of Sarah provides an illustration:

> She was nervous about her first time canvassing, but she told me that she did not feel too bad because she lived near her precinct area and also because she worked at the local school, so she knew many of the people living in that area. (CCAEJ San Bernardino, November 2008)

This comment reinforces the point that neighbors should, when possible, canvass their own neighborhoods. If that is not possible, then organizations should attempt to assign canvassers the same areas repeatedly to make it easier for them to orient themselves and find their targets on their walks. Here is a typical observation:

> The canvassers were given areas that they had not previously canvassed for 2nd contacts. I think Mara would have been more successful if she had conducted 2nd contacts in the areas she had already canvassed . . . Walking lists should be organized with time efficiency in mind; Mara had streets that were far apart. (CARECEN, November 2008)

Our findings suggest that organizations should not assume that canvassers understand the map information they are given. They should build in supervisory safeguards in order to give their canvassers the support and guidance they need so that they may find their targets quickly and therefore conduct their work more effectively.

Once the canvassers visit voters and record the results of their interactions, the organizations need to have some method for inputting and utilizing that data. In the short term, organizations in the middle of a campaign need to be able to print out clean walk lists. These lists are clean in the sense that the names of voters who have been successfully contacted and the names of those known to have moved or passed away have been removed. That way canvassers can focus their efforts on new targeted voters each time they go out. While this may seem simple in theory, it can be complicated in practice. Given that these campaigns are conducted in a very compressed time period, effective data management often requires a staff person to input the data and print out the new walk lists. Sometimes, particularly on the weekend, that person cannot do the inputting overnight, between one canvassing session and another. In those cases, it is best to have canvassers work off their lists from the day before, given that they know what their codes mean and are familiar with the houses they have visited already.

A good example of the importance of short-term data use comes from CCAEJ San Bernardino in November 2008. Some of the canvassing took place on weekday mornings. One of our observers visited the same set of houses three times, all on a Tuesday or Wednesday morning. He reported feeling uneasy revisiting the homes, given that family members had already responded during previous visits that an address was only the voter's mailing address, that the targeted voters were too old or sick to vote, or that the targeted voters were working and therefore not at home. He was concerned that in this instance, the canvassers' persistence may have been counterproductive. Had CCAEJ had the opportunity to look at the non-contacts from that precinct and note the time of day the attempts had been made, perhaps that walk list could have been saved for a weekend shift, thus increasing the chances for success. During campaigns such as this, there are many moving parts that need to be kept in motion simultaneously. Having a regular and effective form of data management in place during a campaign helps GOTV organizations increase their effectiveness.

In the long term, organizations need to be able to use their data to map out previous GOTV campaigns, find out who among their contacts voted, identify targeted volunteer households, and plan subsequent mobilization efforts. Analysis like this requires a different set of data skills from those used in short-term data management, including the ability to access and manipulate statewide voter lists. Luckily, a new source of voter data became available in the state of California while we were engaging in this work—California VoterConnect. This data interface allowed nonprofit organizations to purchase voter lists inexpensively.[11] The interface also helped organizations to determine targeted voters and to format and print canvasser walk lists and maps. The project director at that time was Dan Ancona, who traveled to meet with CVI organizations to train them in how to use the web interface to advance their efforts. This service was invaluable for those organizations, such as PICO, that had very limited resources and staff to engage in data collection and management. Our experience shows that low-cost provision of voter information is key to building GOTV capacity among nonprofit organizations and to supporting and sustaining their long-term data-management needs.

Language Ability

Given the diversity of California voters, we found that canvasser language skills are a critical factor that organizational leaders need to take into consideration when planning their GOTV campaigns. As mentioned previously, APALC and OCAPICA's phone banking efforts showed that multilingual GOTV efforts—in up to nine languages—are not only possible but can be highly effective. Their efforts also show, however, how difficult it is to recruit bilingual (or trilingual) canvassers in that number of languages.[12] One of the key insights from their work is that it is important that canvassers be bilingual, rather than skilled in just one language, so that they can switch into the other language depending on each voter's comfort and preference (E. Lee 2009). We found this skill to be important in all the CVI campaigns:

> The ability to switch languages seamlessly is the asset that served the canvasser best. In the areas that CCAEJ is working[,] this

> skill, [as] I'm witnessing, is invaluable. (CCAEJ San Bernardino, June 2008)

> How conversational the delivery sounded completely depended upon whether the canvassers were speaking to an English-speaking voter or a Spanish-speaking voter. So, if they were speaking with a Spanish-speaking voter, the scripts sounded very conversational, and the ability to engage in unscripted conversation was very good. On the other hand, if speaking to an English-speaking voter, it was more likely not very conversational in the delivery of the script, and the ability to engage in unscripted conversation was not very good. (CCAEJ San Bernardino, June 2008)

> In the first room, I focused on two women. The first woman spoke with ease and didn't even refer to her notes or the script while making Spanish calls. She often engaged in unscripted conversations. She laughed often. However when she spoke to respondents in English she pulled out her script and followed it closely. The second woman seemed to get many more English-speaking respondents. She followed the script closely. Sometimes it was difficult to comprehend her. She did not follow the script as closely when the respondents spoke Spanish. In the second room, I observed two men who appeared to be in their mid-twenties first. They seemed to be more fluent in English. They made both English and Spanish calls sound like robo-calls. They followed the script very closely. I also observed a middle-aged woman who seemed to be most comfortable speaking Spanish. She was very conversational and friendly. She said things like "*anímelo, mándemelo a votar.*" She was very enthusiastic. Another young man sat beside her; he appeared to be in his thirties. This young man seems most comfortable with Spanish calls, often being very conversational. (NALEO, February 2008)

While it is true that our observers reported that few canvassers showed the same degree of comfort canvassing in both languages, they also reported that having the ability to switch languages in response to each voter's preference was critical to the success of a canvassing conversation.

Language ability was also important in the door-to-door campaigns. Although it is nearly impossible to field a canvassing team that can cover the range of languages present in the APALC and OCAPICA efforts, our observations show that fielding bilingual teams in English and Spanish should be standard practice for California voter mobilization organizations, given the demographic makeup of the electorate. If the targeted voters are from a particular ethnoracial group, such as Hmong, then the canvassers' language skills should be appropriate to that community. But many of our organizations were organizing low-propensity voters in general. In California, that means a nontrivial number of the targeted voters are going to be Latino. The Latinos may be English-dominant or Spanish-dominant in their language use. We found that being able to communicate in both languages was crucial in accessing these voters. Our observations showed that organizations had difficulty communicating with Spanish-speaking Latino voters *and* English-dominant Latino and non-Latino voters. On many occasions, according to reports, canvassers could not communicate with targeted voters because of the language barrier, or if they did communicate, it was only in a very limited way:

> The area that needs improvement is the Spanish speaking skills of one of the canvassers. Due to his difficulty with Spanish, the canvasser lacked confidence and clarity in informing the voter about what the June 3rd elections were for. Because of his difficulty with Spanish, María took initiative in speaking with the voters. (CARECEN, June 2008)
>
> This door-to-door session immediately followed a training. Of seven original canvassers, people paired off and drove to their canvassing locations. It took 15 minutes to arrive at the east side of Bakersfield. On the way, and throughout the canvassing session, the canvassers reiterated that they were outside their usual area. They were also unable to communicate very well as they did not speak Spanish and most people in the neighborhood were Spanish-speakers. (PICO, Faith in Action, Bakersfield)

The same was true of Spanish-dominant canvassers. They were less able to communicate effectively with English-dominant voters:

> Of the two canvassers, only one knew a little bit of English. This caused a great problem considering that the two partners split up and worked the block separately. I don't think I have observed any other groups doing this, since I'm pretty sure they were told to stay as a pair during training. (CCAEJ San Bernardino, November 2008)

> The two canvassers in this group knew very little English, practically none. The residents they were encountering were almost all English speakers. There was much confusion because of this and the two canvassers became very intimidated and nervous, to the point where they just asked residents if they were going to vote. Many times they forgot to ask for the registered voter on their list. (CCAEJ San Bernardino, November 2008)

> When encountering an English speaking resident, they [the voters] would often ask who they were and what they wanted. All the canvasser was able to say was, "I'm here for the voting." (CCAEJ San Bernardino, November 2008)

Had these canvassers been paired with English speakers, they could have effectively contacted a much larger number of voters than they did, and the campaign would have been more effective overall.

Canvassers responded to communication problems by developing innovative ways to ensure that they were understood. Saúl, a bilingual canvasser who was less comfortable with English than Spanish, noted whether or not the targeted voter was understanding what he was saying. If he felt they were not, he handed over the script for them to read:

> [When] the script is not receiving the expected responses, [he] will simply show the contact the questionnaire and have them follow along—that way they can read and clarify anything that they didn't understand from Saúl's delivery. (CCAEJ San Bernardino, November 2008)

Translations of an organization's handouts must be provided in the appropriate languages, particularly when the group recruits canvassers with additional language abilities:

> This election season they added Spanish-speaking canvassers but all the forms they had for the canvassers were in English. In addition the training was only done in English[;] a couple of the Spanish-speaking canvassers did not rehearse as well because the scripts were in English. (PICO, Faith in Action, Bakersfield, November 2008)

> None of the material the canvasser had was in Spanish; the script was not in Spanish either, which made it hard for her to give the GOTV message. None of the handouts were in Spanish either. (PICO, Faith in Action, Bakersfield, November 2008)

Because not having the campaign materials available in the appropriate language decreases the possibilities for effective understanding on the part of the canvassers and effective communication between canvassers and targeted voters, groups planning a mobilization campaign should ensure that they match their canvassers' language skills and canvassing materials with those of their targeted voters. The canvassers and the CVI organizations understood that effective communication is at the heart of a successful mobilization campaign. The diversity of the California electorate makes it critical that language skills be at the forefront of organizational planning for these sorts of efforts.

Ongoing Capacity

Our analysis shows the significant amount of organizational capacity and number of resources necessary to mount GOTV campaigns. Because efforts must take place within a compressed time period—our findings suggest within three weeks of Election Day—most of the work needed to run the campaign must occur long before the mobilization is scheduled to begin. Specifically, there are three key areas of organizational capacity that must be maintained between electoral cycles in order to successfully execute a GOTV effort. These are (1) growing and maintaining a volunteer base; (2) hiring and training staff; and (3) integrating GOTV efforts into a broad community-oriented policy program.

Because of the compressed timing of any GOTV campaign, organizations need to have a large and up-to-date list of canvassers that they can access within a short period of time to staff the mobilization effort.

For the best results, as we have seen, these volunteers should be familiar with the organization and its work, be committed to the organization's cause, and be from the targeted neighborhoods where the group will be canvassing. In an ideal world, canvasser recruits should be bilingual and have experience canvassing, which will make them comfortable engaging in mobilization conversations. Finding bilingual, experienced recruits is a tall order. Such a skilled volunteer base must be built and maintained. Only then will it be available when it is needed. Thus, organizations need to work in an ongoing way between campaign cycles to recruit, retain, and foster relationships with their volunteer pools.

Similarly, GOTV staff need to be a regular part of the organization, not temporary workers that get brought in around election time. That regular GOTV staff needs to be involved in expanding and maintaining the volunteer base, as well as engaged in building and nurturing relationships with volunteer leaders. A number of the CVI organizations experienced turnover—due to resignations and unexpected illness—among their GOTV staff. In all cases, the change in staffing occurred in the middle of the planning or execution of the GOTV effort. These events brought home the importance of having the GOTV work not belong to one individual but rather be the product of a team. That way, the campaign becomes identified with the organization and its mission, not the goals and personality of a particular person, which will probably make the work more effective in the long term. At the very least, it will make it much easier for an organization to adapt quickly in the face of the inevitable personnel shifts that will occur.

Finally, to be most effective in turning out voters and influencing policymaking, the mobilization program must be compatible with the organization's broader social and policy goals. SCOPE, for example, considered its GOTV work part of an Integrated Voter Engagement (IVE) approach. This meant that its mobilization program was defined as a central component of a multifaceted strategy designed to help the organization meet its political and programmatic goals. The result was that SCOPE canvassers were able to make clear, direct links between increasing voter turnout and SCOPE's ability to achieve its goals in terms of Green Jobs and improved economic equity for the South Los Angeles community. CARECEN, on the other hand, never developed a narrative that made connections between its voter work and its work providing social services for immigrants. Thus, canvassers could discuss CARECEN services with voters or the importance of voting, but they were not able to show voters the connection between their votes and the achievement of a specific set of political goals that CARECEN was trying to attain. For a GOTV program to be most effective, it must form part of a broader nexus of tactics that the organization engages in during and between electoral cycles. Thus, as our analysis shows, organizations cannot see GOTV work as an effort to engage in only during election years. For an organization to have a substantive impact on voter engagement, its organizing work and capacity building need to continue between election cycles. Only then will it have the capacity to mount an effective campaign come election time.

Conclusion

Our voluminous observer reports made it clear that this kind of outreach work is difficult and that a significant, ongoing organizational infrastructure is necessary to make GOTV campaigns a reality. As can be surmised from a number of the points discussed here, much of the work underlying a campaign happens well before the outreach effort begins. Proper planning in terms of canvasser outreach, supervisor and canvasser training, the creation and provision of multilingual GOTV materials, the design and presentation of maps and walk lists, the assignment of canvassers to particular areas, and so on, is crucial to a successful effort. Most of the published work on GOTV campaigns shows the effectiveness of personal contacts, through either phone banking or door-to-door canvassing; our work supports these findings. What the bulk of previous work does not show, however, is that face-to-face (or live phone) campaigns are not always effective. Our experience with the CVI organizations shows that organizational capacity and long-term planning play a critical role in determining which GOTV campaigns will have the greatest impact.

6

EXPANDING THE ELECTORATE THROUGH PRACTICE: VOTING AND HABIT FORMATION

One of the most important questions regarding voter mobilization is whether its effects endure. Are those who are impelled to vote in a given election likely to vote in subsequent elections? Very often, enduring effects are ascribed to the formation of voting habits, the argument being that people who cast ballots in one election become accustomed to voting: being a voter becomes part of their cognitive schemas. Other explanations are also compatible with enduring mobilization effects. For example, when those classified as low-propensity voters cast ballots in a low-turnout election, they may be reclassified as middle-propensity voters and attract the attention of campaigns eager to communicate with likely voters. The key empirical question is whether those who are randomly induced to vote in a given election are more likely to vote in subsequent elections than those ignored by GOTV campaigns.

With few exceptions, analyses of GOTV experiments have focused on turnout in the targeted election, with little attention being paid to the long-term consequences of mobilization. What evidence there is, however, suggests that there is a habit-formation aspect to voting—that the very act of voting is in itself a positive predictor of future turnout behavior. Using self-reported data from the American National Election Study (ANES), Richard A. Brody and Paul M. Sniderman (1977) use a variety of predictors to model turnout in the 1972 presidential election. They find that "regularity of voting emerges as the most important direct cause of electoral participation in the 1972 election. It towers over the only other factor directly related to turnout, the individual's level of political involvement" (347–348). Donald Green and Ron Shachar (2000) use the ANES panel studies of 1972–76 and 1992–96 to construct various instrumental variable models of the effect of past voting. They find that "turnout in a given presidential election is a powerful determinant of turnout in the subsequent presidential contest" and, further, that the effects are quite large; for example, someone who would ordinarily have a 17 percent probability of voting in 1996 would have an increased probability of voting—50 percent—if he or she voted in one of the two preceding national elections (566).

Green and Shachar consider several competing hypotheses to explain these results. First, they note that voting brings an individual to the attention of political parties and campaigns, which would, in a subsequent election cycle, be more likely to target that individual than a nonvoter with GOTV messages. The ANES-based models include variables controlling for self-reported contacts and discussions, so Green and Shachar reject this possibility as unlikely. While recent work suggests that such self-reports of contact can be remarkably inaccurate (Michelson and García Bedolla 2010), Green and Shachar argue that "it is difficult to attribute effects of this magnitude to political mobilization" (2000, 570). A second possible explanation is that political participation has psychological repercussions, such as an increased sense of political efficacy. Yet the models use all of the psychological orientations included in the ANES surveys and control for such factors. A third, related explanation is that there are unmeasured psychological factors at work, such as the presence or lack of apprehension about the act of voting. The fourth and final explanation put forward is that participation "confirms and reinforces one's self-image as a civic-minded, politically involved citizen. The more one votes, the more one comes to regard going to the polls as 'what people like me do on election day'" (571). In other words, voting becomes part of a person's cognitive schemas through practice.

There are significant limitations to what can be learned about voter turnout and mobilization from survey-based research (Green and Gerber 2008). Despite the strong findings offered in these studies, a robust test of habit formation in turnout requires the implementation of a longitudinal field experiment, such as the CVI. Several efforts to this end have been made by previous researchers. In a small experiment conducted two weeks prior to the May 1970 Democratic primary, Robert E. Kraut and John B. McConahay (1973) interviewed a random sample of Italian Americans living in New Haven, Connecticut, about their political opinions, then tracked their turnout behavior in both the May primary (for a U.S. House seat) and an August primary (for a U.S. Senate seat). Turnout was significantly higher in the treatment group (N = 52) than in the control group (N = 52) for both elections: 48 percent of the treatment group and 21 percent of the control group turned out in May, and 50 percent of the treatment group and 31 percent of the control group turned out in August. A second experiment was conducted by Richard F. Yalch (1975) prior to the aldermanic elections in Chicago in June 1973 and the runoff elections in July 1973. Individuals interviewed prior to the June elections were more likely to vote than those in the control group and were also more likely to vote in the runoff, as were those interviewed only before the second election. Yet the effects did not persist for the national primary in 1974.

Reviewing these early field experiments, Green and Shachar (2000) conclude that it may be that voting has the strongest habit formation effect when elections are similar (e.g., for two local elections or two presidential elections) or that the survey-based evidence is inaccurate. Several more-recent field experiments have helped to clarify which conclusion is more appropriate. Gerber, Green, and Shachar (2003) conducted a large GOTV experiment in New Haven, Connecticut, before the November 1998 general election; they used direct mail and door-to-door canvassing to encourage turnout. Both methods increased turnout in the election, with a treatment-on-treated effect for the door-to-door canvassing of 10.2 percentage points and an effect of 1.5 percentage points for the mailed postcards. The authors then asked whether those mobilized to vote in 1998 were also more likely to vote in the mayoral elections of 1999. Even though the differences between the treatment and the control groups were smaller—1.1 percentage points for the canvassing experiment, for example—they found that the "experimental interventions seem to have left an enduring imprint" (546). More specifically, they found that voting in 1998 raised the likelihood that an individual would vote in 1999, controlling for other predictors of turnout, by 50.4 percentage points.

David Cutts, Edward Fieldhouse, and Peter John (2009) conducted a similar experiment in the United Kingdom. The original GOTV experiment randomly assigned individuals to receive a door-to-door visit or a commercial phone call prior to the 2005 general election (John and Brannan 2008). Both interventions were successful, with treatment-on-treated effects of 6.7 percentage points and 7.3 percentage points, respectively. Cutts, Fieldhouse, and John examined the same voters for any residual effect on voting in the 2006 local elections. Their findings are similar to the findings from New Haven: controlling for other factors, they estimate a habit formation effect of 57.8 percentage points, significant at the .10 level. They note that this changes the calculation of votes per dollar as conventionally estimated in GOTV research, because few "take into account the downstream multiplier effects implied by the habit effect" (2009, 260).

Thus, existing observational and field experiment data point to a considerable habit formation effect among the general public once an individual has been mobilized to vote. As with other GOTV research, however, almost no published work prior to the California Votes Initiative (CVI) examined whether or not these same findings would hold true among low-propensity communities of color. One exception comes from a campaign mobilizing Latino voters in Dos Palos, California, to vote in the 2001 school-board elections (Michelson 2005). While the initial effort for the 2001 school-board election was successful in getting out the vote, there was no lasting effect found from this earlier mobilization in the 2002 June primary election. The data from the CVI thus represent a unique and valuable opportunity to examine whether habit formation operates in similar ways in communities of color as it does in less diverse communities and how the effects may alter our calculations about the cost of increasing turnout.

The CVI experiments provided an unusually good opportunity to study habit formation for several reasons. First, because the targets were low-propensity voters, they tended not to receive contact from other voter mobilization campaigns, making it easier to isolate the mobilization effects of the initial contact.[1] Second, CVI groups did not make a greater effort to contact nonvoters than it did voters mobilized in previous GOTV campaigns (with one exception, noted below). In other words, subsequent campaigns did not use turnout results from earlier elections to determine which potential voters should be placed in treatment and control groups; assignment was random. Third, the CVI experiments constituted a longitudinal study, meaning that we have information about voters over time, elections, and subsequent mobilization campaigns. These factors allow for precise measurement of the degree to which turnout boosted in one election persisted in subsequent elections.

Studying habit formation requires an effective voter mobilization campaign that is fairly large in scale so that sufficient numbers of voters were moved to the polls for us to track over time. Thus, for our analysis, we limited our calculations to include only those experiments for which the overall pool (treatment plus control) was at least 1,000 and for which the treatment-on-treated effect for the initial experiment was statistically significant. As Table 6.1 shows, fifteen CVI experiments met these criteria.[2]

For each of these fifteen experiments, we tracked individuals moved to vote in the initial experiment over subsequent elections. This allowed us to generate a habit formation statistic for the later elections, which we then aggregated to come up with overall estimates for the carryover of the mobilization effort from one election to the next.

Only one campaign, that of CCAEJ in Riverside County, met our criteria for the June 2006 election. In the original June 2006 experiment, the treatment group voted at a rate of 19.6 percent, whereas the control group voted at a rate of 11.1 percent, a difference of 8.5 percentage points. Yet we were unable to accurately test for habit formation effects in subsequent elections. As mentioned in chapter 4, CCAEJ organizers decided to place all individuals successfully contacted in June 2006 into the November 2006 treatment group, effectively negating the random assignment aspect of the experiment for these individuals. Because of that, we had to exclude them from our analysis of habit formation effects. However, we can look at later voting behavior by those in the CCAEJ June 2006 experiment to speak to real-world effects of continued outreach by a community organization.

In the real world, decisions about who to target for mobilization are generally not random. What was the lasting impact on these individuals? When we took CCAEJ's November 2006 campaign into consideration, we found that 995 individuals were in the treatment group for both elections, 78 individuals were assigned to the control group for both elections, and others changed group assignment (i.e., from treatment to

Table 6.1. CVI Campaigns Examined for Habit Formation Effects

Campaign	Original Overall Pool (treatment + control)	Initial Treatment-on-Treated Effect	SE
Door-to-Door Campaigns			
June 2006—CCAEJ Riverside	1,781	43.1	12.5
November 2006—SCOPE	15,367	6.6	2.1
November 2006—Colusa (PICO)	1,275	9.6	5.5
February 2008—LA Voice (PICO)	3,165	10.4	5.6
June 2008—CCAEJ Riverside	5,970	15.7	5.6
June 2008—FIA Bakersfield (PICO)	1,174	8.4	4.1
Phone Bank Campaigns			
November 2006—SVREP	25,862	9.3	3.2
February 2008—NALEO Los Angeles	34,086	12.3	4.7
June 2008—APALC Chinese American	12,216	5.4	1.9
June 2008—APALC Japanese American	2,153	19.9	9.7
June 2008—APALC Korean American	5,336	9.9	4.4
June 2008—OCAPICA Chinese American	3,207	12.6	4.3
June 2008—OCAPICA Filipino American	3,656	16.1	8.4
June 2008—OCAPICA Korean American	4,746	13.2	3.9
June 2008—OCAPICA Vietnamese American	14,862	10.9	5.1

control or control to treatment).[3] Those assigned both times to the control group voted at a rate of 37.2 percent, while those assigned twice to the treatment group voted at a rate of 45.6 percent, a difference of 8.4 percentage points (Table 6.2). At the same time, those assigned to the treatment group for the June election and the control group for the November election voted at a rate of 42 percent, while those assigned to the treatment group in the earlier election and the control group in the latter voted at a rate of 44.1 percent. There is a linear progression to the results that is statistically significant. In other words, having been assigned to the treatment group either once or twice made voters more likely to turn out in November 2006 than being assigned to the control group. Thus, there is evidence that the June 2006 CCAEJ campaign had not only a strong immediate impact on contacted voters but a lasting one as well.

For the remaining fourteen CVI experiments that met our criteria for evaluation for habit formation effects, we followed the procedure

Table 6.2. Cumulative Effects of the June 2006 CCAEJ GOTV Campaign

June 2006 Group Assignment	November 2006 Group Assignment	% Voting, November 2006
Control	Control	37.2 (29/78)
	Treatment	42.0 (124/295)
Treatment	Control	44.1 (108/245)
	Treatment	45.6 (454/995)

established by Gerber, Green, and Shachar (2003). For each successful GOTV effort, turnout in the original field experiment was used to predict turnout in subsequent elections, using the original treatment assignment as an instrumental variable. To clarify, imagine an initial mobilization effort that resulted in turnout in the treatment group that was 10 percentage points higher than that in the control group. In the next election, those in the original treatment group voted at a rate 5 percentage points higher than rate of the original control group. Here, the habit formation statistic is 5/10, or 50 percentage points. Half of the treatment effect persisted into the next election. Instrumental variables allow for more complex estimates of habit formation that take control variables into account, but the underlying calculation remains the same. Turnout for each subsequent election was then modeled twice, once with a relatively simple model and again using available control variables, including voting history, gender, age, and nativity. For these fourteen experiments, assignment to the treatment group for later GOTV campaigns was random, allowing for robust estimates of habit formation.

November 2006

Three campaigns met our criteria for examination of habit formation effects for the November 2006 election, including door-to-door canvassing by SCOPE and by a local PICO affiliate (North Valley Sponsoring Committee) in Colusa and a phone bank carried out by SVREP.

The intent-to-treat effect of the November 2006 SCOPE campaign was 3.0 percentage points, with individuals in the control group voting at a rate of 33.7 percent (1,205/3,578), and individuals in the treatment group voting at a rate of 36.7 percent (4,324/11,789). Did these effects persist into 2008? Given that neither of the two GOTV campaigns conducted by SCOPE in 2008—for the February presidential primary election and the November general election—had a measurable effect on turnout, any observed differences in turnout in the three 2008 elections can safely be attributed to carryover effects from the November 2006 GOTV campaign. In February 2008, the original November 2006 control group voted at a rate of 47.3 percent (1,543/3,261), while the treatment group voted at a rate of 48.9 percent (5,280/10,806), a difference of 1.6 percentage points. Dividing 1.6 by 3.0, the intent-to-treat rate, generates a habit formation statistic of 0.53, indicating that more than half of the original effect persisted into the next election. Following Gerber, Green, and Shachar (2003) to compute 2SLS regression estimates of the experimental effects, we found that mobilization in 2006 raised the probability of voting in February 2008 by 51.0 percentage points (SE = 0.31). The habit effect is smaller but still quite strong for the low-salience June 2008 election. For this later election, the control group voted at a rate of 16.5 percent (516/3,128) and the treatment group at a rate of 17.4 percent (1,803/10,336), a difference of 0.9 percentage points; the habit formation statistic generated is 30 percentage points (0.9/3.0). The corresponding 2SLS estimate is 0.31 (SE = 0.25).

For the next high-salience election, November 2008, those in the original November 2006 control group voted at a rate of 70.1 percent (2,180/3,110), while those in the original treatment group voted at a rate of 73.0 percent (7,545/10,337). This difference of 2.9 percentage points is nearly as large as the original intent-to-treat effect of 2.9 percentage points and generates a habit formation statistic of 97 percentage points (2.9/3.0). 2SLS regression confirms a statistically significant habit formation effect, of 90–91 percentage points, regardless of whether controls are included for voting history and other demographics.[4]

In the Colusa campaign, the original experiment saw an intent-to-treat effect of 6.4 percentage points—the control group voted at a rate of

66.5 percent (653/982), and the treatment group voted at a rate of 72.9 percent (188/258). Despite the lack of a follow-up experiment for the next election, in February 2008, the effect persisted. Turnout was 47.1 percent in February 2008 (474/1007) in the November 2006 control group and 53.4 percent (143/268) in the November 2006 treatment group, a 6.3 percentage point difference. The resulting habit formation statistic is 98.4, indicating that the effect persisted among almost every voter moved to go to the polls in the earlier election. This result is confirmed by 2SLS regression analysis, which generates a coefficient estimate of 1.14 (SE = 0.62). This figure decreases only marginally to 1.13 (SE = 0.58) when we add control variables. In June 2008 and November 2008, however, there is no measurable lasting effect. In the low-salience June primary, the difference in turnout is only 2.2 percentage points; in the November 2008 election, a year after the original experiment, turnout in the control and treatment groups differed by only 0.7 percentage points. In neither case are the differences statistically significant, regardless of whether control variables are included in the model.

The SVREP November 2006 campaign generated an initial intent-to-treat effect of 2.1 percentage points, with the control group voting at a rate of 34.3 percent (2,176/6,350) and the treatment group voting at a rate of 36.4 percent (7,111/19,512). The subsequent differences, however, were modest. In February 2008, the original control group voted at a rate of 39.8 percent (1,517/3,816) and the treatment group at a rate of 39.9 percent (7,188/18,025), a difference of 0.1 percentage points with a generated habit formation effect of 5 percentage points (0.1/2.1). There is no evidence of a lasting habit effect in the June or November 2008 elections.

February 2008

Two campaigns met our criteria for examination of habit formation effects for the February 2008 election, including a door-to-door campaign by the PICO affiliate LA Voice and a phone bank orchestrated by NALEO, also in Los Angeles.

The PICO door-to-door effort resulted in an intent-to-treat effect of 3.8 percentage points, with the control group voting at a rate of 58.9 percent (1,272/2,160) and the treatment group voting at a rate of

62.7 percent (630/1,005). There is no evidence that the effect persisted in either the June or the November 2008 elections; in both cases, there was no true difference in turnout between the original treatment and control groups.

The NALEO phone bank in Los Angeles for February 2008 had an intent-to-treat effect of 2.5 percentage points, with the control group voting at a rate of 43.3 percent (1,470/3,394) and the treatment group at a rate of 45.8 percent (14,054/30,692). Four months later, in June 2008, the control group voted at a rate of 5.7 percent (186/3,267) and the treatment group at a rate of 6.2 percent (1,818/29,541), a difference of 0.5 percentage points, for a habit formation effect of 20 percentage points (0.5/2.5). 2SLS analysis generates a habit formation statistic of 0.18 (SE = 0.17) without covariates or 0.13 (SE = 0.18) when controlling for voting history and demographic variables. In November 2008, the control group voted at a rate of 70.7 percent (1,965/2,781) and the treatment group at a rate of 72.1 percent (18,309/25,405), a difference of 1.4 percentage points, indicating a habit formation statistic of 56 percentage points (1.4/2.5). This effect persists when analyzing the data using 2SLS, with a habit formation statistic for November 2008 of 0.57 (SE = 0.36) without covariates. This reduces slightly to 0.50 (SE = 0.41) when adding control variables.

June 2008

The largest number of campaigns available for us to find evidence of habit formation came from the June 2008 election, when large and statistically significant effects were generated by two door-to-door campaigns—by CCAEJ in Riverside County and by Faith in Action, a PICO affiliate in Bakersfield—and by seven phone bank campaigns orchestrated by APALC and OCAPICA.

Turning first to evidence of habit formation from the CCAEJ June 2008 election campaign, we tracked the November 2008 turnout of those in the original June 2008 experiment. The original experiment for June 2008 had an intent-to-treat effect of 2.1 percentage points, with the control group voting at a rate of 5.4 percent (190/3,489) and the treatment group voting at a rate of 7.5 percent (187/2,481). Of the original pool, 5,489 remained in the November 2008 turnout file. In the November 2008 election, the control group voted at a rate of 59.7 percent (1,910/3,197) and the treatment group at a rate of 60.2 percent (1,380/2,292), a difference of 0.5 percentage points. Dividing 0.5 by 2.1 generates a habit formation statistic of 0.24. Those moved to vote in June 2008 were 24 percentage points more likely to vote in November 2008. 2SLS analysis generates a habit formation statistic of 0.21 (SE = 0.67) without covariates or 0.51 (SE = 0.58) when including voting history, age, and nativity variables.

Even stronger evidence of habit formation comes from the Faith in Action campaign in Bakersfield. The original GOTV effort generated an intent-to-treat effect of 2.9 percentage points, with the control group voting at a rate of 4.2 percent (28/669) and the treatment group at a rate of 7.1 (36/505). In November 2008, the differences persisted, with the control group voting at a rate of 38.4 percent (224/584) and the treatment group at a rate of 43.0 percent (191/444), a difference of 4.6 percentage points, indicating an enormous habit formation effect of 159 percentage points (4.6/2.9). In other words, those assigned to the treatment group for June 2008 were more likely to vote in November 2008 than they were in the election for which they were mobilized. The effect is also apparent when analyzing the data using 2SLS, either with or without various voting history and demographic controls. Without controls the 2SLS effect is estimated at 1.41 (SE = 1.07), with controls at 1.84 (SE = 1.01). Considered together with evidence (reviewed below) regarding the lasting effect of mobilization effects from low-salience (e.g., June 2008) elections on turnout in high-salience (e.g., November 2008) elections, this constitutes further evidence that GOTV contact can change a person's cognitive schemas, making that person a voter, and reminds us that the electoral context is an important factor in this process as well.

Of the national-origin groups targeted by APALC for its June 2008 phone bank effort, three met our criteria for analysis for habit formation: Chinese, Japanese, and Korean Americans. Each national-origin group was randomized separately. In the initial experiment, turnout in the Chinese American pool was increased from 9.8 percent in the control group (804/8,216) to 11.7 percent in the treatment group (469/4,000), an intent-to-treat effect of 1.9 percentage points. In November 2008, the difference decreased slightly, to a 1.1 percentage point intent-to-treat effect. In that election, the control group voted at a rate of 65.2 percent (5,219/8,007) and the treatment group at a rate of 66.3 percent (2,600/3,922). This result generates a habit formation statistic of 58 percentage points (1.1/1.9). Using 2SLS generates a slightly smaller effect of 56.0 percentage points, but with a high standard error (SE = 0.52). Adding covariates for age, gender, and voting history generates a 2SLS estimate of 0.91 (SE = 0.65).

For Japanese Americans, the initial intent-to-treat effect was 3.5 percentage points, with voters in the control group voting at a rate of 12.1 percent (164/1,353) and those in the treatment group voting at a rate of 15.6 percent (125/800). In November 2008, the intent-to-treat effect was 0.7 percentage points, with the control group voting at a rate of 78.1 percent (1,024/1,311) and the treatment group at a rate of 78.8 percent (615/780). This generates a habit formation statistic of 20 percentage points (0.7/3.5), almost identical to the 2SLS statistic of 21 percentage points, albeit again with a high standard error (SE = 0.55). Adding covariates generates a statistic of 0.24 (SE = 0.38).

For Korean Americans the initial experiment generated an intent-to-treat effect of 2.8 percentage points, with the control group voting at a rate of 17.1 percent (485/2,836) and the treatment group at a rate of 19.9 percent (498/2,500). In November 2008, the control group voted at a rate of 66.5 percent (1,828/2,747) and the treatment group at a rate of 67.5 percent (1,641/2,430), a difference of 1.0 percentage points. This generates a habit formation statistic of 36 percentage points (1.0/2.8) or, when we use 2SLS analysis, 35 percentage points (SE = 0.49), or 0.38 (SE = 0.54) with covariates.

Finally, we looked at subsequent turnout for four national-origin groups successfully moved to vote by OCAPICA in the June 2008 election: Chinese Americans, Filipino Americans, Korean Americans, and Vietnamese Americans. We find habit formation effects for two of these national-origin groups—voters of Chinese and Vietnamese ancestry. For the Chinese American subsample, the original experiment increased turnout by 3.8 percentage points, from 8.7 percent in the control group (192/2,217) to 12.5 percent in the treatment group (124/990). In November 2008, the difference persisted slightly, with the control group voting at a rate of 68.8 percent (1,476/2,144) and the treatment group at a rate of 70 percent (675/965), a difference of 1.2 percentage points, indicating a habit formation statistic of 32 percentage points (1.2/3.8). 2SLS generates a similar statistic, 30 percentage points (SE = 51.7), or 21.3 (SE = 54.7) with covariates for age, gender, and voting history. For Vietnamese Americans, the habit formation effect was stronger. In the initial experiment, the intent-to-treat effect was 2.2 percentage points. In November 2008, the turnout difference was 1.5 percentage points: turnout was 58.9 percent in the control group (7,165/12,168) and 60.4 percent in the treatment group (1,464/2,423). This high difference in turnout generates a habit formation statistic of 68 percentage points, which remains 68 (SE = 51.3) percentage points using 2SLS, or 52 (SE = 65.2) with covariates.

Those Filipino and Korean Americans whom OCAPICA moved to the polls seem not to have developed a lasting habit effect. For Filipino Americans, turnout for the November 2008 election by individuals in the original treatment group was actually lower than that of the control group, 76.2 percent (2,339/3,071) compared to 74.3 percent (358/482). There is no evidence of habit formation. For Korean Americans contacted by OCAPICA, turnout for the November 2008 election was slightly higher among individuals in the original treatment group: 67.7 percent (967/1,429), compared to 67.6 percent (2,115/3,129) in the control group, a difference of 0.1 percentage points, indicating a negligible habit formation statistic of 2.3 percentage points.

The national-origin differences we find among the voters mobilized by APALC and OCAPICA speak to the importance of understanding the sociocultural and cognitive differences that exist across voters and how they can affect targeted voters' receptivity to the mobilization conversation. These voters were contacted by the same organization with very consistent messages, yet Asian Americans of different national origins responded differently to the first message and showed variation in terms of their habit formation effects. Clearly, their self-identifications, migration histories, sociocultural contexts, and the electoral context all combined to affect not only their receptivity to the GOTV message but also how well that message stuck over time.

Overall Habit Formation Effects

Calculating the habit formation effects across all fifteen GOTV experiments that fit our criteria across the twenty-four subsequent election-experiment combinations where CVI voters had the opportunity to cast ballots, we find an average habit formation effect of 23 percentage points (Table 6.3). To clarify, individuals first mobilized in June 2006 had the opportunity to demonstrate habit-formation effects in four subsequent CVI elections: November 2006, February 2008, June 2008, and November 2008. Those first mobilized in November 2006 had three subsequent elections in which to demonstrate such effects (the three elections in 2008), et cetera. So for our original 15 experiments there are 24 instances for which habit formation effects can be observed. Eliminating the CCAEJ June 2006 campaign from the analysis owing to that organization's decision to move successfully contacted voters to the next treatment group (instead of allowing for random assignment) generates an even stronger overall habit formation effect of 31 percentage points. Each vote generated by a prior mobilization campaign produced one-third of a vote in the November 2008 presidential election.

We can further refine our understanding of the power of GOTV campaigns to produce a voting habit by examining separately those campaigns conducted for low-salience and high-salience elections and also by looking separately at the habit formation power of door-to-door versus phone bank efforts. Statistics for the high-salience campaigns—for the November 2006 and February 2008 elections—generates an overall habit formation average effect of 24 percentage points in the November 2008 presidential elections. In other words, those voters who had been mobilized during previous high-salience elections were just under one-fourth more likely to vote in November 2008 than those who had not been mobilized.

For the low-salience election campaigns—for June 2006 and June 2008—we find an average habit formation effect of 33 percentage points when including the CCAEJ June 2006 effort and 38 percentage points when looking only at the effect of the June 2008 campaigns on November 2008 voting. Given the general lack of effectiveness of the November 2008 efforts, as noted in chapters 2 and 3, this is somewhat surprising—

Table 6.3. Habit Formation Effects

	November 2006	February 2008	June 2008	November 2008
CCAEJ, June 2006[a]	.24	−.54	.14	−.48
SCOPE, November 2006	—	.53	.30	.97
COLUSA, November 2006	—	.98	—	—
SVREP, November 2006	—	.05	0	0
LA Voice, February 2008	—	—	−.08	−.82
NALEO Los Angeles, February 2008	—	—	.20	.56
CCAEJ Riverside, June 2008	—	—	—	.24
FIA Bakersfield, June 2008	—	—	—	1.59
APALC Chinese American, June 2008	—	—	—	.58
APALC Japanese American, June 2008	—	—	—	.20
APALC Korean American, June 2008	—	—	—	.36
OCAPICA Chinese American, June 2008	—	—	—	.32
OCAPICA Filipino American, June 2008	—	—	—	−.54
OCAPICA Korean American, June 2008	—	—	—	.02
OCAPICA Vietnamese American, June 2008	—	—	—	.68
Overall				.23
Overall (excluding CCAEJ, June 2006)[a]				.31

[a] This experiment was removed from the final analysis because initial contacts were not randomly assigned in later rounds.

but also incredibly important for those working to increase civic participation among these infrequent voters. While door-to-door and phone bank canvassing conducted in the few weeks just prior to the November 2008 election by many of these groups had only negligible effects on turnout, this evidence suggests that turnout in that election was nevertheless significantly influenced by the groups' mobilization efforts in previous campaigns. The result provides strong support for our contention that individuals who have their cognitive schemas affected by a mobilization effort and act on that change solidify their self-identification as a voter through practice.

When looking at the levels of habit formation that result from mobilization during high-salience or low-salience elections, we find that regardless of the level of electoral salience during the first contact, the strongest enduring results are found in later high-salience elections. For example, the long-term effect of SCOPE's November 2006 campaign was only 30 percentage points in June 2008, but it was 53 percentage points in February 2008 and an enormous 97 percentage points in November 2008. Similarly, the effect of NALEO's phone bank in Los Angeles in February 2008 was only 20 percentage points in June 2008 but 56 percentage points in November 2008. In sum, our new voters, having adopted a self-understanding of themselves as electoral participants, were more susceptible to the mobilization messages they received in the high-salience electoral environment of the presidential campaign. The huge effect on turnout in November 2008 attributable to the June 2008 campaign by PICO affiliate Faith in Action in Bakersfield is further evidence of this.

Examining the campaigns separately by tactic, we find an overall habit formation effect for door-to-door campaigns of 26 percentage points when including the CCAEJ 2006 campaign or 46 percentage points without it. For phone bank campaigns the overall effect was 20 percentage points. Consistent with findings that door-to-door campaigns are generally more effective than phone bank campaigns, we also find that door-to-door campaigns produce more powerful habit formation effects. This is not surprising, given that a face-to-face contact can comprise a more meaningful sociocultural interaction than a live phone call. As detailed in chapter 5, we found the door-to-door CVI efforts to be more variable in their outcomes than phone bank efforts conducted in centralized locations, which were more consistently able to increase turnout. What the larger habit formation effect for door-to-door efforts reflects is the more lasting impact resulting from a successful face-to-face mobilization. This impact is not surprising given that the face-to-face conversation is a richer sociocultural interaction.

The enduring impact of voter mobilization has profound implications. First, it suggests that someone who votes in this election is more likely to vote in the next election, whereas someone who skips an election is less likely to vote in the future. Second, habit casts a different light on the usual way of evaluating the costs and benefits of a GOTV campaign. The typical approach is to think only in terms of votes produced in the current election. A more realistic calculation would take into account the future effects of this year's voter mobilization drive. If a campaign generates 1,000 additional votes at a cost of $40,000, the price amounts to $40 per vote for the current election. But if we also include the 310 votes in the next election, the price falls to slightly over $30 per vote ($40,000/1,310). This added efficiency is an important consideration for organizations that have a long-term interest in producing votes. What these habit formation calculations tell us is that increasing turnout in communities whose members have a low propensity to vote not only is possible but has enduring effects. Those living in low-income communities of color will vote, assumptions notwithstanding, and they may even vote at high rates. When made to feel included in a way that moves them to adopt a voter schema, they will vote, particularly in high-salience elections when the perceived importance of doing so is obvious. The enduring effects of voting once make it clear that a socioculturally based cognitive shift happens during the initial mobilization, one that is reinforced by voting practice to produce a remarkably enduring long-term effect. By acting as voters, those previously moved to the polls become voters.

Transforming the Electorate through Practice

Since the CVI campaigns targeted low-propensity voters, it is reasonable to assume that the individuals targeted did not see themselves as voters prior to being contacted. In addition, they tended to live in communities with few regular voters and to belong to social groups that historically have been excluded from formal political participation in the United States. These factors supported their self-identification: voters were not "people like me." Our findings provide strong empirical evidence that mobilization changed those cognitive schemas. Through the narrative sociocultural interaction that formed the initial mobilization, they were moved to identify themselves differently vis-à-vis the polity. Having voted once, those mobilized were much more likely to vote in subsequent elections.

These results speak to the power of practice and, for members of marginal communities, the way that practicing can expand and transform the electorate. These organizations were trying to turn out voters and build their organizational bases. Their staff and their campaigns, along with us, their evaluators, were focused on what proportion of targeted individuals turned out to vote. But if we look at the organizations' efforts from a habit formation standpoint, we can imagine just how transformative their GOTV work was. These individuals, once contacted, were more likely to turn out in subsequent elections. We also know that voter mobilization has significant spillover effects on individuals living in the voter's household (Nickerson 2008). If we extrapolate the long-term result of habit formation combined with spillover effects, the increase in voter turnout grows exponentially over time, resulting in greater and greater numbers of voters. Through their voting practice, the mobilized voters are not only reconstructing how they see themselves as citizens but also expanding citizenship for their households and, in the end, their neighborhoods and communities. GOTV efforts can potentially transform elections and have a tremendous long-term impact on the shape of the American electorate.

CONCLUSION: TRANSFORMING THE AMERICAN ELECTORATE

Carlota had never really talked to anyone about voting. She had just become an American citizen the year before and, as a part of the naturalization process, had registered to vote. The upcoming statewide election was the first contest in which she would be eligible to participate. At first, she was excited about the prospect of voting for the first time in her adult life. Then, when she received the sample ballot, she felt intimidated by the number and complexity of the choices she was being asked to make. She remembered learning about voting for her citizenship test—she knew that Americans choose the president and members of Congress. But this election did not seem similar to those she had read about, and no one in her neighborhood had mentioned it. She thought perhaps this election was for other Americans. When María Elena knocked on her door, Carlota was leaning toward not participating. Her conversation with María Elena changed her mind. The canvasser was of similar age, was from her neighborhood, and was also a naturalized voter. Even though María Elena declined to help her decide who to vote for, emphasizing instead simply the importance of participating, her visit gave Carlota the confidence and the nudge she needed to feel more comfortable with the voting process and more assured about her identity as a voter; that nudge moved her to go to the polls on Election Day. For Carlota, voting has become easier each time she has participated. It now forms part of her cognitive understanding of who she is and what she does every Election Day.

We have seen in this book that the CVI produced many experiences like Carlota's: community canvassers reached out to voters, who changed their voter profiles from low-propensity to regular voters. Our analysis has shown that two-call phone banks are especially effective in creating regular voters, leading to double-digit increases in voter turnout. Door-to-door campaigns also showed strong results, with one effort increasing voter turnout by more than 40 percentage points. Although most GOTV efforts show smaller gains than that, the CVI campaigns demonstrated that low-propensity voters within communities of color can be moved to the polls quite effectively by a well-organized, well-executed, in-person mobilization effort, whether on the phone or on the doorstep.

We find that these sociocultural interactions are effective even though the GOTV conversations have no impact on voters' resources and do little, if anything, to change voters' underlying attitudes toward issues. We contend that this sociocultural interaction may be best conceptualized as a political "speed bump"—a brief disruption to the voters' ongoing conception of themselves in relation to the polity. It is rare for voters within the U.S. political context to have someone knock on their doors or call them at home for the sole purpose of urging them to vote. These sorts of interactions are especially rare in the low-income communities of color where the CVI organizations were conducting their work.[1] That rarity is what helps to make the interaction meaningful. The pause prompted by that interactive bump, we have argued, is sufficient to change some voters' cognition enough for them to see themselves as the type of person who goes to the poll on Election Day.

Our evaluation of the CVI campaigns also showed that indirect efforts were not effective in turning out voters in the targeted communities. Direct mail campaigns may be appealing to groups aiming to get out the vote because they are easy to execute, relatively inexpensive, and make it easy for organizations to say they contacted tens of thousands of voters within a short period of time. Mailings may be effective at influencing vote choice, but they do not compel voters to go to the polls. Thus, the cost for each vote produced by indirect methods can be much higher than that for in-person contact, by phone or by door-to-door canvass. The organizational capacity needed to engage in indirect efforts may be small, but so is the payoff in terms of expanding the electorate.[2]

These indirect efforts are not effective because they do not entail a sociocultural interaction. Only a conversation between the canvasser and the voter is able to shift the voter's cognitive schemas sufficiently to change her or his subsequent behavior. Our strong habit formation findings, showing a more than 30 percentage point increase in participation as a result of the initial GOTV contact, suggest that voting practice does reinforce the individual's identification as a voter long after that initial conversation with a canvasser. We know, too, that voter contact has strong spillover effects within the household—as high as 60 percent— on other household members. In other words, 60 percent of the mobilized voter's propensity to vote in that election is passed on to the other members of the household (Nickerson 2008). As the newly mobilized voters continue to vote, the spillover effects will expand, like ripples in the water, to other voters and households in their communities. The transformative potential of GOTV work is enormous. It has the ability to transform the electorate and redefine citizenship in the United States. We call this governmentality from below.

Theoretical and Methodological Implications

Our Sociocultural Cognition Model, in addition to providing the first systematic theoretical explanation for why and under what circumstances GOTV mobilization works, also has theoretical implications beyond this critical insight. In particular, our model focuses scholarly attention on the cognitive and sociocultural infrastructure underlying individual voting decisions. Looking at that infrastructure is not the usual approach in the political behavior literature to conceptualizing voter interest; rather, voters and potential voters are generally seen as similarly situated. In other words, there is a presumption that voting behavior is an *individual choice*, based on political interest or other predispositions, rather than a structural, socially constructed product rooted in this country's history. What our focus on sociocultural cognition brings to light is the degree to which receptivity to a GOTV visit is in fact a political product resulting from the interaction between individual-level cognition and the sociocultural interaction. That interaction, in turn, is structured in important ways by the individual's multiple self-identifications.

Recently a number of political scientists have advanced arguments about why self-identifications need to become central to studies within their discipline (Huddy 2001). As Rogers Smith (2004, 41) points out,

> Political scientists have tended to think of racial identities as things generated at root by biology and/or economics and/or culture and/or history and/or often unconscious or at least informal social psychological processes and social activities. Precisely because racial identities have been politically constructed in ways that served to legitimate racial inequalities, by making them seem natural and pre-political, even students of politics long did not treat racial identities as substantially created by formal laws and political institutions. Instead, most racial topics seemed more appropriate for other disciplines, both to practitioners of those disciplines and to political scientists.

Smith is talking specifically about racial identifications, but his insights apply to the development of other self-identifications as well, including individuals' self-understandings as voters. Smith, like many other scholars, has argued that ethnoracial, gender, and political identifications are key to political behavior and are fundamentally political products, both shaped by and helping to shape the political process (Dawson 2000; T. Lee 2002; Smith 2004; García Bedolla 2005a; J. Wong 2006). Those understandings form the sociocultural context that frames an individual's cognitive schemas; those schemas can be activated (or not) by the mobilization conversation. Thus, it is the interaction between the individual's preexisting, socioculturally and historically situated self-understandings and the GOTV message that determines what kinds of political behaviors an individual believes it appropriate to engage in. Treating these categorization processes as given, or at least outside the political process, ignores a central and dynamic aspect of the political behavior story.

Therefore, to accurately represent that political behavior story, our model suggests some methodological changes that would have to be made when studying voting behavior. Social cognition theory makes it clear that scholars need to take into greater consideration what is known about how human beings process memory. There is general agreement among cognitive scholars that humans possess short-term (working memory) and long-term memory and that cognitive schemas help to bridge the ground between the two. Schemas "determine what types of information are relevant [to the individual], and therefore what information is noticed, stored, and consequently available for later recall" (Lau and Sears 1986b, 351). Social cognition scholars also agree that forgetting seems to be a common event for individuals, but that forgetting does not mean that the information is no longer available in long-term memory, only that it cannot be retrieved out of short-term memory (Lodge and McGraw 1991; McGraw 2000).

The most pervasive political-science approach to studying political behavior is through the use of surveys, and since surveys depend on accurate and immediate memory retrieval on the part of respondents, we can see how these cognitive insights could affect how we go about understanding the factors underlying individual voting decisions. If individual memory retrieval is consistently inaccurate, then political scientists may need to develop research methodologies to take cognitive variations into account. Most of the schemas work in the field used to be based on surveys (Hastie 1986; Lau and Sears 1986b; McGraw 2000). Perhaps the concept lost popularity because surveys are not the ideal method for capturing the impact of cognitive processes, given the vagaries of memory retrieval. Recent advances in experimental methods in particular may hold promise for the development of methodological approaches for examining these cognitive questions. At the very least, research in social cognition and our analysis of the CVI campaigns show the tremendous cognitive and sociocultural complexity underlying individual decisions to engage in politics. To understand this complexity as fully as possible, political scientists need to take these cognitive and sociocultural factors into account when designing their research. That research, in turn, will need to employ a variety of methodological approaches in order to measure these processes as accurately as possible (Collier, Brady, and Seawright 2010).

Normative Implications: Model Voters, Inclusion, and Representation

Our analysis also has a number of normative implications in terms of democratic citizenship, inclusion, and representation. In *Civic Ideals,*

Rogers Smith (1997) demonstrates how citizenship status in the United States has been restricted based on class, race, and gender. The same point has been made by numerous other scholars looking at the historical development of citizenship in the United States (Jacobson 1998; King 2000; Gardner 2009). Historically, voter identity in the United States has been racialized, classed, and gendered in a uniquely American way.[3] Thus, the American status quo—with the socioeconomically privileged being much more likely to vote—is not automatic; rather, it is a historical artifact, a product of how race, gender, and class have been constructed vis-à-vis electoral politics in the American context. As noted in chapter 1, the fact that in India those of lower socioeconomic status are most likely to vote reminds us that "voter" is a social and political construct.

Because the CVI organizations targeted members of marginal communities in their mobilization efforts, they engaged in a process of rewriting American history. Their efforts suggested the development of a new identification of these voters—as voters—that ran counter to this historical experience. That these campaigns were so successful shows that these low-propensity voters did not engage in voting previously, not because they were not interested or were incapable, but because they had not developed the cognitive voter schema necessary to behave in this fashion. The narrative sociocultural interactions that they participated in with CVI canvassers changed their cognition, and therefore changed their behavior, not only in the particular election for which they were mobilized but also in subsequent elections. Their response to the GOTV conversations illustrates how important the interaction of cognitive processes with sociocultural context is for understanding individual political behavior.

We must be careful not to uncritically assume that the increased political participation that resulted from these GOTV campaigns will lead to a more inclusive, and therefore transformative, politics (Bourdieu 1977; Jones 2006). In an analysis of political participation and democratic theory, Jane Junn (1997) points out that political participation traditionally has been seen as important within democratic theory for two main reasons: (1) the participation of more citizens means that more opinions and preferences are being taken into account, making the final policy outcome more likely to reflect the common good; and (2) participation helps citizens by assisting in their development as citizens of the broader political community. Within these frameworks, greater participation helps the democratic polity to make more equitable, and therefore legitimate, policy decisions, and it also helps individuals to become more confident and effective members of that polity. Zoltan L. Hajnal (2010) documents the bias in both descriptive and substantive representation that results when particular segments of a community, particularly those from ethnoracial groups, fail to participate.

But, as Junn (1997, 388) warns, these assumptions work only if two additional critical assumptions are met. The structures and institutions of democracy must be neutral, not favoring some group or ideology, and the common understanding of agency and citizenship must be fluid. In other words, there cannot be a static (and potentially exclusive) definition of the "model citizen." For Junn, the definition of citizenship "must reflect the composition of all within the political community, including those who differ systematically from the already existing cultural norm. As such, democracy cannot require assimilation to the current model; rather, the conception of the democratic citizen must itself be colored by the diversity of the population." If these assumptions are not satisfied, increased participation will reinforce and legitimate the existing structures of hierarchy and inequality, making it impossible for the political system to substantively address the many inequities there are in the United States.

Within Junn's framework, the question then becomes whether the U.S. democratic system contains a static definition of the model citizen and whether the mobilization campaigns could be seen as having disrupted that definition. Although Americans of whatever sort are not labeled "model citizens" in popular discourse, the category of "likely voter" could serve as a potential proxy. We would argue that "likely voters" are those U.S. citizens whose interests and opinions are considered most relevant to political debates. For example, the vast majority of political polls, during and between electoral cycles, sample only "likely voters."[4] Political analysts in the media focus their attention on the concerns and opinions of "likely voters" and regularly discuss policy proposals in relation to how they will play in the minds of likely voters. Thus, to be a likely voter is to be considered a "model citizen": to be part of the subset of the citizenry

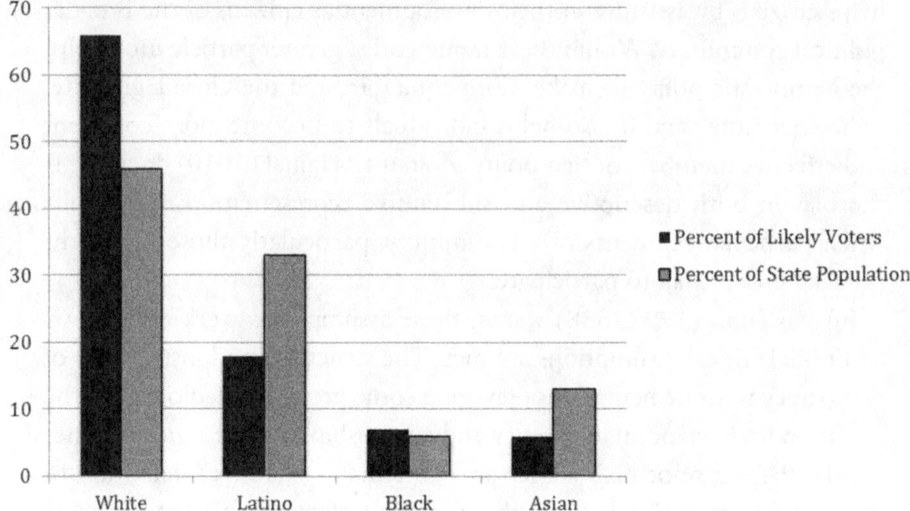

Figure 7.1. Ethnorace of Likely Voters and California Population (%)
Source: Data from "Latino Likely Voters," 2010. The survey findings are based on the pooled results from eight PPIC statewide surveys, fielded from September 2009 to July 2010, including 9,993 likely voters, 4,160 infrequent voters, and 3,232 unregistered adults.

whose opinions are defined as most relevant to democratic politics, both in the course of electoral cycles and also in the process of government policymaking and implementation.

But who exactly are these likely voters? We see in Figure 7.1 that according to the Public Policy Institute of California (PPIC), the state's "likely voters" are not representative of the population as a whole, at least not in terms of ethnoracial characteristics. Whites are significantly overrepresented among likely voters; Latinos and Asians are underrepresented.[5] Figure 7.2 shows that these demographic differences among types of voters cut across race/ethnicity, age, and nativity in notable ways. This set of surveys by PPIC was unique in who were polled: likely voters (defined as respondents who report voting always or nearly always, express an intention to vote in the upcoming election, have followed election news, and state an interest in politics), infrequent voters (defined as those who are registered to vote but do not vote regularly, very much like the individuals targeted by the CVI campaigns), and unregistered potential voters (individuals who are citizens and over eighteen and therefore eligible to vote but who have not registered to vote; Baldassare et al. 2011). In California, we see that likely voters are overwhelmingly white, are much older than less frequent voters, and are very likely to be U.S. born. Nonregistered voters are, by and large, Latino, young, and foreign born; more than two-thirds of nonregistered eligible voters in California are foreign born.

Figure 7.3 shows similar differences between likely voters and other types of voters in California when considering their educational and income levels. Only 17 percent of likely voters have no college education; 70 percent of nonregistered voters have not attended college. The same differences are present in terms of home ownership. Although 64 percent of nonregistered voters are renters, only 26 percent of likely voters are; rather, 74 percent of likely voters are homeowners. Finally, we see that income distribution is also unevenly distributed across different types of

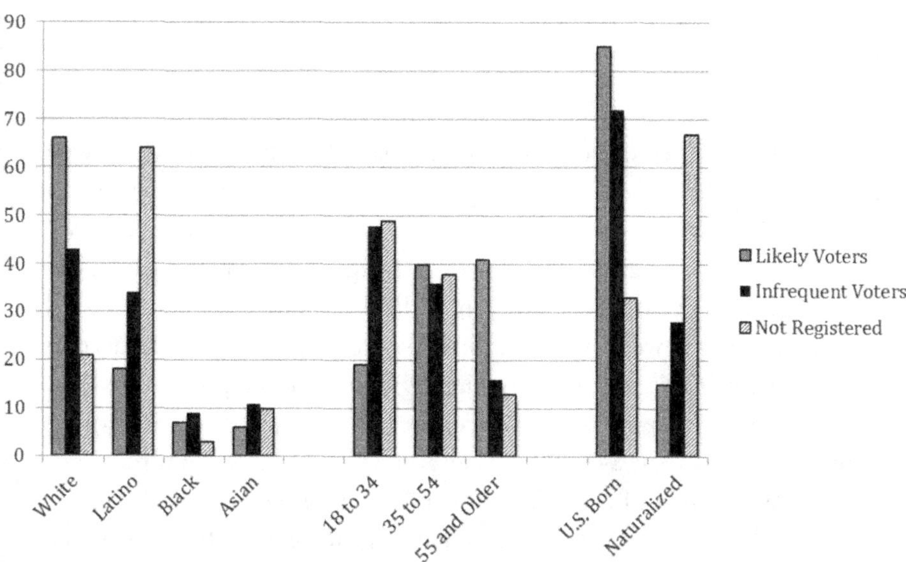

Figure 7.2. Ethnorace, Age, and Citizenship of California Voters by Voter Type (%)
Source: Data from Baldassare et al. 2011. The survey findings are based on the pooled results from eight PPIC statewide surveys, fielded from September 2009 to July 2010, including 9,993 likely voters, 4,160 infrequent voters, and 3,232 unregistered adults.

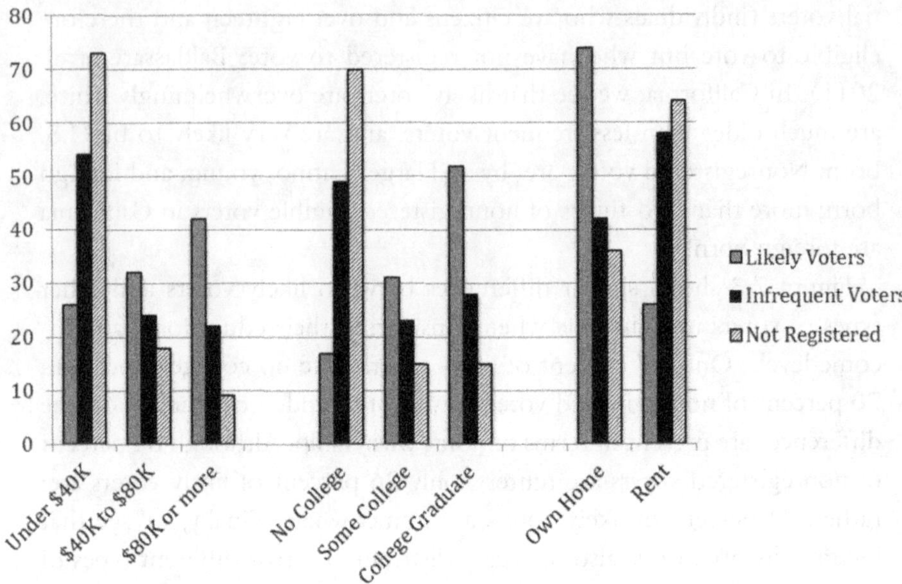

Figure 7.3. Socioeconomic Status, Education, and Home Ownership of California Voters by Voter Type (%)
Source: See Figure 7.2.

voters. Only 26 percent of likely voters make less than $40,000 a year, compared to 73 percent of nonregistered voters. On the upper end of the income scale, only 9 percent of individuals making $80,000 a year or more who are eligible to vote are not registered. Individuals in this income bracket constitute 42 percent of likely voters.

In these figures we can see that infrequent voters, the voters targeted by the CVI campaigns, straddle a demographic middle ground between likely voters and those who are not registered. Over half of the infrequent voters make less than $40,000 a year and 58 percent of them rent their homes. Almost half of them have no college experience, and 28 percent are college graduates. In the area of nativity, however, infrequent voters look more like likely voters than unregistered potential voters. Seventy-two percent of infrequent voters are U.S. born; only 28 percent are naturalized citizens. It seems clear that registering to vote remains a significant hurdle for the integration of foreign-born voters into the political process.

But do these demographic differences lead to political differences in terms of party identification and ideology? Research on the relationship between demographic characteristics and political affiliations and attitudes suggests that they do (Tate 1993; Dawson 2000; Hutchings 2003; Lien, Conway, and Wong 2004; García Bedolla 2005a; Abrajano and Alvarez 2010; J. Wong et al. 2011). African Americans, Latinos, and Asian Americans have been found to have public opinion profiles that vary in significant ways from those of whites. Similarly, the poor have been found to support a different set of policy preferences than the most affluent (Lawless and Fox 2001). Survey data from the PPIC suggest that these differences, at least in terms of partisanship, are represented across people with different commitments to voting (Figure 7.4).

We see in Figure 7.4 that nonregistered voters in California lean more toward the Democratic Party than do likely voters. They, along with

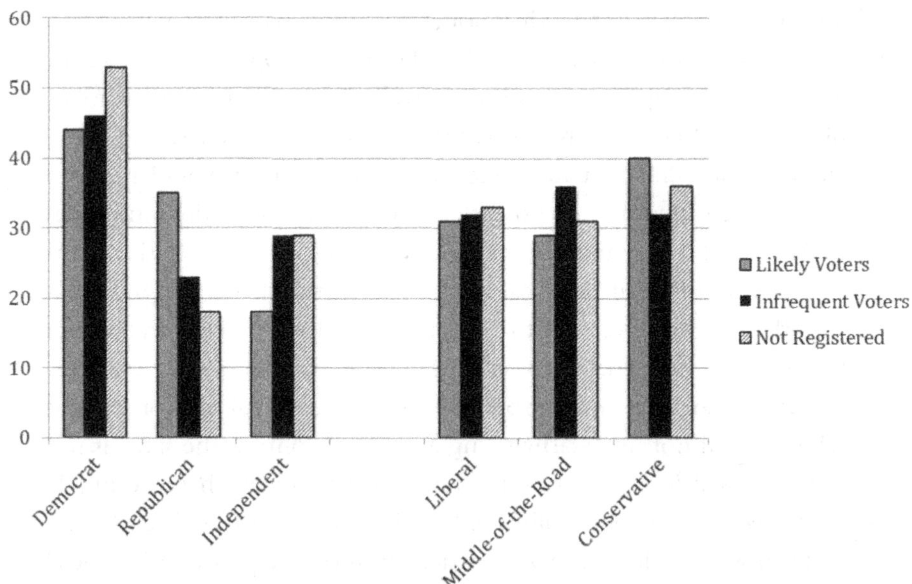

Figure 7.4. Party Identification and Political Ideology in California by Voter Type (%)
Source: See Figure 7.2.
Note: Party identification for the unregistered adults eligible to vote was asked in a question about party "leanings." The "independent" identification for this group represents those who answered "neither" or "don't know" to the question.

infrequent voters, are more inclined than likely voters to be independent of a party—that is, not to have a strong party identification. Zoltan L. Hajnal and Taeku Lee (2011) find the same result among voters nationally, and contend it is the intersection of identity (particularly ethnoracial self-understandings), ideology, and information that explains partisan attachments in the United States. Under conditions of uncertainty and low information about the party system, ethnoracial voters' non-identification may be a "rationally adaptive strategy" (22). From an ideological standpoint, the differences among different kinds of voters in California are not as stark. Compared to infrequent votes, likely voters are significantly more inclined to say they are conservative, but there is only a 4 percentage point difference in levels of conservatism between likely voters and those who are not registered. The PPIC surveys find that liberal identification is similar across all types of voters.

In sum, there are significant differences among likely voters, infrequent voters, and nonregistered potential voters across a number of parameters: ethnorace, nativity, income, education, age, homeownership, party identification, and ideology. We know that the policy proposals preferred by these different groups of voters vary as well (Hajnal 2010). Yet scholars simulating the effect of increased voter participation in Senate and presidential elections find that increased voter participation would have no impact on the outcomes of those elections (Citrin, Schickler, and Sides 2003; Sides, Schickler, and Citrin 2006). Hajnal's (2010) analysis of ethnoracial participation at the local level, on the other hand, suggests that perhaps the national level is not the best place to look for electoral impact on the part of ethnoracial nonvoters.[6] He points out that while ethnoracial voters make up a small proportion of the national electorate, and therefore would not necessarily swing a national contest, the same is not true at the local level, where ethnoracial voters are much more highly concentrated. His overview of more than five decades of local-level turnout data shows that low electoral participation on the part of ethnoracial voters has a significant negative impact on their descriptive and substantive representation at the local level.

If we know, then, that there is a significant turnout differential, particularly at the local level, between ethnoracial voters and whites, and therefore that whites make up a disproportionate number of voters, the question then becomes: Whose interests are better represented in the policymaking process—voters' interests or the interests of all constituents, voters and nonvoters alike? (Lawless and Fox 2001; Griffin and Newman 2008; Hajnal 2010). John D. Griffin and Brian Newman (2005) examine Senate roll-call votes to answer this very question. They test whether Senate roll-call voting more accurately reflects voters' or nonvoters' opinions. They find that "even though Senators may not know with certainty who votes and what their preferences are, their patterns of roll-call voting respond to voters' opinions but not to nonvoters' opinions" (1222). They hypothesize that this relationship exists because voters tend to elect like-minded Senators, because voters are more likely than nonvoters to communicate their desires to their Senators, and because only voters can reelect Senators (1207). Potentially, then, the result is "biases in legislator behavior and ultimately public policy" (1222).

In their book *Minority Report*, Griffin and Newman (2008) analyze the representation of minority-group interests in votes in the House of Representatives and the Senate and in the content of federal public policies. They find that "congressional votes and the content of public policy generally are much more in line with white Americans' preferences. In fact, in many cases minority groups are not better represented even when they make up a larger proportion of electoral districts, suggesting that minorities as individuals are unequally represented" (6). They argue that this political inequality can be alleviated when the issue is of greater interest to minority group members than to whites, when groups have descriptive representation among legislators (a point we return to below), and when turnout is increased. They contend that getting out the vote "can provide a small boost to minorities' relative political representation within certain contexts" but that overall there is a representational bias against minority-group interests in federal legislative institutions and policymaking (7).

Martin Gilens (2005) finds that a similar bias exists among legislators toward the preferences of their most affluent constituents. He notes that existing research examining the relationship between public opinion and policymaking has found "a fairly high level of correspondence between constituency preferences and legislators' behavior," but few studies, he says, have disaggregated policy opinions to consider how that public opinion and policy congruence might vary across the preferences of different social groups (780). Using an original data set of almost 2,000 survey questions on proposed policy changes between 1981 and 2002, Gilens finds that "when Americans with different income levels differ in their policy preferences, actual policy outcomes strongly reflect the preferences of the most affluent but bear virtually no relationship to the preferences of poor or middle-income Americans" (778). That leads him to conclude that "influence over actual policy outcomes appears to be reserved almost exclusively for those at the top of the income distribution" (794).

Although few studies have directly explored the question of the relationship between voter and nonvoter or minority preferences and legislator behavior, the studies that have been conducted suggest a strong bias among legislators toward the policy preferences of white voters, and, more specifically, the most affluent voters. We believe these findings have important implications for questions of democratic inclusion within the U.S. polity. In *Reflexive Democracy*, Kevin Olson (2006) argues that three central democratic values are popular sovereignty, political inclusion, and political equality. Popular sovereignty is "the central value of all democracy": "People should be able to author the laws under which they live." Political inclusion and political equality are related. The first is a presumption that any deviation from full inclusion is difficult for a democracy to justify, and the second, that all those included in a democracy must be equally able to exercise their sovereignty (20). Within Olson's framework, if nonvoters are not represented in legislators' decisionmaking, and if nonvoters represent a particular demographic subset of the population that is excluded from political influence systematically in practice if not by law, then these democratic values are being violated.

Those values are also being violated if we broaden the question to consider differences in degrees of democratic representation across particular sectors of the electorate. Jane Mansbridge (2003) points out that normative political theory needs to do a better job of defining representation, given empirical advances in the field. To that end, she lays out four types of representation: promissory, anticipatory, gyroscopic, and surrogate. Promissory representation is the most traditional conceptualization: the representative is accountable to the constituent to keep the promises made during the authorizing election. Anticipatory representation occurs when a representative tries to please future voters rather than simply carrying out past promises. When voters select representatives who can be expected to behave in ways the voters approve of, even absent any communication from the voters, the representation is gyroscopic. Surrogate representation occurs when an individual's interests are represented by an officeholder who is not from the voter's own district but who believes strongly in a particular set of interests or perspectives that accord with the voter's. Mansbridge emphasizes that these different types are not mutually exclusive; she sees them as "cumulative, not oppositional" (526).

Mansbridge's typology is instructive for our purposes because the different types of representation she lays out require different degrees of communication, interaction, and deliberation between constituents and representatives. Within her model it matters who the voters are and to what degree representatives take their interests into consideration. In promissory representation, the most critical information exchange happens at the election point when the representative makes electoral promises. The potential sanction sits with the subsequent election, when the voter checks to see if the representative has kept his or her promises. The gyroscopic model is similar insofar as what matters is the ideological character and commitments of the representative at election time. No interaction between voter and representative is necessary during the period in office. It is understood that a voter's authority lies in electing the official and, potentially, removing that official from office.

Anticipatory and surrogate representation, on the other hand, require interaction and deliberation between the representative and the voter. In the anticipatory model, representatives not only need to know what voters think now but also need to anticipate what the voters are going to believe at a later point in order to cast their policy votes accordingly. This requires that the representatives have systems for identifying voter preferences, through direct communication, polling, and the like, in order to anticipate future opinions.[7] Surrogate representatives, in a similar way, need to have ways to identify nonconstituents' interests so that they can advocate for them appropriately. Both types of representation "shift our normative focus from the individual to the system, from aggregative democracy to deliberative democracy, from preferences to interests, from the way the legislator votes to the way the legislator communicates, and from the quality of promise-keeping to the quality of mutual education between legislator and constituents" (518).

Voters are more likely than nonvoters to experience promissory and gyroscopic representation because they are the ones choosing the representatives.[8] In addition, since likely voters have a much greater tendency to contact elected officials and a greater tendency to be included in public-opinion polling, their interests tend to be very much overrepresented in both the anticipatory and the surrogate forms of representation (Verba, Schlozman, and Brady 1995; Ramakrishnan and Baldassare 2004). If we see the types of representation as coexisting simultaneously across levels of government and therefore being cumulative, as Mansbridge posits, the lack of representation experienced by nonvoters is therefore cumulative as well.

To satisfy the normative democratic goals of popular sovereignty, political inclusion, and political equality (and therefore adequate representation), it thus becomes critical to change the demographic makeup of the voting population in the United States.[9] That is the work in which the community organizations that formed part of the CVI were engaged. Although these voters were being mobilized to engage in a political system that has been shown to be more responsive to the most affluent, the system has also been shown to be most responsive to *voters.* In addition, the political work that the CVI organizations were engaged in between electoral cycles—building their volunteer networks, fomenting support for their policy programs, and informing elected officials about their members' policy concerns—all strengthen the potential for anticipatory and surrogate representation within the associated ethnoracial communities of low-propensity voters. Mansbridge talks about the importance of considering how elected officials inform and educate constituents within the representative constructs. The CVI work has shown that it is equally important to consider how organizations, through their integrated voter-engagement work, are able to educate and inform elected officials to make them more aware of the challenges and concerns facing these communities. Through these multiple forms of communication, community organizations, and the voters they mobilize and organize, are making their representational relationships more interactive, deliberative, and, ideally, more substantively inclusive.

New voters, then, through their exercise of the franchise, are disrupting the category of model citizen/likely voter. By doing so, they are defining a new model citizen *and* creating new definitions of individual agency and citizenship. Individual agency is defined here (as in *Merriam Webster's Collegiate Dictionary*) as "the capacity, condition, or state of acting or of exerting power." The PPIC survey data presented above show that there is a clear demographic profile for voters in California. That profile historically has not included the low-income communities of color that were the focus of the CVI campaigns. The engagement of those communities in the political process changed the voter profile within those neighborhoods, and our habit formation findings suggest that the changes will have lasting effects on the voter profiles of these communities. We are not saying that the mobilizations will cause a sea change overnight; though an enormous undertaking, resulting in tens of thousands of individual conversations with potential voters, the CVI initiative involved contacts with only a small fraction of the California electorate. Rather, we would like to emphasize that mobilizations of this type are possible within low-income communities of color, as we proved, and, further, that mobilizing low-propensity ethnoracial voters does constitute important political and social change in the American political context.

Building a GOTV-Oriented Choice Architecture

The final lesson to be drawn from the CVI is that nontraditional partnerships can produce important, innovative, and meaningful outcomes. To our knowledge, the CVI represents one of the first times that a private foundation integrated an academic evaluation component into a large-scale community-based voter mobilization campaign. Our job as evaluators was to use rigorous social science methods to help the participating organizations be as effective as possible in their work and also to establish a set of best practices that could be used by other organizations considering embarking on this type of mobilization effort. The collaboration was predicated on a specialized division of labor, with each stakeholder bringing a skill set to this challenging work. In this model, the transparency of the academic publishing process could be used to educate organizers, funders, and the public at large about the impact of the GOTV conversations and the best ways to carry them out.

As with any innovative program, there were some bumps in the road. The participating organizations were accustomed to conducting their own evaluations and were reasonably concerned about allowing a third party detailed knowledge about their inner workings. Similarly, even though the foundation made it clear that future funding was not dependent on outcomes in previous rounds, the organizations were well aware of the fact that, in the nonprofit world, reputation is an important form of currency. Current performance would not affect this particular grant, but a negative outcome could potentially affect an organization's ability to get funding from another foundation in the future. Despite these challenges, the project was quite successful and shows that cross-sector partnerships can produce high-quality information and have real-world impacts.

With our participation in this initiative, we were engaging in a form of what is called "pracademics": academic research that is integrated with political practice (Gillespie and Michelson 2011).[10] As scholars of ethnoracial politics, we share a strong commitment to produce research that is relevant to and helps to empower the communities we study. Recent developments within the American Political Science Association (APSA) suggest that this emphasis on practice is being considered more broadly within our discipline. In addition to having a special issue of the journal *PS: Political Science and Politics* (April 2011) devoted to the topic, the report from APSA's task force on Political Science in the 21st Century discusses the future of the discipline and why it is important that political scientists engage in work that both is politically relevant and addresses the growing levels of domestic and international inequality (APSA 2011). To do this sort of work, academics need to build relationships with community partners, elected officials, social service organizations, and other people and institutions that are developing or implementing policy programs.

The CVI was just such a collaboration, one that provided benefits to all participants. The organizations received guidance and assistance in building their data management and institutional capacities. The broader organizational community received a set of best practices to guide their voter mobilization efforts (Michelson, García Bedolla, and Green 2009). We the academics gained insights into the mobilization process, were given access to local communities, and were provided the opportunity to gather the rich data set that forms the foundation of this book. The funder was able to support this politically important endeavor and to develop and disseminate a set of best practices that could be used by other organizations across the country. Most importantly, as a result of this collaboration, tens of thousands of low-propensity ethnoracial voters were mobilized to participate in the political process, thereby changing the face of the electorate within their respective communities.

These types of cross-institutional partnerships could form the foundation for new kinds of institutional relationships that bridge traditional dividing lines. In an era of dramatic budget deficits and growing social problems, public/private partnerships may hold the key to maintaining our social safety net and infrastructure. On the voter mobilization front, there are populations, such as those mobilized by the CVI, which political campaigns will not necessarily target unless nudged to do so by an outside entity, in the private sector or in the government. In *Nudge*, Richard H. Thaler and Cass R. Sunstein (2008) argue for the creation of a new "choice architecture" to support better choices by individuals. They point out that small changes, or nudges, can have big impacts on individual behavior. They define a nudge as "any aspect of the choice architecture that alters people's behavior in a predictable way without forbidding any options" and argue in favor of "self-conscious efforts, by institutions in the private sector and also by government, to steer people's choices in directions that will improve their lives" (5–6). Although Thaler and Sunstein focus on decisions related to health and wellness, a GOTV conversation easily fits within their definition of a helpful nudge.

If the goal is to create a more inclusive democratic politics within the United States, what we need is a new choice architecture, one designed to enhance voter participation, particularly for infrequent voters and eligible adults who are not registered to vote. Our studies indicate that this new choice architecture would need to include personal mobilization and to be designed explicitly to target those voters who have been the most disenfranchised. Olson (2006, 20) argues "sometimes extra measures must be taken to ensure that all people can exercise their sovereignty." Fostering political participation by all members of the polity may be precisely one of those cases in which extra measures are needed. That these infrequent voters could be mobilized by the CVI suggests that they were not making a conscious or principled decision to sit out of politics. Rather, they did not have the voter schema necessary to move them to the polls. White middle-class and affluent voters are able to develop this schema without outside intervention, probably through their family and community-level political socialization processes. The CVI work shows that this type of cognitive shift is possible for infrequent ethnoracial voters, even absent any change in their resources. By changing the choice architecture within which voters are embedded, it is possible to fundamentally change the demographic makeup of the electorate for the long term. These extra measures are necessary to ensure equal participation, inclusion, and representation for all Americans.

APPENDIX A: DETAILED TABLES

Indirect Experiments
Phone Bank Experiments
Door-to-Door Experiments

Indirect Experiments

Table A2.1: PICO Direct Mail and Leaflet Experiments, June 2006

Site	% Voting, Control Group	% Voting, Treatment Group	N	ITT (SE)
Intervention: Handwritten Letter				
St. Agatha's Church—LA Voice	39.8 (145/364)	38.1 (85/223)	587	−1.7 (4.8)
Intervention: Postcard with Polling-Place Location				
Holy Innocents Church—Long Beach ICO	15.4 (18/117)	17.2 (23/134)	251	1.8 (5.2)
St. Athanasius's Church—Long Beach ICO	10.1 (58/573)	14.3 (73/509)	1,082	4.2* (2.4)
St. Lucy's Church—Long Beach ICO	14.4 (66/458)	13.4 (58/434)	892	−1.1 (2.8)
Intervention: Postcard				
St. Joseph's Church—Sacramento ACT	30.5 (198/646)	36.8 (236/642)	1,288	6.3** (3.2)
St. Charles's Church—Sacramento ACT	34.7 (350/1,010)	35.4 (710/2,008)	3,018	0.7 (2.3)
Holy Innocents Church—Long Beach ICO	15.4 (18/117)	18.2 (31/170)	287	2.9 (5.4)
St. Athanasius's Church—Long Beach ICO	10.1 (58/573)	10.9 (57/524)	1,097	0.8 (2.0)
St. Lucy's Church—Long Beach ICO	14.4 (66/458)	15.3 (60/393)	851	0.9 (2.9)
Our Lady of Talpa Church—LA Voice	33.5 (169/505)	30.8 (322/1,044)	1,549	−2.6 (3.1)
Our Mother of Good Counsel Church — LA Voice	46.5 (217/467)	41.6 (215/517)	984	0.4 (3.7)

Table A2.1. (*Continued*)

Site	% Voting, Control Group	% Voting, Treatment Group	N	ITT (SE)
Resurrection Church—LA Voice	28.2 (227/804)	27.8 (445/1,600)	2,404	−0.4 (2.4)
St. Agatha Church—LA Voice	39.8 (145/364)	42.8 (209/488)	852	3.0 (4.0)
Pooled Direct Mail			14,558	1.1[†] (0.8)
Intervention: Leaflet				
Long Beach—ICO	15.2 (48/315)	24.4 (81/332)	647	9.2** (3.5)
Orange County—OCCCO	17.7 (271/1,530)	18.9 (392/2,080)	3,610	1.1 (1.4)
Pooled Leaflets			4,317	2.2* (1.3)

Note: For an explanation of organizational acronyms, see the acronym list. For all the analyses in this volume, N = the size of the experiment (treatment group + control group). For more on the intent-to-treat (ITT) and treatment-on-treated (TOT) effects see chapter 1.
[†] $p < .10$, * $p < .05$, ** $p < .01$, one-tailed

Table A2.2. PICO Direct Mail and Leaflet Experiments, November 2006

Site	% Voting in Control Group	% Voting in Treatment Group	N	ITT (SE)
Intervention: Postcard with Polling-Place Location				
Visalia—RCI	38.6 (184/477)	31.0 (367/1,185)	1,662	−7.6* (2.6)
Intervention: Postcard				
Fresno—FIC (mixed direct mail & leaflets)	36.5 (77/211)	31.7 (225/709)	920	−4.8 (3.8)
St. Agatha's Church—LA Voice	46.3 (266/575)	45.3 (602/1,328)	1,903	−1.0 (2.5)
Our Lady of Talpa Church—LA Voice	47.1 (259/550)	47.3 (589/1,246)	1,796	0.2 (2.6)
St. Odilia's Church—LA Voice	36.0 (135/375)	38.9 (193/496)	871	2.9 (3.3)
Our Mother of Good Counsel Church—LA Voice	54.0 (305/565)	47.9 (328/685)	1,250	−6.1 (2.8)
Blessed Sacrament Church—LA Voice	45.0 (309/686)	38.9 (355/913)	1,599	−6.1 (2.5)
St. Anne's Church—LA Voice	49.9 (257/515)	48.0 (927/1,933)	2,448	−1.9 (2.5)
Pooled Direct Mail			12,449	−3.2 (1.0)
Intervention: Leaflet				
St. Athanasius's Church—Long Beach ICO	31.8 (147/463)	31.8 (348/1,096)	1,559	0 (2.6)

Table A2.2. (*Continued*)

Site	% Voting in Control Group	% Voting in Treatment Group	N	ITT (SE)
St. Lucy's Church—Long Beach ICO	44.3 (1,159/2,614)	45.1 (421/933)	3,547	0.8 (1.9)
Fullerton (Orange County)—OCCCO	37.3 (202/542)	34.2 (295/863)	1,405	−3.1 (2.6)
Pooled Leaflets			6,511	−0.04 (1.3)

Note: See Table A2.1.
* p < .05, two-tailed

Table A2.3. APALC Direct Mail Experiments, June 2006

National-Origin Group	% Voting in Control Group	% Voting in Treatment Group: mail only	% Voting in Treatment Group: mail and phone bank	N	TOT (SE)
Chinese American	8.0 (965/12,076)	8.2 (279/3,408)	8.8 (143/1,621)	17,105	0.3 (0.5)
Filipino American	9.2 (304/3,298)	8.3 (48/576)	9.5 (78/823)	4,697	−0.9 (1.0)
Korean American	7.6 (412/5,386)	7.9 (79/994)	8.2 (118/1,437)	7,817	0.2 (0.7)
Vietnamese American	8.2 (315/3,829)	7.8 (101/1,294)	6.2 (20/324)	5,447	−0.4 (0.8)
Pooled				35,066	0.01 (0.3)

Note: See Table A2.1. Robust cluster standard errors are by household. None of the TOT estimates from these experiments reach traditional levels of statistical significance. APALC also sent mailers to 646 Cambodian registered voters, but this national-origin group was not included in the field experiments.

Table A2.4. APALC *Easy Voter Guide* Experiments, November 2006

National-Origin Group	% Voting in Control Group	% Voting in Treatment Group: mail only	% Voting in Treatment Group: mail and phone bank	N	TOT (SE)
South Asian American	29.9 (81/271)	40.2 (111/276)	34.2 (166/486)	1,033	4.2* (2.5)
Cambodian American	12.5 (5/40)	5.0 (2/40)	21.4 (55/257)	337	3.8 (3.5)
Chinese American	25.7 (1,961/7,618)	27.8 (762/2,741)	2.3 (310/1,137)	11,496	1.6* (0.8)
Filipino American	32.9 (500/1,520)	33.2 (198/596)	34.9 (204/585)	2,701	0.4 (1.6)
Japanese American	37.1 (385/1,138)	33.6 (130/387)	39.6 (125/316)	1,841	−0.1 (2.1)
Korean American	28.5 (569/1,999)	28.0 (375/1,338)	30.8 (329/1,069)	4,406	0.5 (1.2)
Vietnamese American	23.1 (449/1,947)	24.8 (334/1,349)	22.2 (50/225)	3,521	0.9 (1.4)
Pooled				25,335	1.2* (0.5)

Note: See Table A2.1. Robust cluster standard errors are by household.
*p < .05, one-tailed

Table A2.5. OCAPICA *Easy Voter Guide* Experiments, November 2006

National-Origin Group	Language	% Voting in Control Group	% Voting in Treatment Group: mail only	% Voting in Treatment Group: mail and phone bank	N	TOT (SE)
Chinese American	Mandarin	32.7 (591/1,809)	35.0 (485/1,385)	32.9 (161/489)	3,683	2.3 (1.7)
Chinese American	English	26.5 (498/1,879)	21.3 (67/314)	26.5 (86/324)	2,517	−5.2* (2.6)
Korean American	Korean	32.3 (485/1,501)	35.4 (228/644)	33.7 (386/1,145)	3,290	3.1 (2.3)
Korean American	English	17.7 (153/864)	14.1 (29/206)	14.8 (77/522)	1,592	−3.1 (2.7)
Vietnamese American	Vietnamese	36.1 (2,560/7,083)	36.4 (525/1,443)	38.5 (556/1,445)	9,971	0.2 (1.4)
Vietnamese American	English	24.5 (1,206/4,927)	20.9 (72/345)	26.3 (115/438)	5,710	−3.8* (1.9)
Pooled					26,763	−0.6 (0.9)

Note: See Table A2.1. Robust cluster standard errors are by household.
*p < .05, one-tailed

Phone Bank Experiments

Table A3.1. APALC Phone Bank Experiments, June 2006

National-Origin Group	% Voting in Control Group	% Voting in Treatment Group	Contact Rate (%)	N[a]	ITT	TOT (SE)[b]
South Asian American	5.9 (86/1,453)	8.1 (44/545)	29.7	1,998	2.2	7.2 (4.4)
Chinese American	8.0 (965/12,076)	8.7 (223/2,577)	19.4	14,653	0.7	3.4 (3.1)
Filipino American	9.2 (304/3,298)	9.9 (144/1,454)	20.4	4,752	0.7	3.4 (4.6)
Japanese American	12.4 (268/2,162)	13.6 (83/612)	34.2	2,774	1.2	3.4 (4.5)
Korean American	7.7 (412/5,386)	8.2 (208/2,550)	28.0	7,936	0.5	1.8 (2.3)
Vietnamese American	8.2 (315/3,829)	6.5 (35/537)	13.8	4,366	−1.7	−12.4 (8.6)
Pooled				36,479		2.7* (1.5)

Note: See Table A2.1.

[a]Individuals targeted to receive direct mail but no telephone call are excluded.

[b]Robust cluster standard errors are by household.

*$p < .05$, one-tailed

Table A3.2. APALC Phone Bank Experiments, November 2006

National-Origin Group	% Voting in Control Group	% Voting in Treatment Group	Contact Rate (%)	N[a]	ITT	TOT (SE)[b]
South Asian American	29.9 (81/271)	33.6 (345/1,028)	35.7	1,299	3.7	10.3 (9.7)
Cambodian American	12.5 (5/40)	19.4 (97/499)	27.0	539	6.9	25.8 (23.4)
Chinese American	25.7 (1,961/7,618)	26.8 (1,080/4,026)	36.3	11,644	1.1	3.0 (2.4)
Filipino American	32.9 (500/1,520)	34.7 (708/2,042)	29.9	3,562	1.8	6.0 (5.6)
Japanese American	37.1 (385/1,038)	36.6 (410/1,120)	34.4	2,158	−0.5	−1.4 (6.2)
Korean American	28.5 (569/1,999)	29.9 (775/2,590)	39.1	4,589	1.4	3.7 (3.7)
Vietnamese American	23.1 (449/1,947)	24.3 (138/567)	39.5	2,514	1.2	3.2 (5.2)
Pooled				26,305		3.4* (1.7)

Note: See Table A2.1.

[a]Individuals targeted to receive direct mail but no telephone call are excluded.

[b]Robust cluster standard errors are by household.

*p < .05, one-tailed

Table A3.3. OCAPICA Phone Bank Experiments, November 2006

National-Origin Group	Language	% Voting in Control Group	% Voting in Treatment Group	Contact Rate (%)	N[a]	ITT	TOT (SE)[b]
Chinese American	Mandarin	32.7 (591/1,809)	32.9 (161/489)	40.1	2,298	0.2	0.6 (6.1)
Chinese American	English	26.5 (498/1,879)	26.5 (86/324)	19.8	2,203	0.0	0.2 (13.9)
Korean American	Korean	32.3 (485/1,501)	33.7 (386/1,145)	54.9	2,646	1.4	2.5 (3.4)
Korean American	English	17.7 (153/864)	14.8 (82/555)	38.0	1,419	−2.9	−7.7 (5.4)
Vietnamese American	Vietnamese	36.1 (2,560/7,083)	38.5 (556/1,445)	40.8	8,528	2.4	5.7* (3.5)
Vietnamese American	English	24.5 (1,206/4,927)	27.7 (208/750)	30.4	5,677	3.2	10.7* (5.8)
Pooled					22,771		2.8† (1.9)

Note: See Table A2.1.

[a]Individuals targeted to receive direct mail but no telephone call are excluded.

[b]Robust cluster standard errors are by household.

†$p < .10$, *$p < .05$, one-tailed

Table A3.4. NALEO Phone Bank Experiments, June 2006

Site	% Voting in Control Group	% Voting in Treatment Group	Contact Rate (%)	N[a]	ITT	TOT[b] (SE)
Fresno County	6.4 (558/8,762)	6.1 (441/7,200)	9.2	15,962	−0.3	−2.7 (4.2)
Los Angeles County	19.5 (1,468/7,514)	19.8 (1,872/9,456)	12.4	16,968	0.3	2.1 (5.0)
Orange County	18.5 (1,265/6,830)	19.3 (1,160/6,000)	9.6	12,830	0.8	8.4 (7.3)
Riverside County	14.4 (744/5,182)	15.0 (941/6,285)	10.6	11,467	0.6	5.8 (6.2)
San Bernardino County	8.3 (438/5,265)	8.7 (560/6,449)	9.9	11,714	0.4	3.6 (5.1)
Pooled				68,941		2.1 (2.4)

Note: See Table A2.1.

[a]Analysis includes only single-voter households because of randomization issues in the multivoter households.

[b]None of the TOT estimates reach traditional levels of statistical significance.

Table A3.5. NALEO Phone Bank Experiments, November 2006

Site	% Voting in Control Group	% Voting in Treatment Group	Contact Rate (%)	N	ITT	TOT[a] (SE)
Fresno County	20.8 (554/2,667)	23.1 (1,230/5,324)	41.4	7,991	2.3	1.2 (2.2)
Los Angeles County	49.4 (726/1,470)	47.0 (4,596/9,789)	25.9	11,259	−2.4	−4.5 (5.3)
Orange County	39.0 (1,015/2,600)	39.3 (2,276/5,792)	29.4	8,392	0.3	−0.4 (3.3)
Riverside County	34.5 (689/1,996)	37.4 (2,079/5,556)	21.0	7,552	2.9	11.8* (5.4)
San Bernardino County	17.7 (623/3,527)	17.5 (997/5,685)	19.9	9,212	−0.2	−2.5 (4.0)
Pooled				44,406		0.7 (1.5)

Note: See Table A2.1.

[a]Because of randomization issues, TOT estimates include covariates for voting history and whether or not the targeted voter lived in a multivoter household.

* $p < .05$, one-tailed

Table A3.6. NALEO Phone Bank Experiments, City of Los Angeles, March 2007

	% Voting in Control Group	% Voting in Treatment Group: basic script	Contact Rate: basic script (%)	ITT	% Voting in Treatment Group: informational script	Contact Rate: informational script (%)	ITT
Single-voter households	14.4 (34/236)	16.8 (215/1,283)	39.4	2.4	16.6 (203/1,222)	40.8	2.2
Multivoter households	19.3 (66/342)	20.7 (302/1,459)	42.3	1.4	22.5 (353/1,571)	48.5	3.2
All Voters	17.3 (100/578)	18.9 (517/2,742)	41.0	1.6	19.9 (556/2,793)	45.3	2.6

Note: See Table A2.1. Reliable TOT estimates cannot be calculated because of the different contact rates for each script. Results are presented separately for single-voter and multivoter households because of randomization issues.

Table A3.7. SVREP Phone Bank Experiment, November 2006

Site	% Voting in Control Group	% Voting in Treatment Group	Contact Rate (%)	N	ITT	TOT (SE)[a]
Los Angeles	34.3 (2,176/6,350)	36.4 (7,111/19,512)	23.5	25,862	2.1	9.3** (3.2)

Note: See Table A2.1.

[a]Robust cluster standard errors are by household.

**p < .01, one-tailed

Table A3.8. NALEO Phone Bank Experiments, February 2008

Site	% Voting in Control Group	% Voting in Treatment Group	Contact Rate (%)	N	ITT	TOT (SE)[a]
Kern County	34.8 (180/517)	33.5 (1,584/4,734)	21.1	5,251	−1.3	−6.4 (11.0)
Los Angeles County	43.3 (1,470/3,394)	45.8 (14,054/30,692)	20.2	34,086	2.5	12.3** (4.7)
Riverside County	36.7 (219/596)	38.0 (2,069/5,439)	21.7	6,035	1.3	6.0 (10.2)
San Bernardino County	38.8 (212/547)	38.4 (1,853/4,831)	28.1	5,378	−0.4	−1.4 (8.3)
Pooled				50,750		7.0* (3.6)

Note: See Table A2.1.

[a]Robust cluster standard errors are by household.

*$p < .05$, **$p < .01$, one-tailed

Table A3.9. OCAPICA Phone Bank Experiments, June 2008

National-Origin Group	% Voting in Control Group	% Voting in Treatment Group	Contact Rate (%)	N	ITT	TOT (SE)[a]
South Asian American	7.0 (195/2,797)	8.9 (44/495)	34.5	3,292	1.9	5.5 (4.5)
Chinese American	8.7 (192/2,217)	12.5 (124/990)	30.6	3,207	3.8	12.6** (4.3)
Filipino American	9.0 (286/3,161)	12.5 (62/495)	21.6	3,656	3.5	16.1* (8.4)
Korean American	11.4 (372/3,265)	15.8 (234/1,481)	33.5	4,746	4.4	13.2** (3.9)
Vietnamese American	22.4 (2,774/12,395)	24.6 (608/2,467)	20.7	14,862	2.2	10.9* (5.1)
Pooled				29,763		11.1** (2.1)

Note: See Table A2.1.

[a]Robust cluster standard errors are by household.

*p < .05, **p < .01, one-tailed

Table A3.10. APALC Phone Bank Experiments, June 2008

National-Origin Group	% Voting in Control Group	% Voting in Treatment Group	Contact Rate (%)	N	ITT	TOT (SE)[a]
South Asian American	8.4 (23/273)	9.8 (117/1,200)	35.5	1,473	1.4	n/a[b]
Chinese American	9.8 (804/8,216)	11.7 (469/4,000)	36.2	12,216	1.9	n/a
Filipino American	10.5 (224/2,143)	11.9 (227/1,900)	27.4	4,043	1.4	n/a
Japanese American	12.1 (164/1,353)	15.6 (125/800)	17.6	2,153	3.5	n/a
Korean American	17.1 (486/2,836)	19.9 (498/2,500)	28.0	5,336	2.8	n/a
Vietnamese American	8.5 (133/1,567)	9.6 (153/1,600)	32.6	3,167	1.1	n/a
Pooled (first call only)				28,388		4.0
Second Call	14.0[c] (56/400)	19.5 (293/1,501)	44.3	1,901	5.5	13.0** (4.9)

Note: See Table A2.1.

[a]Robust cluster standard errors are by household.

[b]Reliable TOT estimates cannot be calculated for the first call because some individuals in the treatment group also received a second call.

[c]The campaign also contacted eight individuals in the control group during the second round of calls.

**$p < .01$, one-tailed

Table A3.11. APALC Phone Bank Experiments, November 2008

National-Origin Group	% Voting in Control Group	% Voting in Treatment Group	Contact Rate (%)	N	ITT	TOT (SE)[a]
Asian Indian American	68.7 (697/1,015)	73.2 (625/854)	23.9	1,869	4.5	18.9* (9.8)
Chinese American	64.1 (4,286/6,684)	65.9 (3,380/5,131)	31.8	11,815	1.8	5.5* (3.1)
Filipino American	71.4 (272/381)	70.6 (1,963/2,779)	17.2	3,160	−0.8	−4.4 (15.5)
Japanese American	71.8 (893/1,244)	73.3 (747/1,019)	24.5	2,263	1.5	6.2 (8.1)
Korean American	65.4 (870/1,330)	64.5 (2,043/3,167)	25.0	4,497	−0.9	−3.6 (6.8)
Vietnamese American	61.0 (781/1,280)	63.3 (990/1,565)	26.8	2,844	2.3	8.5 (7.2)
Pooled				26,448		5.3* (2.4)

Note: See Table A2.1.

[a]Robust cluster standard errors are by household.

*$p < .05$, one-tailed

Table A3.12. OCAPICA Phone Bank Experiments, November 2008

National-Origin Group	% Voting in Control Group	% Voting in Treatment Group	Contact Rate (%)	N	ITT	TOT (SE)[a]
South Asian American	74.4 (1,746/2,348)	76.7 (690/900)	29.0	3,248	2.3	8.0[†] (6.2)
Chinese American	68.6 (2,774/4,046)	69.3 (1,248/1,800)	26.6	5,846	−4.7	2.9 (5.4)
Filipino American	78.6 (612/779)	75.3 (678/900)	16.9	1,679	−3.3	−19.1 (13.1)
Korean American	68.5 (1,483/2,166)	66.3 (1,193/1,800)	33.7	3,966	−2.2	−6.5 (5.0)
Vietnamese American	61.1 (6,225/10,196)	59.9 (1,975/3,300)	22.0	13,496	−1.2	−5.5 (5.0)
Pooled				28,235		−1.9 (2.6)

Note: See Table A2.1.

[a]Robust cluster standard errors are by household.

[†]$p < .10$, one-tailed

Table A3.13. NALEO Phone Bank Experiments, November 2008

Site	% Voting in Control Group	% Voting in Treatment Group	Contact Rate (%)	N	ITT	TOT (SE)[a]
Fresno County	45.9 (2,292/4,992)	47.8 (3,584/7,500)	17.1	12,492	1.9	11.0* (5.8)
Bakersfield (Kern County)	54.5 (1,475/2,707)	54.1 (4,055/7,500)	16.9	10,207	−0.4	−2.5 (7.1)
Los Angeles County	66.6 (17,822/26,759)			66,759		
Optimistic script		66.1 (13,216/20,000)	11.8		−0.5	−4.4 (4.0)
Pessimistic script		66.4 (13,271/20,000)	18.2		−0.2	−1.4 (2.6)
Orange County	47.5 (3,132/6,594)	48.3 (6,039/12,500)	17.8	19,094	0.8	4.6 (4.8)
Riverside County	63.5 (3,315/5,224)	61.7 (3,001/4,866)	44.3	10,090	−1.8	−4.0 (2.4)
San Bernardino County	60.2 (3,412/5,664)	60.0 (2,999/5,000)	45.3	10,664	−0.2	−0.6 (2.3)
Pooled				129,306		−1.2 (1.2)

Note: See Table A2.1.

[a]Robust cluster standard errors are by household.

*$p < .05$, one-tailed

Table A3.14. PICO Phone Bank Experiments, November 2006

Site	% Voting in Control Group	% Voting in Treatment Group	Contact Rate (%)	N	ITT	TOT (SE)[a]
Colusa—NVSC	62.2 (280/450)	64.6 (880/1,363)	45.6	1,813	2.4	0.6 (3.6)
Arbuckle—NVSC	40.2 (99/246)	46.7 (244/522)	47.3	768	6.5	13.8 (9.8)
Williams—NVSC	50.2 (109/217)	50.9 (258/507)	35.0	724	0.7	1.9 (12.7)
St. Edward's Church—Stockton PACT	36.3 (69/190)	39.9 (154/386)	36.9	576	3.6	9.7 (12.9)
St. Agatha's Church—LA Voice	46.3 (266/575)	45.6 (607/1,332)	23.3	1,907	−0.7	−3.0 (12.1)
Our Lady of Talpa Church—LA Voice	47.1 (259/550)	47.0 (279/1,232)	26.6	1,782	−0.1	−0.4 (10.8)
St. Odilia's Church—LA Voice	36.0 (135/375)	42.2 (211/500)	21.0	875	6.2	29.5 (17.9)
Our Mother of Good Counsel Church—LA Voice	54.0 (305/565)	49.1 (387/789)	17.0	1,354	−4.9	−29.0 (17.8)
Blessed Sacrament Church—LA Voice	45.0 (309/686)	38.5 (354/919)	23.1	1,605	−6.5	−28.3 (12.7)
Resurrection Church—LA Voice	51.8 (185/357)	49.0 (659/1,345)	24.5	1,702	−2.8	−11.5 (13.1)
San Bernardino—ICUC	34.1 (93/273)	32.2 (176/547)	33.6	820	−1.9	−5.6 (12.8)
Pooled				13,926		−0.05 (2.7)

Note: See Table A2.1.

[a]None of the TOT coefficient estimates reach traditional levels of statistical significance. Robust cluster standard errors are by household.

Table A3.15. PICO Nonsocial Network Phone Bank Experiments, 2008

Site	% Voting in Control Group	% Voting in Treatment Group	Contact Rate (%)	N	ITT	TOT (SE)[a]
February 2008						
Stockton Hmong—PACT	30.7 (58/189)	23.6 (48/203)	25.1	392	−7.1	−28.0 (18.7)
San Bernardino—ICUC	31.7 (780/2,458)	30.4 (743/2,444)	21.6	4,902	−1.3	−6.2 (6.2)
June 2008						
Anaheim—OCCCO[b]	7.2 (48/668)	7.6 (58/763)	8.8	1,431	0.4	n/a
San Bernardino—ICUC	10.0 (82/823)	9.4 (181/1,921)	31.4	2,744	−0.6	−1.7 (4.1)
November 2008						
Stockton Hmong—PACT	53.8 (538/1,001)	53.1 (561/1,057)	21.1	2,058	−0.7	−3.2 (12.4)
Hollywood[c]—LA Voice	76.6 (236/308)	79.9 (255/319)	35.7	627	3.3	9.3 (9.9)
St. Odilia Youth Group—LA Voice	77.5 (117/151)	81.5 (123/151)	37.8	302	4.0	10.5 (13.1)

Note: See Table A2.1.

[a]None of the TOT coefficient estimates reach traditional levels of statistical significance. Robust cluster standard errors are by household.

[b]The group was randomized at the precinct level.

[c]Specifically, Hollywood's Human Development Overlay District.

Table A3.16. PICO Social Network Phone Bank Experiments, 2008

Site	% Voting in Control Group	% Voting in Treatment Group	Contact Rate (%)	N	ITT	TOT (SE)[a]
February 2008						
St. Lucy's Church—Long Beach ICO	39.4 (172/436)	44.9 (122/272)	59.2	708	5.5	12.8 (8.5)
Group A (friends)		49.5 (46/93)	48.4		10.1	20.7 (13.1)
Group B (fellow congregants)		44.0 (40/91)	63.7		4.6	7.1 (9.5)
Group C (neighbors)		40.9 (36/88)	65.9		1.5	2.2 (8.7)
June 2008						
St. Lucy's Church—Long Beach ICO	6.7 (31/463)	6.5 (29/447)	32.7	910	−0.2	−0.6 (5.3)
Group A (friends)		9.1 (6/66)	100.0		2.4	n/a
Group B (fellow congregants)		7.5 (6/80)	100.0		0.8	n/a

Note: See Table A2.1.

[a]For the February 2008 experiment, robust cluster standard errors are for groups A and B only; cluster information is not available for group C. TOT estimates cannot be calculated for the June 2008 efforts.

Door-to-Door Experiments

Table A4.1. CARECEN Door-to-Door Experiments, 2006–2008

Date	% Voting in Control Group	% Voting in Treatment Group	Contact Rate (%)	N	ITT	TOT (SE)[a]
June 2006, pooled[b]						2.2 (1.8)
No phone number	14.5 (113/780)	14.7 (125/851)	36.4	1,631	0.2	0.6 (3.9)
With phone number	20.6 (424/2,063)	21.8 (729/3,352)	45.8	5,415	1.2	2.6 (2.0)
November 2006	52.5 (821/1,565)	52.2 (2,391/4,583)	52.9	6,148	−0.3	−0.5 (2.9)
February 2008	54.1 (860/1,589)	54.6 (1,959/3,591)	49.8	5,180	0.5	0.9 (3.2)
June 2008	20.4 (372/1,827)	22.3 (928/4,168)	48.0	5,995	1.9	4.0 (2.6)
November 2008	64.9 (1,214/1,871)	65.0 (2,819/4,334)	23.0	6,205	0.1	0.7 (6.0)

Note: See Table A2.1.

[a]None of the TOT coefficient estimates reach traditional levels of statistical significance. Robust cluster standard errors are by household.

[b]Households are randomized separately in the June 2006 experiment, creating separate experiments for those with and without valid telephone numbers in the voter file.

Table A4.2. SCOPE Door-to-Door Experiments, 2006–2008

Date	% Voting in Control Group	% Voting in Treatment Group	Contact Rate (%)	N	ITT	TOT (SE)[a]
June 2006	16.8 (3,041/815)	17.6 (974/5,530)	34.6	7,345	0.8	2.6 (3.3)
November 2006	33.7 (1,205/3,578)	36.7 (4,324/11,789)	45.3	15,367	3.0	6.6** (2.1)
February 2008	58.0 (1,728/2,979)	59.7 (3,580/5,994)	50.4	8,973	1.7	3.4 (2.3)
November 2008	88.2 (2,782/3,155)	88.5 (12,282/13,881)	59.0	17,036	0.3	0.5 (1.1)

Note: See Table A2.1.
[a]Robust cluster standard errors are by household.
**p < .01, one-tailed

Table A4.3. CCAEJ Door-to-Door Experiments, 2006–2008

Site and Date	% Voting in Control Group	% Voting in Treatment Group	Contact Rate (%)	N	ITT	TOT (SE)[a]
Riverside						
June 2006	11.1 (39/350)	19.6 (281/1,431)	19.7	1,781	8.5	43.1** (12.5)
November 2006	53.4 (321/601)	53.5 (993/1,857)	19.5	2,458	0.1	0.4 (15.7)
June 2008	5.5 (190/3,489)	7.5 (187/2,481)	13.3	5,970	2.0	15.7** (5.6)
November 2008	65.2 (1,492/2,290)	64.3 (3,223/5,010	24.1	7,300	−0.9	−3.4 (5.7)
San Bernardino						
November 2006	45.0 (799/1,776)	46.3 (2,477/5,352)	25.5	7,128	1.3	5.1 (6.4)
June 2008	9.3 (227/2,435)	9.4 (188/2,009)	31.3	4,444	0.1	0.1 (3.2)
November 2008	53.2 (803/1,510)	54.7 (3,272/5,986)	23.7	7,496	1.5	6.3 (7.3)

Note: See Table A2.1.
[a]Robust cluster standard errors are by household.
**$p < .01$, one-tailed

Table A4.4. AACU Door-to-Door Experiments, 2006–2007

Site and Date	% Voting in Control Group	% Voting in Treatment Group	Contact Rate (%)	N	ITT	TOT (SE)[a]
November 2006						
Los Angeles County	41.6 (4,731/11,378)	42.6 (524/1,230)	7.1	12,608	1.0	14.4 (25.4)
Riverside County	41.8 (4,157/9,935)	40.5 (501/1,236)	15.9	11,171	−1.3	−8.2 (14.5)
San Bernardino County	36.2 (3,329/9,187)	35.5 (436/1,229)	18.8	10,416	−0.7	−4.0 (10.6)
Pooled				34,195		−3.4 (8.1)
March 2007						
Los Angeles	11.7 (606/5,188)	11.2 (580/5,184)	35.0	10,393	−0.5	−1.4 (2.0)

Note: See Table A2.1.

[a]Robust cluster standard errors are by household. None of the TOT coefficient estimates reach traditional levels of statistical significance.

Table A4.5. PICO Door-to-Door Experiments, November 2006

Site	% Voting in Control Group	% Voting in Treatment Group	Contact Rate (%)	N	ITT	TOT (SE)[a]
Colusa—NVSC	66.5 (653/982)	72.9 (188/258)	66.8	1,240	6.4	9.6* (5.5)
Sacramento ACT	35.5 (77/217)	39.7 (93/234)	32.9	451	4.2	12.9 (15.4)
Bakersfield—RCI	44.1 (317/719)	42.8 (203/474)	22.4	1,193	−1.3	−5.6 (15.4)
Fullerton—OCCCO	37.3 (202/542)	34.2 (295/863)	47.6	1,405	−3.1	−6.5 (6.6)
Pooled				4,289		3.1 (3.9)

Note: See Table A2.1.
[a]Robust cluster standard errors are by household.
*$p < .05$, one-tailed

Table A4.6. PICO Door-to-Door Experiments, February 2008

Site	% Voting in Control Group	% Voting in Treatment Group	Contact Rate (%)	N	ITT	TOT (SE)[a]
Winters—NVSC	46.5 (60/129)	58.2 (92/158)	90.5	287	11.7	12.9* (6.6)
St. Joseph's Church—Sacramento ACT	30.4 (24/79)	35.2 (31/88)	46.6	167	4.8	10.4 (16.3)
Burbank High School, precinct 45716—Sacramento ACT	45.2 (19/42)	41.7 (20/48)	14.6	90	−3.5	−24.5 (76.2)
Burbank High School, 4 precincts[b]—Sacramento ACT	25.1 (49/195)	32.2 (110/342)	21.1	537	7.1	47.2 (46.8)
Christ Temple, precinct 51116—Sacramento ACT	36.5 (19/52)	44.6 (25/56)	23.2	108	8.1	34.9 (43.5)
Christ Temple, precinct 51400—Sacramento ACT	21.5 (14/65)	40.3 (27/67)	10.4	132	18.8	179.56 (102.51)
St. Mark's Church—Sacramento ACT	46.3 (31/67)	39.2 (29/74)	43.2	141	−7.1	−16.4 (22.5)
North Sacramento —Sacramento ACT	27.6 (16/58)	21.7 (13/60)	15.0	118	−5.9	−39.5 (59.5)
Next Generation—Sacramento ACT	28.1 (18/64)	41.7 (30/72)	66.7	136	13.6	20.3 (14.2)
Hmong—Sacramento ACT	34.7 (41/118)	44.8 (56/125)	38.4	243	10.1	26.2 (17.8)
Green House—Sacramento ACT	43.4 (33/76)	47.4 (36/76)	40.8	152	4.0	9.7 (23.2)
Lodi—CBC	28.0 (59/211)	27.5 (53/193)	15.5	404	−0.5	−3.2 (31.6)

Table A4.6. (*Continued*)

Site	% Voting in Control Group	% Voting in Treatment Group	Contact Rate (%)	N	ITT	TOT (SE)[a]
Stockton—PACT	32.7 (32/98)	37.5 (45/120)	20.0	218	4.8	24.2 (33.5)
Modesto—CBC	53.1 (60/113)	57.7 (60/104)	40.4	217	4.6	11.4 (20.1)
Fresno—FIC	34.1 (177/519)	34.3 (180/525)	22.5	1,044	0.2	0.8 (15.9)
Mt. Zion—Bakersfield RCI	39.6 (110/278)	40.5 (102/252)	15.5	530	0.9	5.9 (30.5)
Compassion Christian Church—Bakersfield RCI	44.4 (8/18)	34.5 (10/29)	37.9	47	−9.9	−26.3 (42.3)
Emmanuel Church—Bakersfield RCI	44.0 (33/75)	45.9 (17/37)	37.8	112	1.9	5.1 (26.5)
EBFCA (East Bakersfield Faith Community Alliance)—Bakersfield RCI	26.1 (12/46)	25.5 (27/106)	13.2	152	−0.6	−4.7 (59.0)
LA Voice	58.9 (1,272/2,160)	62.7 (630/1,005)	36.6	3,165	3.8	10.4* (5.6)
Orange County—OCCCO	38.1 (99/260)	41.6 (67/161)	32.9	421	3.5	10.7 (14.7)
San Bernardino County—ICUC	51.5 (669/1,298)	53.1 (693/1,306)	31.5	2,604	1.6	4.8 (6.9)
Pooled[c]				10,356		9.0** (3.4)

Note: See Table A2.1.

[a]Robust cluster standard errors are by household, except for the four precincts canvassed by Burbank High School, for which the standard errors are clustered by precinct.

[b]The target group was randomized at the precinct level.

[c]Pooled statistic does not include the precinct-randomized experiment (Burbank High School, 4 precincts) or one experiment for which a reliable standard error could not be calculated (Christ Temple, precinct 51400).

*$p < .05$, ** $p < .01$, one-tailed

Table A4.7. PICO Door-to-Door Experiments, June 2008

Site	% Voting in Control Group	% Voting in Treatment Group	Contact Rate (%)	N	ITT	TOT (SE)[a]
Door-to-Door Experiments Randomized by Precinct						
The Rock—Sacramento ACT	15.8 (373/2,365)	15.2 (166/1,092)	9.0	3,457	−0.6	n/a[b]
Burbank High School—Sacramento ACT	14.5 (218/1,508)	17.0 (285/1,680)	8.0	3,188	2.5	n/a
Sacrifice of Praise—Sacramento ACT	11.2 (103/920)	15.1 (161/1,064)	12.9	1,984	3.9	n/a
Long Beach—ICO	16.3 (445/2,729)	14.2 (402/2,822)	9.3	5,551	−1.9	n/a
Pooled: 4 precinct-level experiments (16 precincts total)				14,180		0.9 (13.9)
Door-to-Door Experiments Randomized by Household						
Anderson (Shasta County)—NVSC	32.1 (205/639)	31.6 (238/753)	20.1	1,392	−0.5	−2.4 (15.2)
Hmong—Sacramento ACT	28.2 (60/213)	23.2 (51/220)	42.3	433	−5.0	−11.8 (13.6)
Cristo Rey—Sacramento ACT	37.0 (225/608)	36.9 (225/610)	38.5	1,218	−0.1	−0.3 (8.9)
St. Edwards—Stockton PACT	47.7 (295/618)	52.1 (328/630)	5.6	1,248	4.4	77.9 (61.3)
Tsia's List—Stockton PACT	19.8 (83/419)	18.5 (78/421)	26.6	840	−1.3	−4.8 (12.3)
Modesto, precinct 95354—CBC	11.3 (71/628)	10.7 (67/626)	80.2	1,254	−0.6	−0.8 (2.2)

Table A4.7. (*Continued*)

Site	% Voting in Control Group	% Voting in Treatment Group	Contact Rate (%)	N	ITT	TOT (SE)[a]
Modesto, precinct 95351—CBC	11.1 (70/629)	11.3 (72/639)	89.0	1,268	0.2	0.2 (2.0)
Central Baptist Modesto—CBC	9.8 (68/691)	12.2 (84/686)	16.0	1,377	2.4	15.0 (10.7)
Fresno, precinct 74—FIC	8.6 (21/243)	7.5 (19/254)	36.2	497	−1.1	−3.2 (8.0)
Fresno, precinct 150—FIC	8.8 (30/342)	11.0 (38/345)	17.7	687	2.2	12.7 (14.7)
Fresno, precinct 206—FIC	9.5 (16/169)	8.9 (31/349)	14.3	518	−0.6	−4.1 (21.4)
Fresno, precinct 208—FIC	20.6 (41/199)	23.1 (46/199)	79.4	398	2.5	3.2 (6.8)
Bakersfield, ward 1—ICUC	4.2 (28/669)	7.1 (36/505)	34.9	1,174	2.9	8.4* (4.1)
Bakersfield, ward 2—ICUC	5.6 (28/501)	7.5 (37/495)	25.1	996	1.9	7.5 (7.3)
San Bernardino—ICUC	10.9 (26/239)	7.7 (18/235)	35.7	474	−3.2	−9.0 (8.2)
Pooled: 19 Experiments randomized at the household level				13,773		1.0 (1.3)

Note: See Table A2.1.

[a]Robust cluster standard errors are by household or precinct, depending on the randomization.

[b]TOT estimates are not calculated for individual experiments randomized at the precinct level because the large standard errors (due to the small number of clusters) make such estimates unreliable.

*p < .05, one-tailed

Table A4.8. PICO Door-to-Door Experiments, November 2008

Site	% Voting in Control Group	% Voting in Treatment Group	Contact Rate (%)	N	ITT	TOT (SE)
Precinct-Level Experiments						
St. Peter's Church—Sacramento ACT	76.4 (980/1,282)	76.0 (877/1,154)	31.4	2,436	−0.4	n/a[a]
Samuel Jackman Middle School—Sacramento ACT	65.4 (408/624)	70.9 (516/728)	19.6	1,352	5.5	n/a
Burbank High School—Sacramento ACT	60.0 (716/1,193)	68.6 (1,930/2,815)	13.6	4,008	8.6	n/a
Long Beach—ICO	60.2 (505/839)	56.4 (403/714)	12.3	1,553	−3.8	n/a
Pooled: 4 precinct-level experiments (14 precincts total)				9,349		14.6 (21.4)
Household-Level Experiments						
Hmong North—Sacramento ACT	54.6 (113/207)	64.6 (144/223)	47.1	430	10.0	21.2* (11.5)
Hmong South—Sacramento ACT	52.5 (259/493)	50.0 (259/518)	29.0	1,011	−2.5	−8.8 (13.4)
Lodi Latinos—PACT	73.6 (129/169)	77.8 (137/176)	20.5	345	4.2	7.4 (23.7)
Thessalonians 1 Baptist Church—Stockton PACT	51.8 (128/247)	53.4 (126/236)	24.6	483	1.6	6.4 (22.9)
Thessalonians 2 Baptist Church—Stockton PACT	53.0 (114/215)	46.8 (102/218)	2.8	433	−6.2	−226.5[b] (233.1)

Table A4.8. *(Continued)*

Site	% Voting in Control Group	% Voting in Treatment Group	Contact Rate (%)	N	ITT	TOT (SE)
Central United 2—Stockton PACT	60.2 (65/108)	64.7 (86/133)	90.2	241	4.5	5.0 (7.7)
Corinthian—Stockton PACT	26.1 (12/46)	35.4 (17/48)	77.1	94	9.3	12.1 (12.5)
Cuff Area—Stockton PACT	62.4 (143/229)	63.3 (152/240)	49.6	469	0.9	1.8 (11.2)
St. Edward's Church 1—Stockton PACT	47.1 (89/189)	53.3 (106/199)	40.7	388	6.2	15.2 (14.5)
St. Edward's Church 2—Stockton PACT	45.7 (58/127)	48.6 (69/142)	11.3	269	2.9	25.9 (62.8)
West Stockton—PACT	81.7 (107/131)	85.6 (113/132)	74.2	263	3.9	5.3 (6.4)
Coswell, South Modesto—CBC	86.7 (202/233)	73.9 (150/203)	70.0	436	−12.8	−18.3 (6.3)
Modesto, precinct 95351—CBC	77.5 (421/543)	71.6 (212/296)	86.8	839	−5.9	−6.8 (4.2)
West Modesto—CBC	61.0 (740/1,214)	65.4 (337/515)	63.5	1,729	4.4	7.1 (4.5)
Pinedale, precinct 206—Fresno FIC	51.7 (91/176)	51.5 (283/550)	35.8	726	−0.2	−0.7 (14.9)
Fresno, precinct 208—FIC	57.0 (102/179)	47.6 (108/227)	37.9	406	−2.4	−24.8 (17.8)

Table A4.8. *(Continued)*

Site	% Voting in Control Group	% Voting in Treatment Group	Contact Rate (%)	N	ITT	TOT (SE)
Fresno, precinct 276—FIC	80.4 (127/158)	85.7 (138/161)	25.5	319	5.3	20.9 (18.5)
Bakersfield Hispanic—FIA	56.8 (54/95)	59.6 (59/99)	66.7	194	2.8	4.1 (11.6)
Believers in Jesus—Bakersfield FIA	57.8 (59/102)	59.4 (63/106)	57.5	208	1.6	2.8 (13.7)
Compassion 1—Bakersfield FIA	52.9 (64/121)	42.7 (56/131)	53.4	252	−10.2	−19.0 (13.7)
Compassion 2—Bakersfield FIA	52.9 (54/102)	50.4 (64/127)	42.5	229	−2.5	−6.0 (16.8)
Compassion 3—Bakersfield FIA	42.6 (20/47)	46.9 (23/49)	53.1	96	4.3	8.3 (21.5)
EBFCA[c]—Bakersfield FIA	35.6 (48/135)	33.6 (44/131)	30.5	266	−2.0	−6.4 (22.9)
Emmanuel—Bakersfield FIA	38.7 (43/111)	46.8 (52/111)	35.1	222	8.1	23.1 (22.2)
Mt. Zion 1—Bakersfield FIA	39.4 (84/213)	44.6 (95/213)	19.7	426	5.2	47.8 (49.7)
Mt. Zion 2—Bakersfield FIA	39.1 (81/207)	44.7 (98/219)	23.3	426	5.6	30.4 (28.5)
St. Joseph's Church—Bakersfield FIA	37.1 (52/140)	43.9 (61/139)	41.0	279	6.8	16.4 (16.7)
Hollywood[d]—LA Voice	76.6 (236/308)	79.9 (255/319)	35.7	627	3.3	9.3 (9.9)

Table A4.8. *(Continued)*

Site	% Voting in Control Group	% Voting in Treatment Group	Contact Rate (%)	N	ITT	TOT (SE)
St. Odilia Youth Group—LA Voice	77.5 (117/151)	81.5 (123/151)	37.7	302	4.0	10.5 (13.1)
Anaheim—OCCCO	57.9 (252/435)	57.2 (251/439)	29.2	874	−0.7	−2.6 (14.0)
San Bernardino—ICUC	89.0 (2,001/2,248)	89.7 (2,081/2,321)	26.9	4,569	0.7	2.4 (3.7)
Pooled: 30 experiments randomized at the household level				17,418		1.1 (1.7)
LA Voice Individual-List Experiments[c]						
Amalia	86.2 (25/29)	87.9 (29/33)	84.8	62	1.7	2.0 (11.0)
Bianca	80.0 (28/35)	78.9 (30/38)	34.2	73	−1.1	−3.1 (32.4)
Celine	69.7 (23/33)	82.9 (29/35)	91.4	68	13.2	14.4 (12.9)
David	74.1 (20/27)	81.5 (22/27)	55.6	54	7.4	13.3 (23.3)
Elsa	88.2 (15/17)	80.0 (12/15)	46.7	32	−8.2	−17.6 (30.4)
Frances	78.1 (25/32)	81.1 (30/37)	29.7	69	3.0	9.9 (34.4)
Gloria	67.9 (19/28)	83.3 (25/30)	60.0	58	15.4	25.8 (21.7)

Table A4.8. (*Continued*)

Site	% Voting in Control Group	% Voting in Treatment Group	Contact Rate (%)	N	ITT	TOT (SE)
Hector	75.4 (46/61)	78.3 (47/60)	41.7	121	2.9	7.0 (18.5)
Isabella	86.7 (52/60)	88.7 (55/62)	75.8	122	2.0	2.7 (8.2)
Janelle	82.2 (106/129)	79.7 (102/128)	72.7	257	−2.5	−3.4 (7.6)
Katrina	83.6 (56/67)	90.1 (64/71)	62.0	138	6.5	10.6 (10.8)
Laura	83.3 (20/24)	66.7 (16/24)	66.7	48	−16.6	−25.0 (20.7)
Mariana	75.0 (12/16)	83.3 (15/18)	44.4	34	8.3	18.8 (30.4)
Nancy	81.5 (22/27)	87.5 (21/24)	70.8	51	6.0	8.5 (16.9)
Tomas	67.6 (23/34)	68.8 (22/32)	62.5	66	1.2	1.8 (20.3)
Vivian	73.1 (19/26)	63.0 (17/27)	18.5	53	−10.1	−54.6 (78.2)
Pooled: 16 individual lists, 11 positive, 5 negative						

Note: See Table A2.1.

[a]TOT estimates are not calculated for individual experiments randomized at the precinct level because the large standard errors (due to the small number of clusters) make such estimates unreliable.

[b]Standard error is not reliable; this experiment is not included in the pooled results.

[c]East Bakersfield Faith Community Alliance.

[d]Specifically, Hollywood's Human Development Overlay District.

[e]The names assigned to the individual lists in this table are pseudonyms for the actual LA Voice canvassers.

*$p < .05$, one-tailed

APPENDIX B: FORMS

location: ________________	date:______________	observer: ________________

CANVASSER TRAINING ASSESSMENT FORM

Complete this form during or immediately following your observation.

Training session led by (name):________________________	Other trainers/staff present (names): ______________ ______________________________

Time your observation took place:	Starting Time: ____:_____		Ending Time: ____:_____	
Total number of canvassers present:	# male:	# female:	# arrived late:	# left early:

How long did each of the following activities last? Indicate the number of minutes, or record N/A if it did not occur. Record minutes based on time actually spent in these activities; do not include time spent preparing for the activities, gathering materials, or other housekeeping.
PLEASE NOTE: Length of time is not equivalent to quality; these measures are merely a quantifiable data point that will help inform our overall understanding of the canvassing.

Explanation of overall mobilization effort: __________ minutes

Description of script and instructions on how to speak to voters: __________ minutes

How to fill out control sheet (or use computer interface): __________ minutes

Legal limits/what not to say to voters: __________ minutes

Canvasser/voter rehearsal & role playing: __________ minutes

Answering questions from canvassers: __________ minutes

Eliciting feedback from canvassers: __________ minutes

Other: ________ minutes (Topic: ____)

Based on your immediate reaction, what would you say were the strengths of this training session? Please give specific examples.

Based on your immediate reaction, what would you say are the weaknesses or areas that need to be improved? Please give specific examples.

location: ________________	date:______________	observer: ________________

PHONE CANVASSING ASSESSMENT FORM

Complete this form during or immediately following your observation.

Canvassing session supervised by (name):______________________	Other group staff present (names): ______________ ______________________________

Time your observation took place:	Starting Time: ____:_____		Ending Time: ____:_____	
Total number of canvassers present:	# male:	# female:	# arrived late:	# left early:

How long did each of the following activities last? Indicate the number of minutes, or record N/A if it did not occur. These observations should be limited to conversations with targeted voters. PLEASE NOTE: Length of time is not equivalent to quality; these measures are merely a quantifiable data point that will help inform our overall understanding of the training program.

Average length of canvassing conversation: __________ minutes (average of __________ calls)

Average length of time spent delivering prepared script: __________ minutes

Overall, did the delivery of these prepared scripts sound conversational?

☐ **very conversational** ☐ **fairly conversational**

☐ **not very conversational** ☐ **not conversational at all (sounded scripted)**

Average length of time spent delivering focused GOTV message: __________ minutes

Average length of time spent in unscripted conversation with voters: __________ minutes

Overall, how well did canvassers seem able to engage in unscripted conversation and answer questions from voters?

☐ **very well** ☐ **fairly well** ☐ **not very well** ☐ **poorly**

Based on your immediate reaction, what would you say were the strengths of this canvassing session? Please give specific examples.

Based on your immediate reaction, what would you say are the weaknesses or areas that need to be improved? Please give specific examples.

location: ________________	date:____________	observer: ________________

DOOR-TO-DOOR CANVASSING ASSESSMENT FORM

Complete this form during or immediately following your observation.

Canvassing session supervised by (name):________________________	Other group staff present (names): ____________ ________________________________

Time your observation took place:	Starting Time: ____:_____		Ending Time: ____:_____	
Total number of canvassers present:	# male:	# female:	# arrived late:	# left early:

How long did each of the following activities last? Indicate the number of minutes, or record N/A if it did not occur. These observations should be limited to conversations with targeted voters. PLEASE NOTE: Length of time is not equivalent to quality; these measures are merely a quantifiable data point that will help inform our overall understanding of the canvassing.

Average length of canvassing conversation: __________ minutes (average of _________ conversations)

Average length of time spent delivering prepared script: __________ minutes

Overall, did the delivery of these prepared scripts sound conversational?
□ very conversational □ fairly conversational
□ not very conversational □ not conversational at all (sounded scripted)

Average length of time spent delivering focused GOTV message: _________ minutes

Average length of time spent in unscripted conversation with voters: _________ minutes

Overall, how well did canvassers seem able to engage in unscripted conversation and answer questions from voters?
□ very well □ fairly well □ not very well □ poorly

Based on your immediate reaction, what would you say were the strengths of this canvassing session? Please give specific examples.

Based on your immediate reaction, what would you say are the weaknesses or areas that need to be improved? Please give specific examples.

location: ________________	date: ______________	observer: ________________

CANVASSER INFORMATION FORM

The purpose of this form is to help the program evaluators determine the best tactics for voter turnout. All information provided here will remain confidential and is for evaluation purposes only. The information will not be shared with anyone who is not part of the project evaluation team.

Please complete this form once, immediately following one of your walks.

Canvasser name: ______________________

Time your walking took place: Starting Time: ____:_____ Ending Time: ____:_____

Have you ever done door-to-door canvassing before?

□ **Yes** □ **No**

If YES, how many times?

□ **1 – 5** □ **6 – 10** □ **More than 10**

How long have you been involved with CCAEJ?

□ **1 – 5 years** □ **6 – 10 years** □ **More than 10 years**

Did you know any of the voters you contacted today? If so, please write how many: ________________

How long have you lived in this neighborhood?

□ **1 – 5 years** □ **6 – 10 years** □ **More than 10 years**

What language do you prefer to speak? (circle one or more)

ENGLISH **SPANISH** **OTHER** ___________________

What language did you use for most of your contacts today?

ENGLISH **SPANISH** **BOTH**

How do you prefer to describe yourself in terms of your race/ethnicity? (You may mark more than one)

□ **White, not Latina/o** □ **Latina/o** □ **African American** □ **Asian American**

□ **Other (please write in)** ___________________________________

What is your age? ____________________

Please circle your gender **FEMALE** **MALE**

THANK YOU VERY MUCH!!!

Sitio: ______________	Fecha: ______________	Observador: ______________

INFORMACIÓN SOBRE EL VOLUNTARIO

La información coleccionada aquí se va a usar para ayudar a los que están evaluando este programa a determinar cuáles son las tácticas más eficaces para mobilizar a la gente para votar. Toda la información proveada aquí se matendrá completamente privada. Nadie además de los evaluadores tendrá acceso a esta información.

Favor de rellenar esta forma solamente una vez, al término de una caminata

Nombre de voluntario/a: ______________________

Hora de la caminata: La hora que empezó: ____:_____ La hora que acabó: ____:_____

¿Ha ido de puerta a puerta para hablar con votantes en otra ocasión?

□ Sí □ No

¿Si lo ha hecho antes, cuántas veces (no incluyendo ésta vez)?

□ 1 a 5 □ 6 a 10 □ Más de 10

¿Por cuánto tiempo ha estado Ud. involucrado/a con la organización CCAEJ?

□ 1 a 5 años □ 6 – 10 años □ Más de 10 años

¿Ud. conoció a algunos de los votantes que contactó hoy? Favor de escribir cuántos: ______________

¿Por cuánto tiempo ha vivido Ud. en esta vecindad?

□ 1 a 5 años □ 6 a 10 años □ Más de 10 años

¿En qué idioma prefiere hablar Ud.? (Puede marcar uno o más de uno)

INGLÉS ESPAÑOL OTRO ______________

¿Cuál idioma usó Ud. con más frecuencia cuando estaba hablando con votantes hoy?

INGLÉS ESPAÑOL LOS DOS IDIOMAS

¿Qué término prefiere usar Ud. para describirse racial or étnicamente? (Puede marcar más de uno)

□ Blanco, no Latina/o □ Latina/o □ Negra/o □ Asiática/o

□ Otro (favor de escribirlo) ______________________________

¿Qué edad tiene Ud.? ______________

Favor de marcar su sexo MUJER HOMBRE

¡¡¡MUCHÍSIMAS GRACIAS!!!

NOTES

Chapter 1. Constructing Voters: The Sociocultural Cognition Model and Voter Mobilization

1. By randomized field experiments we mean that the treatment and control groups were selected randomly. Organizations targeted treatment groups for contact and provided us with contact information. That information was merged with validated voter turnout data provided by the relevant county registrars. We calculated the statistical impact of each campaign by running a 2SLS regression with "contact" as an explanatory variable and "assignment to the treatment group" as an instrumental variable. A more detailed description of our methodology may be found at the end of this chapter.

2. The CVI efforts included a number of additional experiments in which, because of problems with randomization, the provision of contact information, or a lack of organizational capacity to carry out the campaign, we were unable to evaluate the groups' efforts. The experiments included in this analysis are the successful experiments for which the randomization was completed correctly, for which we have valid contact information from the groups, and for which we are therefore able to have confidence in our calculations of their respective success.

3. This organization requested that it remain anonymous; its name is a pseudonym.

4. The California Public Interest Research Group (CalPIRG) was also one of the CVI-funded groups. But since it did not conduct any randomized field experiments as part of its voter engagement work, its efforts do not form part of this study.

5. Two statewide elections in 2006, one set of municipal elections in Los Angeles in 2007, and two primary elections and one presidential election in 2008 give the total of six.

6. In chapter 2 we shall see that we tested the effectiveness of indirect methods of contact (i.e., mailers and leaflets) and found that they did not have a significant impact on turnout. Our theoretical model thus focuses on explaining those GOTV interac-

tions that did significantly change voter behavior—live conversations on the phone or on voters' doorsteps.

7. Kathleen McGraw (2000, 810) argues that the term "schema" has lost favor among political cognition researchers because of its imprecision and has been replaced with "associative network models." Given the continued use of "schema" in social and cognitive psychology, and given its usefulness for our purposes here, we choose to use the term, and we attempt to define it with sufficient specificity to make it useful as our "metaconstruct."

8. We should note that many of the organizations included issue surveys as part of their GOTV scripts. Although it is possible that these short questionnaires changed voters' conceptions of their interests, it remains the case that the voter turnout portion of those scripts did not focus on the issues per se but rather on voter turnout in general, as was required by the nonpartisan nature of these campaigns. Because these mobilization campaigns were funded by the James Irvine Foundation, a private foundation, the funds for this project could not be used for any partisan purposes or issue-based voter mobilization. The foundation was vigilant about this and stated it in their messages to the participating organizations and watched for it in their supervision of these GOTV efforts.

9. It is the interactive aspect of the narrative component that is central to our argument. Indirect mailers, if they contain a written message, could be seen as a type of narrative. But without any sort of social interaction to accompany the narrative (and without social persuasion), this narrative form is insufficient to shift cognition and therefore change voter behavior. We expand on this argument in chapter 2.

10. Another possible explanation is that even though the canvassers are instructed to use a particular script, they embellish the text sufficiently that it dilutes any potential messaging effects. Given the significant variation that we found in how canvassers deliver the script at the door (and, at times, on the phone), this may be an important issue, making it difficult to accurately test messaging effects. More detail about this phenomena may be found in chapter 5.

11. Some may argue that the election of Barack Obama as president of the United States precludes an argument based on the continued exclusion of ethnoracial minorities from the U.S. polity. We support Eduardo Bonilla-Silva's (2009) contention that Obama's election, rather than representing a break with the U.S. racial order, was in fact a product of it.

12. We ran the analyses both ways (with and without covariates) and found no significant differences in the results. The covariate data are available as part of the publicly available CVI data set which can be accessed at http://isps.research.yale.edu/data/D065.

13. We shall see in chapter 3 that those organizations that asked phone canvassers to use their cell phones to make calls encountered many of the quality-control issues we discovered in door-to-door campaigns.

Chapter 2. Voters *Will* Throw Away Jesus: Indirect Methods and Getting Out the Vote

Portions of this chapter appeared in Lisa García Bedolla and Melissa R. Michelson, "What Do Voters Need to Know? Testing the Role of Cognitive Information in Asian American Voter Mobilization," *American Politics Research* 37 (2) 2009: 254–274, copyright © 2009 by Lisa García Bedolla and Melissa R. Michelson. Reprinted by permission of Sage Publications.

1. Recent experiments looking at the effects of mailings that include social persuasion messages have shown these kinds of indirect approaches to be effective. But as we discuss in chapter 1, we would argue that the mechanism at work is the social aspect of the message rather than the mailing itself. That social persuasion mimics the narrative interaction that we contend underlies the impact of direct mobilization tactics.

2. In fact, Neil Malhotra et al. (2011) find a heterogeneous effect of "cold" text messages when looking separately at voters with different vote histories and find no statistically significant effects on low-propensity voters.

3. In experimental research, it is standard practice that the N equals the treatment plus the control groups. That is the practice used in this publication and the way we define the N in all of our experimental analyses.

4. We should note that direct mail with a social persuasion component has been found to have a significant impact on turnout. Green and Gerber (2008) caution against campaign strategists using this tactic, however, given the strong potential backlash. Both their study and other studies (Panagopoulos 2009b) resulted in voter complaints about the mailings.

5. Much of the work on African American religion and participation emphasizes the relationship between religious affiliation and African American group identification (Dawson 2000; Harris 2001). The relationship between religious affiliation and group identification has not been as well established for other ethnoracial groups, but it is possible that a relationship does exist, making the differentiation between the impact of religious identification and the impact of ethnoracial identification difficult to discern. Readers should keep this in mind when considering the impact of PICO's work in these communities of color.

6. Berinsky's definition of the relationship between participation and cognition is quite different from the one we are advancing here. In his formulation, voters do not have to develop a schema per se but rather the cognitive capacity to make a voting decision. This is an important factor, particularly for vote choice, but in our minds not the one that is central to voter turnout.

7. In California, a decline-to-state voter is any registered voter who chooses not to affiliate with a political party when he or she registers to vote. Decline-to-state voters can request a ballot of any political party that has notified the secretary of state that it will permit decline-to-state registered voters to help nominate their candidates. Decline-to-state voters cannot request more than one party's ballot.

8. Details from the individual national-origin group experiments may be found in appendix A.

9. See Michelson, García Bedolla, and Green 2007 for additional details about OCAPICA's voter education and mobilization efforts for the November 2006 campaign.

Chapter 3. Calling All Voters: Phone Banks and Getting Out the Vote

Portions of this chapter appeared in Melissa R. Michelson, Lisa García Bedolla, and Margaret McConnell, "Heeding the Call: The Effect of Targeted Two-Round Phonebanks on Voter Turnout," *Journal of Politics* 71 (4) 2009: 1549–1563. Reprinted with permission. Copyright 2009 by Cambridge University Press.

1. We should note that APALC's and OCAPICA's phone canvassers had target numbers to reach each shift, so this distinction between the expectations of volunteer and paid canvassers is not a hard and fast one. In addition, Nickerson's work on call quality included other ways of making volunteers sound like paid canvassers, such as warning them to stick strictly to their scripts, while APALC and OCAPICA staff encouraged callers to be conversational.

2. Underscoring the results from the 2002 experiment by Ramírez are the results of NALEO's continued efforts outside of California to use robocalls to move low-propensity Latino voters to the polls, which have produced only negligible increases in turnout. NALEO has found that such calls are useful for cleaning lists of telephone numbers. Producing lists for live volunteers that include a reduced proportion of non-working phone numbers and working fax numbers saves volunteer time. Our focus here is on live calls only.

3. As we mentioned in chapter 1, the CVI organizations attempted a number of additional experiments that, for a variety of reasons, were not able to be analyzed. Our data here come from those experiments for which we have verified randomization and contact information.

4. APALC also worked to mobilize Cambodians in this campaign, but the number of registered voters in this group was too small to allow for a field experiment. For the sake of clarity, we have removed them from the analysis. (See note on Table A2.3).

5. Detailed results from the individual national-origin group experiments may be found in appendix A.

6. Outreach coordinators decided not to divide up the message for these two national-origin groups because the relatively small size of their lists made it unlikely that we would find statistically discernable variation from the messaging.

7. This raises the question of the demographic characteristics of those doing the canvassing and how that might affect their ability to mobilize voters. Here we ran into a difficulty of real-world research. Although, for the 2008 elections, we asked the participating organizations to provide us with demographic and experiential information on their canvassers (i.e., race/ethnicity, gender, age, previous canvassing experience, experience with the participating organization, etc.), the organizations were inconsis-

tent in their compliance with our request. For that reason, we do not engage in any analysis or inference based on the canvasser information we do have. Any conclusions we make, given the incomplete data, would be speculative at best. Copies of the forms we distributed to the CVI groups requesting this information may be found in appendix B.

8. In this experiment, multivoter households were included in the random assignment in some counties. But only one phone call was placed to households with more than one registered voter in the treatment groups. A successful contact was defined narrowly as a live conversation with the intended targeted individual. Not all counties in this experiment, however, included multivoter households in their randomized assignment. Our analysis is adjusted accordingly.

9. Detailed results may be found in appendix A. Several smaller phone bank campaigns took place in the June 2006 election, but their small sample sizes, and resulting large standard errors, make it difficult for us to be confident that they had a significant effect on turnout. They include a phone bank carried out by CARECEN targeting low-propensity Latino voters in the Pico-Union/Westlake community of Los Angeles, as well as a number of small campaigns by various PICO affiliates.

10. Since the county-level efforts were separate, we randomized by county and made our calculations separately as well. To gauge the effectiveness of this voter mobilization campaign, households (defined by a common address) were randomly assigned to treatment or control groups. Statistical analysis was conducted separately for each of the counties and then pooled in our final analysis.

11. Detailed results may be found in appendix A.

12. Only 2.8 percent of the treatment group was contacted via door-to-door canvassing; these individuals are excluded from our analysis. The results from the door-to-door campaign are available from the authors upon request.

13. SVREP's experiment consisted of two rounds of random assignments, designed to test for spillover effects both within households and between neighbors. First, 478 precincts were randomly assigned to treatment and control groups. This resulted in 432 treatment precincts and 46 control precincts. We then drop from the analysis those targeted for door-to-door canvassing and those for whom either contact or voting information was missing. This brings the total number in the experiment to 25,862, including 19,512 targeted voters in the treatment group and 6,350 individuals in the control group.

14. The tactic of making follow-up calls to self-identified likely voters has been used previously, including in a field experiment aimed at young voters in New Jersey conducted by the Public Interest Research Group (PIRG) in 2003 (see Michelson, García Bedolla, and McConnell 2009). In that experiment, in a preelection phase, calls were made to ask contacted individuals whether they intended to vote. In the GOTV phase, individuals were randomized without regard to the outcome of the preelection set of calls, and no change was made to the treatment in light of those earlier contacts. Post hoc comparisons revealed that those contacted only through

messages in the preelection phase or who did not plan to vote or who refused to indicate whether or not they intended to vote were unaffected by the Election Day GOTV calls. Those who had previously indicated an intention to vote, by contrast, were significantly influenced. For these voters, turnout increased from 16.9 percent in the control group to 27.5 percent in the treatment group, an intent-to-treat effect of 10.6 percentage points. The treatment-on-treated effect is 7.8 percentage points (SE = 2.3).

15. NALEO, in contrast, chose to call back all contacted voters rather than focusing exclusively on those voters who, in the first call, expressed an intention to vote.

16. This included 78 individuals in the treatment group and 321 individuals in the control group.

17. This result, and the similar results that other groups had when asking this question, supports our proposition that voting is the socially desirable answer, one that is tied to normative understandings of what constitutes good citizenship.

18. OCAPICA also engaged in media outreach to promote the June 2008 election. A quarter-page vote flyer was published in the *Nguoi Viet* newspaper (circulation 17,548) on Sunday, May 25. The "Power of the Ballot" song was played five times on Little Saigon Radio (around 150,000 listeners) from May 31 to June 3, and the upcoming elections were mentioned in morning, afternoon, and evening weather and traffic reports for a week before the election. The song also aired four times on Radio Bolsa (around 170,000 listeners) from May 29 to June 3. Most callers to the OCAPICA Voter Hotline said that they had learned of the hotline from radio announcements. The OCAPICA effort was also covered by VHN-TV and aired during the station's news and community announcements coverage.

19. Detailed results may be found in appendix A.

20. To obtain these estimates, we first calculated the number of votes produced in the second round, using the turnout rate for the control group (14.0 percent) to determine how many individuals in the pool would have voted in the absence of a second round of calls: 0.140 × 1501 = 210. We subtract this from the number of individuals in the pool who did actually vote to obtain the vote gain: 293 − 210 = 83. Similar calculations for each national-origin group in the first round generate an estimate of 235 overall votes gained: ([117 − (0.084 × 1,200)] + [469 − (0.098 × 4,000)] + [227 − (0.105 × 1,900)] + [125 − (0.121 × 800)] + [498 − (0.171 × 2,500)] + [153 − (0.085 × 1,600)]) = 235. We subtract from this estimate the votes generated by the second call: 235 − 83 = 152 votes generated during the first round.

21. The distinction between absentee and polling-place voters is an important one among Asian Americans given that it is estimated that as many as half of Asian American registered voters vote absentee. Thus it was important for both of the organizations focused on Asian Americans, APALC and OCAPICA, to have strategies in place that took into account the special challenges entailed in attempting to mobilize these voters.

22. Details for each experiment may be found in appendix A.

23. We must stress that these GOTV campaigns were nonpartisan. However, the partisan nature of an election is, we would argue, an important part of the electoral context and should be taken into consideration. This is especially true among Asian American targeted voters, of whom there were more Republican registrants than there were for any other ethnoracial group targeted by CVI mobilization efforts.

24. Because of the small size of the text-message group, we do not provide a separate analysis of these results.

25. Details may be found in appendix A.

26. PICO affiliates attempted several small phone bank efforts for the June 2006 election. Unfortunately, our data from those campaigns are incomplete, which prevents us from including these efforts in our analysis. Yet it is important to note that those earlier efforts probably contributed to PICO's ability to conduct phone banks in November 2006.

27. Details for these experiments may be found in appendix A.

28. Details may be found in appendix A.

Chapter 4. Knock, Knock, Who's There? Door-to-Door Canvassing and Getting Out the Vote

1. There were four canvassing treatment groups for the 1954 study: one contacted in person by students, one contacted in person by party canvassers, one contacted by phone, and one contacted in person by students and also sent a piece of what Eldersveld calls "mail propaganda"(158). Another group of voters was sent only mail.

2. As we noted in chapter 2, a more appropriate methodological approach would have been for the authors to calculate intent-to-treat effects for the original treatment and control groups and then treatment-on-treated effects that took into account the contact rate (this is the failure-to-treat problem).

3. These effect sizes are from the corrected data published in Gerber and Green 2005 but do not differ greatly from the originals.

4. The group name African American Churches United is a pseudonym for a CVI group that has asked to remain anonymous.

5. As we mention in a note to chapter 3, above, the participating organizations were inconsistent in providing us with demographic information about their canvassers; this is a reflection of the many challenges involved in conducting research in the real world. In addition, those groups that did provide us with canvasser information did not necessarily record which canvassers carried out which contact, making it impossible for us to connect canvassers with their contacted voters. Although we assume that the gender, age, ethnoracial background, and experience of a canvasser factors significantly into the outcome of a GOTV visit, our data do not allow us to analyze the impact of canvasser characteristics in a systematic or rigorous fashion. An example of the forms we used to elicit this information may be found in appendix B.

6. CARECEN also conducted a small phone canvassing effort for this election,

but there were inconsistencies in how the calling was carried out. For that reason, we limit our analysis to the door-to-door campaign.

7. Even though we cannot say specifically the extent of this problem, we would assume that it was an issue. Given the demographic makeup of Latino voters in Los Angeles, who are more likely to be native born and English monolingual than the population at large, it is reasonable to assume that the language issue made it impossible for CARECEN canvassers to communicate with a nontrivial number of voters. Thus, even though a contact may have been made, the quality of that contact is questionable.

8. For a description of the *Easy Voter Guides,* see chapter 2.

9. Despite CARECEN's use of follow-up contact attempts in this iteration, its inconsistency in making and recording the follow-up contacts led us to analyze this campaign as a "one contact" mobilization effort.

10. These targeted voters, even though they are low-propensity voters, know that stating an intention to vote is the socially desirable answer. This observation is consistent with our findings in chapter 3. The very high percentage in this case (96 percent) also suggests that targeted voters' need to give the socially desirable answer is even greater face-to-face than over the phone. It also suggests that the filtering aspect of the question (which we discuss in Michelson, García Bedolla, and McConnell 2009) may have been missing and that those stating a desire to vote did not, in fact, always possess a strong disposition to do so. That, in turn, may have muted the impact of the second contact.

11. The second-round contact was a reminder card that canvassers were asked to deliver to voters. Given the large number of second-round contacts reported by CARECEN across a three-day period (amounting to fully 67 percent of those they had contacted in the previous four weeks), we believe it unlikely that the majority of those contacts included a face-to-face interaction. The more likely scenario is that canvassers left the cards at the voters' homes, possibly with family members, without necessarily speaking to the actual voter, but still coded the voter as contacted. Therefore, we do not characterize this campaign as a true "two contact" effort.

12. Most of the CVI groups paid their canvassers some amount for their work; some paid more than others. SCOPE was the only group to employ a hard distinction between the paid and the volunteer teams and to have each canvass at different times. We considered conducting an analysis to compare paid versus unpaid canvassing but were unable to do so in a meaningful way because strong volunteer canvassers were often recruited into the paid street teams. Also, some paid canvassers worked on the weekends, blurring the lines between the two types of canvassing.

13. Proposition 87 was a proposal to tax oil revenue in California to pay for research and development in alternative energy production.

14. For more details on the social networking aspects of the SCOPE experiment, see Sinclair, McConnell, and Michelson, forthcoming.

15. By focusing on Green Jobs, SCOPE was asking that local government locate manufacturing related to new clean energy production in South Los Angeles and that government create preferences for local residents for hiring in the new companies.

16. After the CVI was concluded, these communities and surrounding areas voted to incorporate (as of July 2011) into the new Jurupa Valley.

17. Details from the CCAEJ experiments may be found in appendix A.

18. In addition, after the randomization of the November pool it was discovered that thirteen individuals placed into the control group lived on the same block as a CCAEJ leader; these individuals were moved into the treatment group and targeted for mobilization but were excluded from the analysis since their assignment to the treatment group was not random.

19. The "others" are individuals for whom there was no race information. That information was provided by Political Data, Inc., a for-profit data company that collects race data from numerous proprietary sources. This information was not publicly available in the county voter files. Because Political Data, Inc., does not disclose how it ascertains this information (particularly how it identifies African American voters), we cannot vouch for its accuracy.

20. This is another example of the real-world difficulties that academics can encounter when engaging in this sort of work. CCAEJ had limited resources and capacity for recording contacts for us, which limited the amount of detailed information we obtained.

21. This is not to say that Riverside canvassers did not face their challenges, including being attacked by geese. But in general there were more reports of questionable neighborhoods in the San Bernardino observations.

22. Detailed results may be found in appendix A.

23. AACU's experience is a cautionary tale for organizations purchasing voter lists from commercial vendors. AACU was promised a list consisting only of older African American voters. The vendor in question did not deliver, but AACU did not know that until canvassers went into the field, and by then it was too late to make adjustments.

24. Details for the individual experiments may be found in appendix A.

25. Unfortunately, because of our inability to recruit a Hmong-speaking observer in Sacramento, we do not have field reports from this campaign to help explain the difference in results.

Chapter 5. Notes from the Field: Running an Effective Mobilization Campaign

1. This analysis would not have been possible without the tireless dedication of our field research team: Kim Danh, Joanna Do, Elizabeth Fernández, Aida Frias, Olivia García-Quiñones, Alisha Glass, Christy Glass, María Elena Guadamuz, Marisol Gutiérrez, Jacqueline Guzmán, Lisa Hahn, Jennifer Hernández, Angela Ju, Nhi Khoan, Amanda Knockaert, Mzilikazi Kone, Christine Lee, Stephanie Loera, Margaret McConnell, Xavier Medina, Thien-Huong Ninh, Susan Phay, Jonathan Sarpolis, Betsy Sinclair, David Tran, Diane Tran, Titi Mary Tran, Yamissette Westerband, Jaehee Yoon, and Arely Zimmerman. We thank them for all their efforts on behalf of this project.

2. Although the organization names are real, we use pseudonyms to identify all of the canvassers and staff members we discuss in this chapter.

3. Some of the PICO affiliates, such as ICUC, had always used large numbers of youth as canvassers. We did notice, however, that there seemed to be an even larger number in November 2008, and many of our observers noted the congregations' need to find more volunteers to do their canvassing work.

4. CARECEN staff were aware that this was a potential risk of the group leader model when they implemented it, so the result did not catch them by surprise. They wanted to test it out it to see if it could be an effective strategy for them.

5. AGENDA stands for Action for Grassroots Empowerment and Neighborhood Development Alternatives. This membership organization forms part of SCOPE and is the entity that coordinates SCOPE's voter mobilization work, along with other activities. AGENDA was formed after the 1992 civil unrest in Los Angeles—the six days of rioting and looting that followed the Rodney King verdict, resulting in fifty-three deaths and numerous injuries. SCOPE's organizing area was one of the core parts of Los Angeles affected by the civil unrest. AGENDA was created in response to this unrest in order to address declining civic participation levels and economic disinvestment in South Los Angeles.

6. SCOPE, for example, taped critical information for the canvasser to the front of each canvasser's clipboard. All the canvassers had to do to access that information was to flip up their walk sheets. Yet it is more awkward and disruptive to the conversation to look at notes while speaking to a voter in person than it is to look at this sort of information while talking with a targeted voter on the phone.

7. Since language fluency and the use of culturally appropriate communication styles were so critical for these multilingual phone banks, we asked the observers to be certain to comment on these factors in their reports. Some callers, if they were less fluent in one of their languages, were said to have a limited vocabulary with which to deliver the mobilization message, especially when doing so required going off the script to answer voters' questions. Having a sufficient vocabulary, therefore, was seen as a positive factor when rating the caller's ability to communicate the mobilization message effectively.

8. None of these canvassers was strictly alone, of course, since they were being observed. By "alone" we mean one canvasser and one observer, rather than a pair of canvassers and one observer. Even though the canvassers were not truly alone, our observers did note this difference in terms of their staying on script. It is possible that the variability would have been even greater had our observers not been there. At the very least, our observer reports make it clear that having someone else from the organization present did seem to improve consistency in canvassers' delivery of the GOTV message.

9. APALC and OCAPICA used the same system for assigning the language to make calls in. Given that more than half of Asian Americans are foreign born (as we mention above) and that the foreign born tend to be older than the native born, both groups decided to contact voters under thirty-five in English and those over thirty-

five in their presumed native language. Since almost all of the callers were bilingual (and even trilingual), they were instructed to begin the conversation in the target language but to switch as necessary, following the voter's cues.

10. Pointing out the confusion about codes could lead readers to question the validity of the contact data we received from these organizations. We are confident that although there were some errors in reporting, the size of these experiments—which targeted thousands of voters—allows us to have robust and accurate calculations even though there was a small amount of reporting error.

11. In 2011, California VoterConnect was merged into Catalist, a national voter-data company.

12. As academics, we also learned how difficult it is to recruit and train bilingual field observers in this number of languages.

Chapter 6. Expanding the Electorate through Practice: Voting and Habit Formation

1. It is possible that CVI-contacted voters became middle-propensity voters as a result of participation and therefore may have ended up on campaign radars. Given our experiences in the targeted communities, however, where there is a general lack of political advertising or mobilization efforts, and given the overall lower level of voter outreach that occurs in California politics, we find this explanation unlikely.

2. Because the CVI ended with the November 2008 election, we were unable to track successful GOTV efforts from that round for effects on turnout in later elections. That will be the focus of future research.

3. CCAEJ insisted that all voters *contacted* in June 2006 be included in the treatment in November 2006. Voters in the treatment group in June but not successfully contacted in that campaign could have been randomly assigned in November to either the treatment or the control group.

4. Since we are comparing the treatment group's behavior to the control group's behavior in the same election—namely, the extremely high-salience election of November 2008—our calculations control for any increase in mobilization that resulted from that unique electoral context. In other words, it is the remaining difference (if any) between the two groups' behavior in November 2008 that we are attributing to habit formation.

Conclusion: Transforming the American Electorate

1. Much more frequent are visits or telephone calls (or mailers) that encourage registered voters to make a particular choice on the ballot, either in favor of a particular candidate or for or against a ballot initiative. While these are also shown by previous field experiments to move voters to the polls, they contain an underlying message that is very different, in that voters are being valued for their ability to help someone win; in other words, the individual making the outreach effort is asking for

action from the voter on behalf of a candidate or political party rather than conveying a neutral/nonpartisan message designed simply to help the individual voter have a voice.

2. Important exceptions, as noted in chapter 2, include mailers that include social persuasion or vote-monitoring components.

3. A clear example of an alternative construction is India, where the poor are most likely to vote even though they may not necessarily receive redistributive government services as a result (Keefer and Khemani 2004).

4. Polling organizations can vary substantially in how they define likely voters. More important for our purposes is that they tend to focus on all registered voters for reported poll results much less often than they focus on likely voters.

5. This underrepresentation is partly due to the large number of noncitizens that make up both populations. But even taking that into account, a gap still exists between these groups and whites in terms of their proportion of the electorate.

6. John Sides, Eric Schickler, and Jack Citrin (2006) acknowledge that they find important state-level variation in their analysis, which suggests that national estimates are not the best way to determine these effects.

7. For an acknowledgment that voters are often poor predictors of their own future opinions, see Arnold 1992.

8. This is without taking into consideration the fact that minority voters are less likely to have their representatives of choice, given the majoritarian nature of the U.S. political system (see Tate 2003).

9. Zoltan Hajnal (2010) argues for a mainly institutional approach to addressing this problem. We believe he underestimates the importance of mobilization in changing the face of the electorate and, potentially, in creating the political will necessary to accomplish the institutional changes he suggests.

10. Other scholars call this approach to scholarship "design research": it is research that produces usable knowledge for practitioners while at the same time advancing scholarly knowledge within a particular discipline.

REFERENCES

Abdelai, Rawl, Yoshiko M. Herrera, Alastair Iain Johnston, and Rose McDermott. 2006. "Identity as a Variable." *Perspectives on Politics* 4 (4): 695–711.

Abrajano, Marisa, and R. Michael Alvarez. 2010. *New Faces, New Voices: The Hispanic Electorate in America*. Princeton, NJ: Princeton University Press.

Abrajano, Marisa, Jonathan Nagler, and R. Michael Alvarez. 2005. "A Natural Experiment of Race-Based and Issue Voting: The 2001 City of Los Angeles Elections." *Political Research Quarterly* 58 (2): 203–218.

Abramson, Paul R., and John H. Aldrich. 1982. "The Decline of Electoral Participation in America." *American Political Science Review* 76 (3): 502–521.

Adams, William C., and Dennis J. Smith. 1980. "Effects of Telephone Canvassing on Turnout and Preferences: A Field Experiment." *Public Opinion Quarterly* 44 (3): 389–395.

Addonizio, Elizabeth. 2006. "A Social Approach to Voter Mobilization and Election Day." Unpublished manuscript. Institution for Social and Policy Studies, Yale University.

Aldrich, John H. 1993. "Rational Choice and Turnout." *American Journal of Political Science* 37 (1): 246–278.

Allen, Richard L., Michael C. Dawson, and Ronald E. Brown. 1989. "A Schema-Based Approach to Modeling an African-American Racial Belief System." *American Political Science Review* 83 (2): 421–441.

Alvarez, R. Michael 1997. *Information and Elections*. Ann Arbor: University of Michigan Press.

Alvarez, R. Michael, and Lisa García Bedolla. 2003. "The Foundations of Latino Voter Partisanship: Evidence from the 2000 Elections." *Journal of Politics* 65 (1): 31–49.

Alvarez, R. Michael, and Jonathan Nagler. 1998. "Economics, Entitlements, and Social Issues: Voter Choice in the 1996 Presidential Election." *American Journal of Political Science* 42 (4): 1349–1363.

American Political Science Association (APSA). 2011. *Political Science in the 21st Century*. Task Force Report. Washington, DC: American Political Science Association. http://www.apsanet.org/21stcentury/ [last accessed December 30, 2011].

Appadurai, Arjun. 2002. "Deep Democracy: Urban Governmentality and the Horizon of Politics." *Public Culture* 14 (1): 21–47.

Arceneaux, Kevin, and David W. Nickerson. 2010. "Comparing Negative and Positive Campaign Messages." *American Politics Research* 38 (1): 54–83.

Arnold, Douglas R. 1992. *The Logic of Congressional Action*. New Haven: Yale University Press.

Axelrod, Robert. 1973. "Schema Theory: An Information Processing Model of Perception and Cognition." *American Political Science Review* 67 (4): 1248–1266.

Azari, Julia, and Ebonya Washington. 2006. "Results from a 2004 Leafleting Field Experiment in Miami-Dade and Duval Counties, Florida." Unpublished manuscript. Institution for Social and Policy Studies, Yale University.

Bagozzi, Richard, and Kyu-Hyun Lee. 2002. "Multiple Routes for Social Influence: The Role of Compliance, Internalization, and Social Identity." *Social Psychology Quarterly* 65 (3): 226–247.

Baldassare, Mark, Dean Bonner, Sonja Petek, and Jui Shrestha. 2011. "California's Likely Voters." *Just the Facts*. San Francisco: Public Policy Institute of California. Available at http://www.ppic.org/main/series.asp?i=12.

Bandura, Albert. 1989. "Human Agency in Social Cognitive Theory." *American Psychologist* 44 (9): 1175–1184.

Bartels, Larry M. 2000. "Partisanship and Voting Behavior, 1952–1996." *American Journal of Political Science* 44 (1): 35–50.

Berinsky, Adam J. 2005. "The Perverse Consequence of Electoral Reform in the United States." *American Politics Research* 33 (4): 471–491.

Bolland, John M. 1985. "The Structure of Political Cognition: A New Approach to Its Meaning and Measurement." *Political Behavior* 7 (3): 248–265.

Bonilla-Silva, Eduardo. 2009. *Racism without Racists: Color-Blind Racism and the Persistence of Racial Inequality in America*. New York: Rowman and Littlefield.

Borgatti, Stephen P., and Pacey C. Foster. 2003. "The Network Paradigm in Organizational Research: A Review and Typology." *Journal of Management* 29 (6): 991–1013.

Bourdieu, Pierre. 1977. *Outline of a Theory of Practice*. New York: Cambridge University Press.

Brekhus, Wayne H., David L. Brunsma, Todd Platts, and Priya Dua. 2010. "On the Contributions of Cognitive Sociology to the Sociological Study of Race." *Sociology Compass* 4 (1): 61–76.

Brewer, Marilynn B. 2001. "The Many Faces of Social Identity: Implications for Political Psychology." *Political Psychology* 22 (1): 115–125.

Brewer, Mark. 2005. "The Rise of Partisanship and the Expansion of Partisan Conflict within the American Electorate." *Political Research Quarterly* 58 (2): 219–229.

Brody, Richard A., and Paul M. Sniderman. 1977. "From Life Space to Polling Place." *British Journal of Political Science* 7 (3): 337–360.

Brubaker, Rogers, and Frederick Cooper. 2000. "Beyond 'Identity.'" *Theory and Society* 29 (1): 1–47.

Brubaker, Rogers, Mara Loveman, and Peter Stamatov. 2004. "Ethnicity as Cognition." *Theory and Society* 33 (1): 31–64.

Campbell, Angus, Philip E. Converse, Warren E. Miller, and Donald F. Stokes. 1960. *The American Voter*. New York: Wiley.

Chávez, Maria L., Brian Wampler, and Russ Burkhart. 2006. "Left Out: Trust and Social Capital among Migrant Seasonal Farmworkers." *Social Science Quarterly* 87 (5): 1012–1029.

Citrin, Jack, Eric Schickler, and John Sides. 2003. "What If Everyone Voted? Simulating the Impact of Increased Turnout in Senate Elections." *American Journal of Political Science* 47 (1): 75–90.

Clark, Susan S., Mara Wold, and Harriet Mayeri. 1997. "Fall 1996 Election Study." Key to Community Voter Involvement Project, Santa Clara County [California] Library Reading Program. http://literacynet.org/slrc/vip/ [last accessed December 30, 2011].

Cohen, Cathy J. 1999. *The Boundaries of Blackness: AIDS and the Breakdown of Black Politics*. Chicago: University of Chicago Press.

Collier, David, Henry E. Brady, and Jason Seawright. 2010. "Outdated Views of Qualitative Methods: Time to Move On." *Political Analysis*. 18(4): 506–513.

Collins, Patricia Hill. 2000. *Black Feminist Thought: Knowledge, Consciousness and the Politics of Empowerment*, 2nd ed. New York: Routledge.

Conover, Pamela Johnston, and Stanley Feldman. 1984. "How People Organize the Political World: A Schematic Model." *American Journal of Political Science* 28 (1): 95–126.

———. 1991. "Where Is the Schema? Critiques." *American Political Science Review* 85 (4): 1364–1369.

Conway, M. Margaret. 1991. *Political Participation in the United States*, 2nd ed. Washington, DC: Congressional Quarterly Press.

Crenshaw, Kimberlé. 1991. "Mapping the Margins: Intersectionality, Identity, Politics, and Violence against Women of Color." *Stanford Law Review* 43: 1241–1299.

Cummings, Jonathon N., and Rob Cross. 2003. "Structural Properties of Work Groups and Their Consequences for Performance." *Social Networks* 25: 197–210.

Cutts, David, Edward Fieldhouse, and Peter John. 2009. "Is Voting Habit Forming? The Longitudinal Impact of a GOTV Campaign in the UK." *Journal of Elections, Public Opinion, and Parties* 19 (3): 251–263.

Dale, Alison, and Aaron Strauss. 2009. "Don't Forget to Vote: Text Message Reminders as a Mobilization Tool." *American Journal of Political Science* 53 (4): 787–804.

Dawson, Michael. 1994. *Behind the Mule: Race and Class in African American Politics*. Princeton, NJ: Princeton University Press.

———. 2000. *Black Visions: The Roots of Contemporary African-American Political Ideologies.* Chicago: University of Chicago Press.

Dettori, Giuliana, and Francesca Morselli. 2008. "Accessing Knowledge through Narrative Context." In Michael Kendall and Brian Samways, eds., *Learning to Live in the Knowledge Society*, 253–260. International Federation for Information Processing (IFIP), vol. 281. Boston: Springer.

Duncan, Lauren D. 2005. "Personal Political Salience as a Self-Schema: Consequences for Political Information Processing." *Political Psychology* 26 (6): 965–976.

Eldersveld, Samuel J. 1956. "Experimental Propaganda Techniques and Voting Behavior." *American Political Science Review* 50 (1): 154–165.

Eliasoph, Nina, and Paul Lichterman. 2003. "Culture in Interaction." *American Journal of Sociology* 108 (4): 735–794.

Fiorina, Morris P. 1981. *Retrospective Voting in American Elections.* New Haven: Yale University Press.

Fiske, Susan T., and Patricia W. Linville. 1980. "What Does the Schema Concept Buy Us?" *Personality and Social Psychology Bulletin* 6 (4): 543–557.

Foucault, Michel. 2004a. *The Birth of Biopolitics: Lectures at the Collège de France, 1978–1979.* Translated by Graham Burchell. New York: Palgrave.

———. 2004b. *Security, Territory, Population: Lectures at the Collège de France, 1977–1978.* Translated by Graham Burchell. New York: Palgrave.

Fournier, Patrick, André Blais, Richard Nadeau, Elisabeth Gidengil, and Neil Nevitte. 2003. "Issue Importance and Performance Voting." *Political Behavior* 25 (1): 51–67.

Fraga, Luis R., John A. García, Rodney E. Hero, Michael Jones-Correa, Valerie Martinez-Ebers, and Gary M. Segura. 2006. "Su Casa Es Nuestra Casa: Latino Politics Research and the Development of American Political Science." *American Political Science Review* 100 (4): 515–521.

Franklin, Charles H., and John E. Jackson. 1983. "The Dynamics of Party Identification." *American Political Science Review* 77 (4): 957–973.

Frey, Valerie A., and Santiago Suárez. 2006. "¡Mobilización Efectiva de Votantes! Analyzing the Effects of Bilingual Mobilization and Notification of Bilingual Ballots on Latino Turnout." Unpublished manuscript. Institution for Social and Policy Studies, Yale University.

García Bedolla, Lisa. 2005a. *Fluid Borders: Latino Power, Identity and Politics in Los Angeles.* Berkeley: University of California Press.

———. 2005b. "Resources and Civic Engagement: The Importance of Social Capital for Latino Political Incorporation." *Harvard Journal of Hispanic Policy* 17: 41–54.

———. 2006. "Rethinking Citizenship: Noncitizen Voting and Immigrant Political Engagement in the United States." In Taeku Lee, Karthick Ramakrishnan, and Ricardo Ramírez, eds., *Transforming Politics, Transforming America: The Political and Civic Incorporation of Immigrants in the United States*, 51–70. Charlottesville: University of Virginia Press.

———. 2007. "Intersections of Inequality: Understanding Marginalization and Privilege in the Post Civil-Rights Era." *Politics and Gender* 3 (2): 232–248.

———. 2009. *Latino Politics.* Cambridge, UK: Polity.

García Bedolla, Lisa, and Melissa R. Michelson. 2009. "What Do Voters Need to Know? Testing the Role of Cognitive Information in Asian American Voter Mobilization." *American Politics Research* 37 (2): 254–274.

Gardner, Martha. 2009. *The Qualities of a Citizen: Women, Immigration, and Citizenship, 1870–1965.* Princeton, NJ: Princeton University Press.

Gerber, Alan S., and Donald P. Green. 2000a. "The Effect of a Nonpartisan Get-Out-the-Vote Drive: An Experimental Study of Leafletting." *Journal of Politics* 62 (3): 846–857.

———. 2000b. "The Effects of Canvassing, Direct Mail, and Telephone Contact on Voter Turnout: A Field Experiment." *American Political Science Review* 94 (3): 653–663.

———. 2001. "Do Phone Calls Increase Turnout? A Field Experiment." *Public Opinion Quarterly* 65 (1): 75–85.

———. 2005. "Correction to Gerber and Green (2000), Replication of Disputed Findings, and Reply to Imai (2005)." *American Political Science Review* 99 (2): 301–313.

Gerber, Alan S., Donald P. Green, and Michael N. Green. 2003. "Partisan Direct Mail and Voter Turnout: Results from Randomized Field Experiments." *Electoral Studies* 22: 563–579.

Gerber, Alan S., Donald P. Green, and Christopher W. Larimer. 2008. "Social Pressure and Voter Turnout: Evidence from a Large-Scale Field Experiment." *American Political Science Review* 102: 33–48.

Gerber, Alan S., Donald P. Green, and David W. Nickerson. 2001. "Testing for Publication Bias in Political Science." *Political Analysis* 9 (4): 385–392.

Gerber, Alan S., Donald P. Green, and Ron Shachar. 2003. "Voting May Be Habit Forming: Evidence from a Randomized Field Experiment." *American Journal of Political Science* 47 (3): 540–550.

Gilens, Martin. 2005. "Inequality and Democratic Responsiveness." *Public Opinion Quarterly* 69 (5): 778–796.

Gillespie, Andra, and Melissa R. Michelson. 2011. "Participant Observation and the Political Scientist: Possibilities, Priorities, and Practicalities." *PS: Political Science and Politics* 44 (2): 261–265.

Gimpel, James, Wendy Cho, and Daron Shaw. 2005. "Turning Out the Vote in Texas." Paper presented at the annual meeting of the American Political Science Association, Washington, DC.

Goldberg, David Theo. 2002. *The Racial State.* Malden, MA: Blackwell.

Gosnell, Harold. 1927. *Getting Out the Vote: An Experiment in the Stimulation of Voting.* Chicago: University of Chicago Press.

Green, Donald P. 2004. "Mobilizing African-Americans Using Direct Mail and Commercial Phone Banks: A Field Experiment." *Political Research Quarterly* 57 (2): 245–255.

Green, Donald P., and Peter M. Aronow. 2011. "Analyzing Experimental Data Using Regression: When Is Bias a Practical Concern?" Social Science Research Network. http://ssrn.com/abstract=1466886 [last accessed May 31, 2011].

Green, Donald P., and Alan S. Gerber. 2008. *Get Out the Vote: How to Increase Voter Turnout*, 2nd ed. Washington, DC: Brookings Institution.

Green, Donald P., Alan S. Gerber, and David W. Nickerson. 2003. "Getting Out the Vote in Local Elections: Results from Six Door-to-Door Canvassing Experiments." *Journal of Politics* 65 (4): 1083–1096.

Green, Donald P., Christopher W. Larimer, and Celia Paris. 2010. "When Social Pressure Fails: The Untold Story of Null Findings." Paper presented at the annual meeting of the Midwest Political Science Association, Chicago.

Green, Donald P., and Melissa R. Michelson. 2009. "ACORN Experiments in Minority Voter Mobilization." In Robert Fisher, ed., *"The People Shall Rule": ACORN, Community Organizing, and the Struggle for Economic Justice*, 235–248. Nashville, TN: Vanderbilt University Press.

Green, Donald P., and Ron Shachar. 2000. "Habit-Formation and Political Behavior: Evidence of Consuetude in Voter Turnout." *British Journal of Political Science* 30 (4): 561–573.

Green, Donald P., and Lynn Vavreck. 2006. "Assessing the Turnout Effects of Rock the Vote's 2004 Television Commercials: A Randomized Field Experiment." Paper presented at the annual meeting of the Midwest Political Science Association, Chicago.

Griffin, John D., and Brian Newman. 2005. "Are Voters Better Represented?" *Journal of Politics* 67 (4): 1206–1227.

———. 2008. *Minority Report: Evaluating Political Equality in America.* Chicago: University of Chicago Press.

Gutiérrez, David G. 1995. *Walls and Mirrors: Mexican Americans, Mexican Immigrants, and the Politics of Ethnicity.* Berkeley: University of California Press.

Ha, Shang E., and Dean S. Karlan. 2009. "Get-Out-the-Vote Phone Calls: Does Quality Matter?" *American Politics Research* 37 (2): 353–369.

Hajnal, Zoltan L. 2010. *America's Uneven Democracy: Turnout, Race, and Representation in City Politics.* New York: Cambridge University Press.

Hajnal, Zoltan L., and Taeku Lee. 2011. *Why Americans Don't Join the Party: Race, Immigration, and the Failure (of Political Parties) to Engage the Electorate.* Princeton, NJ: Princeton University Press.

Hamill, Ruth, Milton Lodge, and Frederick Blake. 1985. "The Breadth, Depth, and Utility of Class, Partisan, and Ideological Schemata." *American Journal of Political Science* 29 (4): 850–870.

Hammack, Phillip L. 2008. "Narrative and the Cultural Psychology of Identity." *Personality and Social Psychology Review* 12 (3): 222–247.

Hancock, Ange-Marie. 2007. "When Multiplication Doesn't Equal Quick Addition: Examining Intersectionality as a Research Paradigm." *Perspectives on Politics* 5 (1): 63–79.

Haney-López, Ian F. 1996. *White by Law: The Legal Construction of Race.* New York: New York University Press.

Harris, Fredrick C. 1999. "Will the Circle Be Unbroken? The Erosion and Transformation of African American Civic Life." In R. K. Fullinwider, ed., *Civil Society, Democracy, and Civic Renewal,* 317–338. Lanham, MD: Rowman and Littlefield.

———. 2001. *Something Within: Religion in African American Political Activism.* New York: Oxford University Press.

Harris, Milton, and Artur Raviv. 2002. "Organization Design." *Management Science* 48 (7): 852–865.

Harris-Lacewell, Melissa, and Jane Junn. 2007. "Old Friends and New Alliances: How the 2004 Illinois Senate Race Complicates the Study of Race and Religion." *Journal of Black Studies* 38 (1): 30–50.

Haste, Helen. 2004. "Constructing the Citizen." *Political Psychology* 25 (3): 413–439.

Hastie, Reid. 1986. "A Primer of Information-Processing Theory for the Political Scientist." In Lau and Sears 1986a, 11–39.

Hero, Rodney E. 2003. "Social Capital and Racial Inequality in America." *Perspectives on Politics* 1 (1): 113–122.

Hitlin, Steven. 2003. "Values as the Core of Personal Identity: Drawing Links between Two Theories of Self." *Social Psychology Quarterly* 66 (2): 118–137.

Holland, Dorothy, William Lachicotte, Jr., Debra Skinner, and Carole Cain. 1998. *Identity and Agency in Cultural Worlds.* Cambridge, MA: Harvard University Press.

Howard, George S. 1991. "Culture Tales: A Narrative Approach to Thinking, Cross-Cultural Psychology, and Psychotherapy." *American Psychologist* 46 (3): 187–197.

Howard, Judith A. 2000. "Social Psychology of Identities." *Annual Review of Sociology* 26: 367–393.

Huddy, Leonie. 2001. "From Social to Political Identity: A Critical Examination of Social Identity Theory." *Political Psychology* 22 (1): 127–156.

Hutchings, Vincent L. 2003. *Public Opinion and Democratic Accountability: How Citizens Learn about Politics.* Princeton, NJ: Princeton University Press.

Jacobson, Matthew Frye. 1998. *Whiteness of a Different Color: European Immigrants and the Alchemy of Race.* Cambridge, MA: Harvard University Press.

Janowitz, Morris, and Dwaine Marvick. 1956. *Competitive Pressure and Democratic Consent: An Interpretation of the Politics of the 1952 Presidential Election.* Ann Arbor: University of Michigan Press.

John, Peter, and Tessa Brannan. 2008. "How Different Are Telephoning and Canvassing? Results from a Get Out the Vote Field Experiment in the UK 2005 General Election." *British Journal of Political Science* 38 (3): 565–574.

Jones, Steven J. 2006. *Antonio Gramsci.* New York: Routledge.

Jones-Correa, Michael. 1998. *Between Two Nations: The Political Predicament of Latinos in New York City.* Ithaca, NY: Cornell University Press.

Junn, Jane. 1997. "Assimilating or Coloring Participation? Gender, Race, and Democratic Participation." In Cathy J. Cohen, Kathleen Jones, and Joan Tronto, eds.,

Women Transforming Politics: An Alternative Reader, 387–397. New York: New York University Press.

Kahne, Joseph, David Crow, and Nam-Jin Lee. Forthcoming. "Different Pedagogy, Different Politics: High School Learning Opportunities and Youth Political Engagement." *Political Psychology.*

Keefer, Philip, and Stuti Khemani. 2004. "Why Do the Poor Receive Poor Services?" *Economic and Political Weekly* 39 (9): 935–943.

Kim, Claire J. 2000. *Bitter Fruit: The Politics of Black-Korean Conflict in New York City.* New Haven: Yale University Press.

King, Desmond. 2000. *Making Americans: Immigration, Race, and the Origins of the Diverse Democracy.* Cambridge, MA: Harvard University Press.

Knoke, David. 1990. "Networks of Political Action: Towards Theory Construction." *Social Forces* 68 (4): 1041–1063.

Kraut, Robert E., and John B. McConahay. 1973. "How Being Interviewed Affects Voting: An Experiment." *Public Opinion Quarterly* 37 (3): 398–406.

Kuklinksi, James H., Robert C. Luskin, and John Bolland. 1991. "Where Is the Schema? Going Beyond the 'S' Word in Political Psychology." *American Political Science Review* 85 (4): 1341–1356.

Kymlicka, Will, and Wayne Norman. 1994. "Return of the Citizen: A Survey of Recent Work on Citizenship Theory." *Ethics* 104 (2): 352–381.

"Latino Likely Voters in California." 2010. *Just the Facts.* San Francisco: Public Policy Institute of California. Available at http://www.ppic.org/main/series.asp?i=12.

Lau, Richard R., and David O. Sears, eds. 1986a. *Political Cognition.* Hillsdale, NJ: Erlbaum.

———. 1986b. "Social Cognition and Political Cognition: The Past, the Present, and the Future." In Lau and Sears 1986a, 347–366.

Lawless, Jennifer L., and Richard L. Fox. 2001. "Political Participation of the Urban Poor." *Social Problems* 48 (3): 362–285.

Lawy, Robert. 2003. "Transformation of Person, Identity and Understanding: A Case Study." *British Journal of Sociology of Education* 24 (3): 331–345.

Lee, Carol D. 2008. "2008 Wallace Foundation Distinguished Lecture—The Centrality of Culture to the Scientific Study of Learning and Development: How an Ecological Framework in Education Research Facilitates Civic Responsibility." *Educational Researcher* 37 (5): 267–279.

Lee, Carol D., Margaret Beale Spencer, and Vinay Harpalani. 2003. "'Every Shut Eye Ain't Sleep': Studying How People Live Culturally." *Educational Researcher* 32 (5): 6–13.

Lee, Eugene. 2009. "Getting Out the Asian American Vote: Achieving Double-Digit Increases in Turnout during the 2006 and 2008 Elections." Los Angeles: American Pacific Legal Center; Orange, CA: Orange County Asian Pacific Islander Community Alliance.

Lee, Taeku. 2002. *Mobilizing Public Opinion: Black Insurgency and Racial Attitudes in the Civil Rights Era.* Chicago: University of Chicago Press.

Leighley, Jan E. 2001. *Strength in Numbers? The Political Mobilization of Racial and Ethnic Minorities.* Princeton, NJ: Princeton University Press.

Lewis-Beck, Michael S., Richard Nadeau, and Angelo Elias. 2008. "Economics, Party, and the Vote: Causality Issues and Panel Data." *American Journal of Political Science* 52 (1): 84–95.

Lieberman, Matthew D., Darren Schreiber, and Kevin N. Ochsner. 2003. "Is Political Cognition Like Riding a Bicycle? How Cognitive Neuroscience Can Inform Research on Political Thinking." *Political Psychology* 24 (4): 681–704.

Lien, Pei-te, Margaret M. Conway, and Janelle Wong. 2004. *The Politics of Asian Americans: Diversity and Community.* New York: Routledge.

Lipsitz, George 1998. *The Possessive Investment in Whiteness: How White People Benefit from Identity Politics.* Philadelphia: Temple University Press.

Lodge, Milton, and Ruth Hamill. 1986. "A Partisan Schema for Political Information Processing." *American Political Science Review* 80 (2): 505–520.

Lodge, Milton, and Kathleen M. McGraw. 1991. "Where Is the Schema? Critique." *American Political Science Review* 85 (4): 1357–1364.

Luhtanen, Riia, and Jennifer Crocker. 1992. "A Collective Self-Esteem Scale: Self-Evaluation of One's Social Identity." *Personality and Social Psychology Bulletin* 18 (3): 302–318.

Malhotra, Neil, Melissa R. Michelson, Todd Rogers, and Ali Adam Valenzuela. 2011. "Text Messages as Mobilization Tools: The Conditional Effects of Habitual Voting and Election Salience." *American Politics Research* 39 (4): 664–681.

Malhotra, Neil, Melissa R. Michelson, and Ali Adam Valenzuela. Forthcoming. "Emails from Official Sources Can Increase Turnout." *Quarterly Journal of Political Science.*

Mansbridge, Jane. 2003. "Rethinking Representation." *American Political Science Review* 97 (4): 515–528.

Matland, Richard E., and Gregg R. Murray. 2012. "An Experimental Test of Mobilization Effects in a Latino Community." *Political Research Quarterly.* 65 (1): 192–205.

McAdam, Douglas, Sidney Tarrow, and Charles Tilly. 2001. *The Dynamics of Contention.* New York: Cambridge University Press.

McFarland, Daniel, and Heli Pals. 2005. "Motives and Context of Identity Change: A Case for Network Effects." *Social Psychology Quarterly* 68 (4): 289–315.

McGraw, Kathleen. 2000. "Contributions of the Cognitive Approach to Political Psychology." *Political Psychology* 21 (4): 805–832.

Michelson, Melissa R. 2003. "Getting Out the Latino Vote: How Door-to-Door Canvassing Influences Voter Turnout in Rural Central California." *Political Behavior* 25 (3): 247–263.

———. 2005. "Meeting the Challenge of Latino Voter Mobilization." *Annals of Political and Social Science* 601 (September): 85–101.

———. 2006. "Mobilizing the Latino Youth Vote: Some Experimental Results." *Social Science Quarterly* 8 (5): 1188–1206.

Michelson, Melissa R., and Lisa García Bedolla. 2010. "Survey Says: Numbers Don't Lie, but People Do." Paper presented at the annual meeting of the Midwest Political Science Association, Chicago.

Michelson, Melissa R., Lisa García Bedolla, and Donald P. Green. 2007. "New Experiments in Minority Voter Mobilization: A Report from the California Votes Initiative." San Francisco: James Irvine Foundation. Available at www.irvine.org.

———. 2008. "New Experiments in Minority Voter Mobilization: The Second in a Series of Reports on the California Votes Initiative." San Francisco: James Irvine Foundation. Available at www.irvine.org.

———. 2009. "New Experiments in Minority Voter Mobilization: The Third and Final Report on the California Votes Initiative." San Francisco: James Irvine Foundation. Available at www.irvine.org.

Michelson, Melissa R., Lisa García Bedolla, and Margaret A. McConnell. 2009. "Heeding the Call: The Effect of Targeted Two-Round Phonebanks on Voter Turnout." *Journal of Politics* 71 (4): 1549–1563.

Michelson, Melissa R., and David W. Nickerson. 2011. "Voter Mobilization." In James S. Druckman, Donald P. Green, James H. Kuklinski, and Arthur Lupia, eds., *Cambridge Handbook of Experimental Political Science*, 228–240. New York: Cambridge University Press.

Miller, Arthur H. 1991. "Where Is the Schema? Critiques." *American Political Science Review* 85 (4): 1369–1377.

Miller, Arthur H., and Thomas F. Klobucar. 2003. "The Role of Issues in the 2000 U.S. Presidential Election." *Presidential Studies Quarterly* 33 (1): 101–124.

Miller, Arthur H., Martin P. Wattenberg, and Oksana Malanchuk. 1986. "Schematic Assessments of Presidential Candidates." *American Political Science Review* 80 (2): 521–540.

Miller, Roy E., David A. Bositis, and Denise L. Baer. 1981. "Stimulating Voter Turnout in a Primary: Field Experiment with a Precinct Committeeman." *International Political Science Review* 2 (4): 445–460.

Morris, James P., Nancy K. Squires, Charles S. Taber, and Milton Lodge. 2003. "Activation of Political Attitudes: A Psychophysiological Examination of the Hot Cognition Hypothesis." *Political Psychology* 24 (4): 727–745.

Nasir, Na'ilah. 2002. "Identity, Goals, and Learning: Mathematics in Cultural Practice." *Mathematical Thinking and Learning* 4 (2–3): 213–247.

Nasir, Na'ilah, and Victoria M. Hand. 2006. "Exploring Sociocultural Perspectives on Race, Culture, and Learning." *Review of Educational Research* 76 (4): 449–475.

Nasir, Na'ilah, Milbrey W. McLaughlin, and Amina Jones. 2009. "What Does It Mean to Be African American? Constructions of Race and Academic Identity in an Urban Public High School." *American Educational Research Journal* 46 (1): 73–114.

Ngai, Mae M. 2004. *Impossible Subjects: Illegal Aliens and the Making of Modern America*. Princeton, NJ: Princeton University Press.

Nickerson, David W. 2006. "Volunteer Phone Calls Can Increase Turnout." *American Politics Research* 34 (3): 271–292.

———. 2007. "Quality Is Job One: Volunteer and Professional Phone Calls." *American Journal of Political Science* 51 (2): 269–282.

———. 2008. "Is Voting Contagious? Evidence from Two Field Experiments." *American Political Science Review* 102 (1): 49–57.

———. 2011. "Social Networks and Political Context." In James N. Druckman, Donald P. Green, James H. Kuklinksi, and Arthur Lupia, eds., *Handbook of Experimental Political Science*, 273–288. New York: Cambridge University Press.

Nickerson, David W., Ryan D. Friedrichs, and David C. King. 2006. "Partisan Mobilization Campaigns in the Field: Results from a Statewide Turnout Experiment in Michigan." *Political Research Quarterly* 59 (1): 85–97.

Oakes, Penelope. 2002. "Psychological Groups and Political Psychology: A Response to Huddy's 'Critical Examination of Social Identity Theory.'" *Political Psychology* 23 (4): 809–824.

Olson, Kevin. 2006. *Reflexive Democracy: Political Equality and the Welfare State.* Cambridge, MA: MIT Press.

———. 2008. "Constructing Citizens." *Journal of Politics* 70 (1): 40–53.

O'Malley, Pat, Lorna Weir, and Clifford Shearing. 1997. "Governmentality, Criticism, Politics." *Economy and Society* 26: 501–517.

Overton, Spencer. 2007. "Voter Identification." *Michigan Law Review* 105 (4): 631–682.

Panagopoulos, Costas. 2009a. "Partisan and Nonpartisan Message Content and Voter Mobilization: Field Experimental Evidence." *Political Research Quarterly* 62 (1): 70–77.

———. 2009b. "Thank You for Voting: Gratitude and Prosocial Behavior." Paper presented at the annual meeting of the Midwest Political Science Association, Chicago.

Panagopoulos, Costas, and Donald P. Green. 2011. "Spanish-Language Radio Advertisements and Latino Voter Turnout in the 2006 Congressional Elections: Field Experimental Evidence." *Political Research Quarterly* 64 (3): 588–599.

Parker, Chris. 2009. *Fighting for Democracy: Black Veterans and the Struggle against White Supremacy in the Postwar South.* Princeton, NJ: Princeton University Press.

Pérez, Myrna. 2008. *Voter Purges.* New York: Brennan Center for Justice, New York University School of Law. http://www.brennancenter.org/content/resource/voter_purges [last accessed May 30, 2011].

Peterson, David A. M. 2005. "Heterogeneity and Certainty in Candidate Evaluations." *Political Behavior* 27 (1): 1–24.

Putnam, Robert D. 1995. "Bowling Alone: America's Declining Social Capital." *Journal of Democracy* 6 (1): 65–78.

———. 2000. *Bowling Alone: The Collapse and Revival of American Community.* New York: Simon and Schuster.

Ramakrishnan, Karthick, and Mark Baldassare. 2004. *The Ties That Bind: Changing Demographics and Civic Engagement in California*. San Francisco: Public Policy Institute of California.

Ramírez, Ricardo. 2005. "Giving Voice to Latino Voters: A Field Experiment on the Effectiveness of a National Nonpartisan Mobilization Effort." *Annals of the American Academy of Political and Social Science* 601: 66–84.

Rappaport, Julian. 1993. "Narrative Studies, Personal Stories, and Identity Transformation in the Mutual Help Context." *Journal of Applied Behavioral Science* 29 (2): 239–256.

———. 2000. "Community Narratives: Tales of Terror and Joy." *American Journal of Community Psychology* 28 (1): 1–24.

Reicher, Stephen. 2004. "The Context of Social Identity: Domination, Resistance, and Change." *Political Psychology* 25 (6): 921–945.

Rosenstone, Steven, and John Mark Hansen. 1993. *Mobilization, Participation, and Democracy in America*. New York: Macmillan.

Rosenstone, Steven, and Raymond Wolfinger. 1978. "The Effect of Registration Laws and Voting Turnout." *American Political Science Review* 72 (1): 22–45.

Rudolph, Thomas J., and J. Tobin Grant. 2002. "An Attributional Model of Economic Voting: Evidence from the 2000 Election." *Political Research Quarterly* 55 (4): 805–823.

Rudolph, Thomas J., and Elizabeth Popp. 2007. "An Information Processing Theory of Ambivalence." *Political Psychology* 28 (5): 563–585.

Scargle, Jeffrey D. 2000. "Publication Bias: The 'File-Drawer' Problem in Scientific Inference." *Journal of Scientific Exploration* 14 (1): 91–106.

Schildkraut, Deborah J. 2007. "Defining American Identity in the Twenty-First Century: How Much 'There' Is There?" *Journal of Politics* 69 (3): 597–615.

Schlozman, Kay Lehman, Sidney Verba, and Henry E. Brady. 1995. "Participation's Not a Paradox: The View from American Activists." *British Journal of Political Science* 25 (1): 1–36.

Scottham, Krista Maywalt, and Ciara P. Smalls. 2009. "Unpacking Racial Socialization: Considering Female African American Primary Caregivers' Racial Identity." *Journal of Marriage and Family* 71: 807–818.

Sides, John, Eric Schickler, and Jack Citrin. 2006. "If Everyone Had Voted, Would Bubba and Dubya Have Won?" *Presidential Studies Quarterly* 38 (3): 521–539.

Sinclair, Betsy, Margaret A. McConnell, and Melissa R. Michelson. Forthcoming. "Local Canvassing and Social Pressure: The Efficacy of Grassroots Voter Mobilization." *Political Communication*.

Smith, Rogers. 1997. *Civic Ideals: Conflicting Visions of Citizenship in U.S. History*. New Haven: Yale University Press.

———. 2004. "Identities, Interests, and the Future of Political Science." *Perspectives on Politics* 2 (2): 301–312.

Sterling, T. D., W. L. Rosenbaum, and J. J. Weinkam. 1995. "Publication Decisions Revisited: The Effect of the Outcome of Statistical Tests on the Decision to Publish and Vice Versa." *American Statistician* 4 (1): 108–112.

Stets, Jan E., and Michael M. Harrod. 2004. "Verification across Multiple Identities: The Role of Status." *Social Psychology Quarterly* 67 (2): 155–171.

Stryker, Sheldon, and Peter J. Burke. 2000. "The Past, Present, and Future of Identity Theory." *Social Psychology Quarterly* 63 (4): 284–297.

Tate, Katherine. 1993. *From Protest to Politics: The New Black Voters in American Elections.* Cambridge, MA: Harvard University Press.

———. 2003. *Black Faces in the Mirror: African Americans and Their Representatives in the U.S. Congress.* Princeton, NJ: Princeton University Press.

Thaler, Richard H., and Cass R. Sunstein. 2008. *Nudge: Improving Decisions about Health, Wealth and Happiness.* New Haven: Yale University Press.

Todd, Jennifer. 2005. "Social Transformation, Collective Categories, and Identity Change." *Theory and Society* 34: 429–463.

Trivedi, Neema. 2005. "The Effect of Identity-Based GOTV Direct Mail Appeals on the Turnout of Indian Americans." *Annals of the American Academy of Political and Social Science* 601 (1): 115–122.

van Alstyne, Marshall. 1997. "The State of Network Organization: A Survey of Three Frameworks." *Journal of Organizational Computing and Electronic Commerce* 7 (2): 83–151.

Verba, Sidney, and Norman H. Nie. 1972. *Participation in America: Political Democracy and Social Equality.* Chicago: University of Chicago Press.

Verba, Sidney, Norman Nie, and Jae-on Kim. 1978. *Participation and Political Equality: A Seven-Nation Comparison.* Chicago: University of Chicago Press.

Verba, Sidney, Kay Lehman Schlozman, and Henry E. Brady. 1995. *Voice and Equality: Civic Voluntarism in American Politics.* Cambridge, MA: Harvard University Press.

Wilcox, Clyde. 1990. "Religious Sources of Politicization among Blacks in Washington, D.C." *Journal for the Scientific Study of Religion* 29 (3): 387–394.

Wilcox, Clyde, and Leopoldo Gomez. 1990. "Religion, Group Identification, and Politics among American Blacks." *Sociological Analysis* 51 (3): 271–185.

Williams, Lewis, Ronald Labonte, and Mike O'Brien. 2003. "Empowering Social Action through Narratives of Identity and Culture." *Health Promotion International* 18 (1): 33–40.

Wolfinger, Raymond E., Ben Highton, and M. Mullin. 2005. "How Postregistration Laws Affect the Turnout of Citizens Registered to Vote." *State Politics and Policy Quarterly* 5 (1): 1–23.

Wolfinger, Raymond E., and Jonathan Hoffman. 2001. "Registering and Voting with Motor Voter." *PS: Political Science and Politics* 34 (1): 85–92.

Wolfinger, Raymond E., and Steven J. Rosenstone. 1980. *Who Votes?* New Haven: Yale University Press.

Wong, Cara, and Grace E. Cho. 2005. "Two-Headed Coins or Kandinskys: White Racial Identification." *Political Psychology* 26 (5): 699–720.

Wong, Janelle. 2005. "Mobilizing Asian American Voters: A Field Experiment." *Annals of the American Academy of Political and Social Science* 601 (1): 102–114.

———. 2006. *Democracy's Promise: Immigrants and American Civic Institutions.* Ann Arbor: University of Michigan Press.

Wong, Janelle, Karthick Ramakrishnan, Taeku Lee, and Jane Junn. 2011. *Asian American Political Participation: Emerging Constituents and Their Political Identities.* New York: Russell Sage.

Wortham, Stanton. 2004. "The Interdependence of Social Identification and Learning." *American Educational Research Journal* 41 (3): 715–750.

Yalch, Richard F. 1975. "Attribution Theory and Voter Choice." In Mary Jane Schlinger, ed., *Advances in Consumer Research*, vol. 2, 783–792. Duluth, MN: Association for Consumer Research.

INDEX

Page numbers in *italics* refer to tables and figures.